AF255602

DISCOVERING KANO JOURNEY TO AN ANCIENT NIGERIAN EMIRATE

By Virgil Taylor

Copyright © 2025 By Virgil Taylor

All rights reserved

No part of this publication may be reproduced, distributed, or transmitted in any form or by any means, including photocopying, recording, or other electronic or mechanical methods, without the prior written permission of the publisher, except in the case of brief quotations embodied in critical reviews and certain other noncommercial uses permitted by copyright law.

ISBN: 978-1-968593-11-7

Nigeria

SOKOTO
KATSINA
JIGAWA
YOBE
BORNO
ZAMFARA
KEBBI
KANO
KADUNA
BAUCHI
GOMBE
NIGER
ADAMAWA
KWARA
PLATEAU
ABUJA (F.C.T)
OYO
NASSARAWA
TARABA
OSUN
KOGI
BENUE
OGUN
ONDO
EDO
EBONYI
ENUGU
LAGOS
EKITI
DELTA
IMO
CROSS RIVER
BAYELSA
RIVERS
AKWA IBOM
ANAMBRA
ABIA

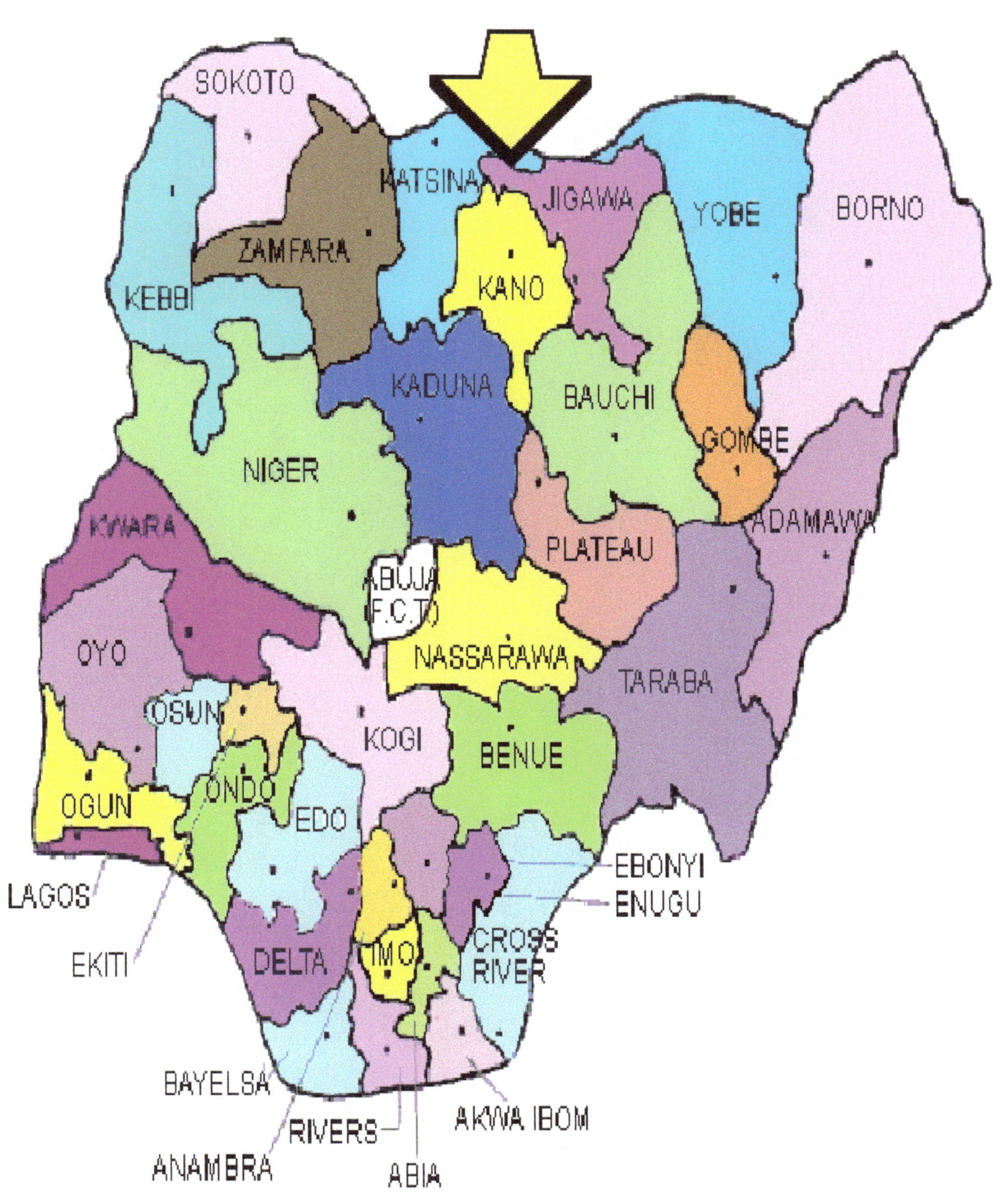

TABLE OF CONTENTS

ABOUT THE AUTHOR

Virgil Taylor is an artist, writer, and poet who studies African art, culture and history. His research into his ancestry revealed maternal ties to the Fulani and Yoruba tribes of Nigeria. Over the past decade, he has traveled across Africa to study its various cultures. Virgil's focus on African material culture has led to his detailed study of art, customs, and the history of the continent also known as Alkebulan, the mother of mankind.

ACKNOWLEDGMENTS

I would like to express my sincere gratitude to all who contributed to the success of my journey to Kano—special thanks to my friends and advisors for their invaluable advice, guidance, and support. I am particularly grateful to my brother Carl for his help and loving counsel throughout this project. I extend my heartfelt appreciation to Professors Nwando Achebe and Kabir Ahmed; this journey would not have been possible without your tremendous support and counsel, for which I am forever indebted.

To Arc Ahmad Abba Yusuf, I cannot adequately express my gratitude for your generosity, time, and friendship during my visit to Kano. I also want to thank His Highness Muhammadu Sanusi II, Emir of Kano, for the kindness and graciousness extended to me during my audience at Gidan Rumfa, the Palace of the Emir.

Additionally, I acknowledge the efforts of the team members at Aspire Book Publishing, who worked diligently to bring this book to fruition. I would like to thank the photographers that took the pictures used on the back cover of the book, Derrien Shelton and Mark Sullivan.

I am eternally grateful to the love of my life, Roz, for her unwavering encouragement and understanding throughout this journey. Lastly, I thank my family, to my children Shawn and Allen; Dad loves you both beyond measure. To my grandsons Cameron, Brayden, Bryce, and Karson, you are my legacy and my heart; Grandpa loves you all more than I can express.

PREMISE

"Kano was never just a destination. It was a calling — part curiosity, part heritage, part need to witness a world seldom seen beyond searches by those curious about Nigeria or found in travel brochures. I arrived with my camera phone, my DJI gimbal *(I learned on earlier trips big cameras are a liability, so I opt for smaller, more discrete devices),* and a promise to myself: to listen, to learn, and to share the story of this ancient city through my images and impressions…

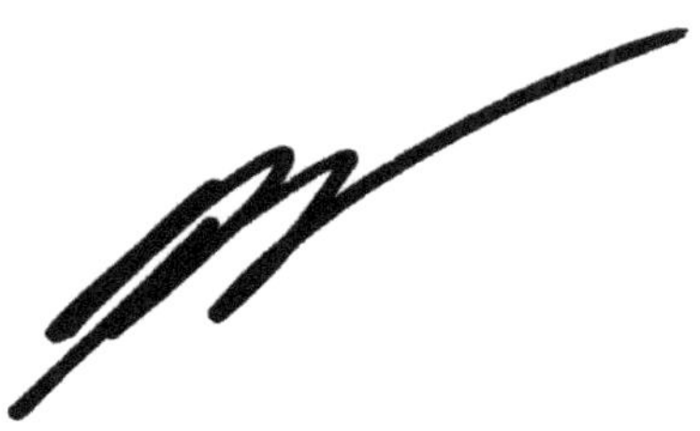

INTRODUCTION

I had been planning my visit to Kano, Nigeria, for months. Last year, I learned about the Durbar Festivals held annually throughout northern Nigeria at the end of Ramadan. I was immediately intrigued and began researching the 'Kano Durbar', digging deeper into the history, rituals, and vibrant displays that make it one of the most spectacular festivals in the world.

The more I learned, the more captivated I became. It wasn't just the grand parades of decorated horses and finely dressed riders but the centuries-old traditions and the powerful sense of community that struck me. As I researched, I learned that on my Mother's side, Yoruba and Fulani are part of our lineage, both tribes of Nigeria; perhaps this is part of the reason I've been so compelled to visit this land… I further discovered that Kano hosts the largest and most iconic festival — the Durbar of Kano, which has drawn visitors and dignitaries from across the globe for centuries. That's when I decided to travel to Kano and experience the largest and most regal of Durbars firsthand.

This book is a pictorial story of that journey — a journey not just to see the festival but to immerse myself in the pulse of Kano itself. As I explored the ancient city, I was drawn into its vibrant streets, rich heritage, and the uniqueness of its people. This book is not just about the Durbar (which I never actually witnessed); it is about all I discovered during my journey — from the dazzling colors of the city's marketplaces to the politeness and friendliness of the many people I met.

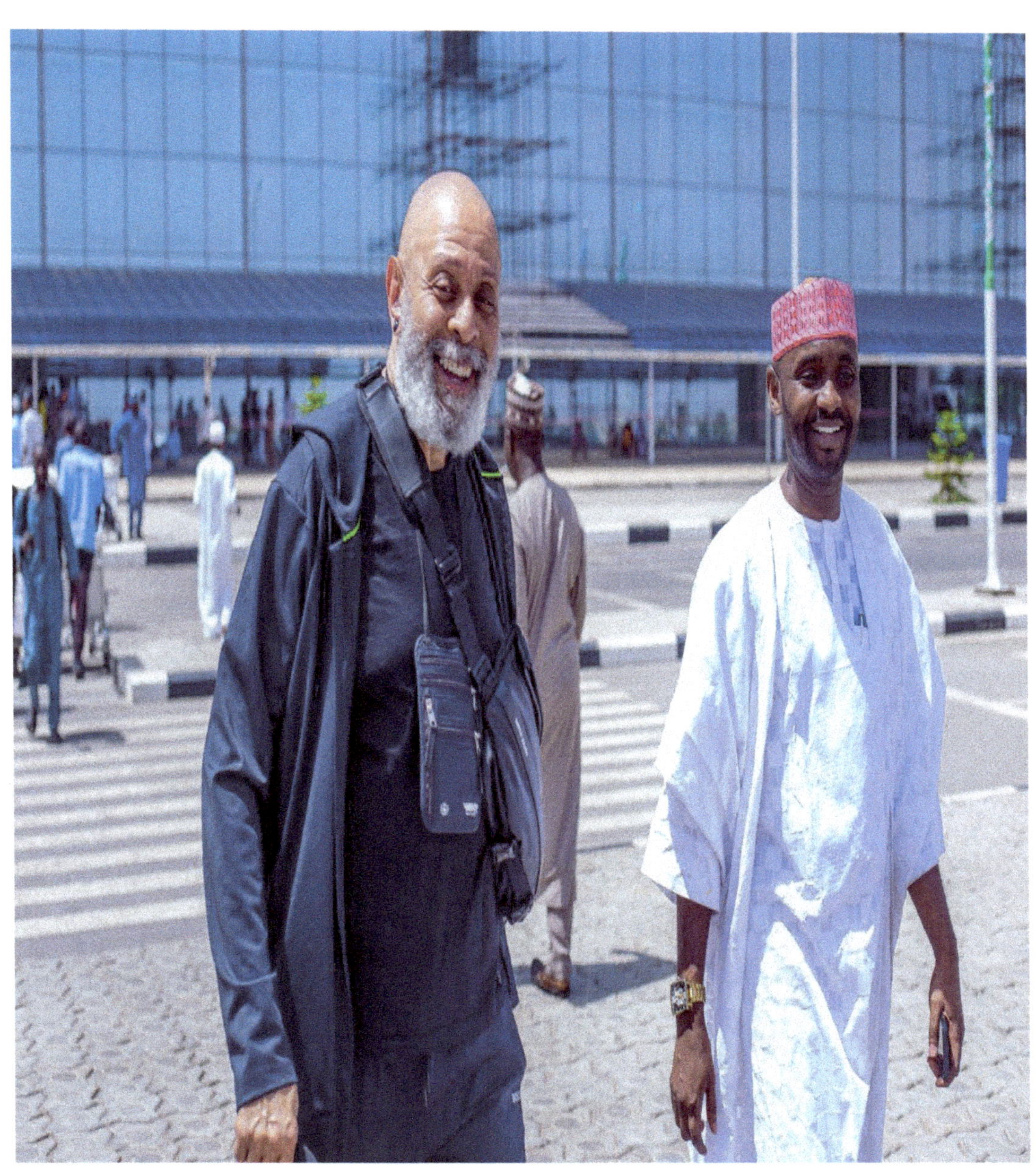

ARRIVAL

After months of anticipation, I finally landed in Kano, Nigeria, with a sense of excitement and wonder. The flight had been long, but the thought of stepping into a city rich with culture and history made the weariness worth it. I had imagined this moment countless times during my research — the busy airport, the streets full of life, the first glimpse of the city's vibrant soul.

However, my arrival wasn't as smooth as I had imagined.

Clearing immigration proved to be a challenge. This wasn't my first trip to Africa, so I had some idea of how challenging immigration could be, but Nigerian immigration was an experience like no other. The lines were long, the process antiquated and disorganized, and I found myself caught in a whirlwind of poorly managed chaos. My passport and Visa on Arrival application were scrutinized, and the same questions were asked time and again; I began to wonder if there was something I had missed in the planning. The moving from one immigration officer to another only heightened my apprehension. What I thought would be a reasonably quick process dragged on, and with each passing minute, my frustration grew, as did my discomfort.

Eventually, after sometime, I was finally cleared to enter the country. The immense feeling of relief was soon overshadowed by the new reality that awaited me before I could leave the terminal. An immigration officer seemed to be escorting me to the exit. Still, before we could reach the doors to the exit, we were approached by several other men. I was uncertain of their identities; I could only assume they were officials because not all wore uniforms. I was led into a room where a discussion unfolded. Unable to speak the language, I naturally didn't understand what they were saying. It appeared they were arguing. Finally, the official escorting me indicated that we were leaving. He guided me out of the terminal, and I sensed he intended to inform me that I owed him money.

Thankfully, as we emerged from the terminal, we were met by my host, who was an authority from the Emirate designated by His Highness, the Emir of Kano, to see to it that I was attended to during my visit… my host and his staff welcomed me with open arms. Their smiles were comforting, and it felt good to finally have such kind, reassuring faces around me after the immigration stress. The immigration officer who'd been escorting me quietly departed… I breathed a sigh of relief to be among friendly faces.

But as we exchanged pleasantries and I settled into the rhythm of my arrival, I soon learned that the trip would not unfold the way I had expected.

As we made our way from the airport, my host broke the news — the Durbar Festival, the reason I had traveled to Kano, had been canceled. The grand celebration I had so carefully researched and planned was no longer happening.

I sat in the car, taken aback, with disappointment settling in. The festival that had drawn me here, the event I had envisioned myself witnessing in all its glory, would not come to pass.

ADJUSTING EXPECTATIONS

When I found out the Durbar Festival was canceled, I was disappointed. But I was also exhausted from the long journey that had taken me through Adis Ababa, Ethiopia. Finally, I was in Nigeria... and though I was very disappointed, I trusted my host. So, I went to my hotel to rest and recover before deciding what to do next.

Kano had a temperature of 105°F on the day of my arrival. Coming from the Midwest, such high temperatures were extreme to me and, needless to say, uncomfortable. The Bristol Palace Hotel in Kano provided my accommodation for the upcoming days. The air conditioning in the lobby and the large, well-appointed room was pleasing, and I was thankful *(things we take for granted at home can mean a lot when traveling to places we're unfamiliar with)*. After showering, I enjoyed the quiet the room provided. I was delighted to discover that many television programs were in English; this was a huge bonus! So, I settled in and relaxed.

DAY 1

Kano, Nigeria, is a Muslim state, and I arrived at the end of Ramadan, one of Islam's most holy holidays. Unbeknownst to me, the Islamic holiday Eid al-Fitr begins at the end of Ramadan. I would soon learn this meant there would be several days of merry-making and celebrations. Ramadan began at sundown on Friday, February 28, and technically ended at sundown on Sunday, March 30.

Ramadan fasting ends with Eid al-Fitr, the Festival of Breaking the Fast. Theoretically, Eid al-Fitr is a two-to-three-day festival that officially ends Ramadan. Somehow, those two to three days stretched until April 9, my last day in Kano. To say the people enjoy these holidays would be an understatement. Eid al-Fitr is one of two Eids celebrated annually on the Islamic calendar.

In communities with larger Muslim populations like Kano, Eid al-Fitr is regarded as a national holiday, resulting in the closure of schools and businesses and enabling families, neighbors, and friends to celebrate together.

My first full day in the activities and celebrations was Sunday, March 30. After driving through the city, where scores of people filled the streets, we arrived at Gidan Shettima, a building constructed during pre-colonial Kano to house one of the top-ranking slaves of the Emir. Today, it is tradition for the Governor of Kano to receive His Highness the Emir at 'Shettima's House' on the first day of Sallah. The following pictures show the crowds arriving to see His Excellency Alhaji Abba Kabir Yusuf, Governor of Kano, and His Highness Muhammadu Sanusi II, Emir of Kano, as they arrive at Gidan Shettima.

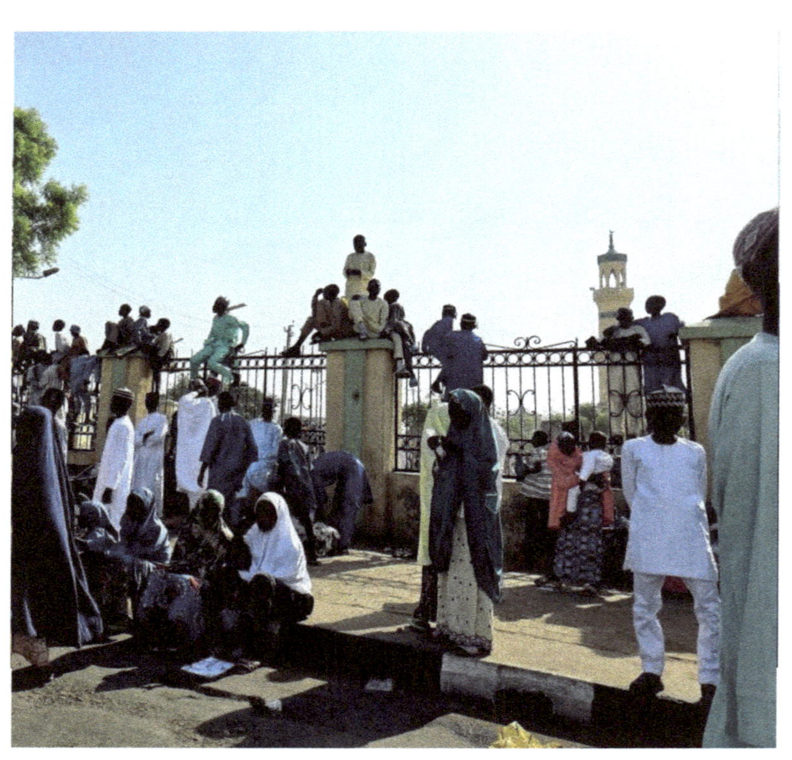

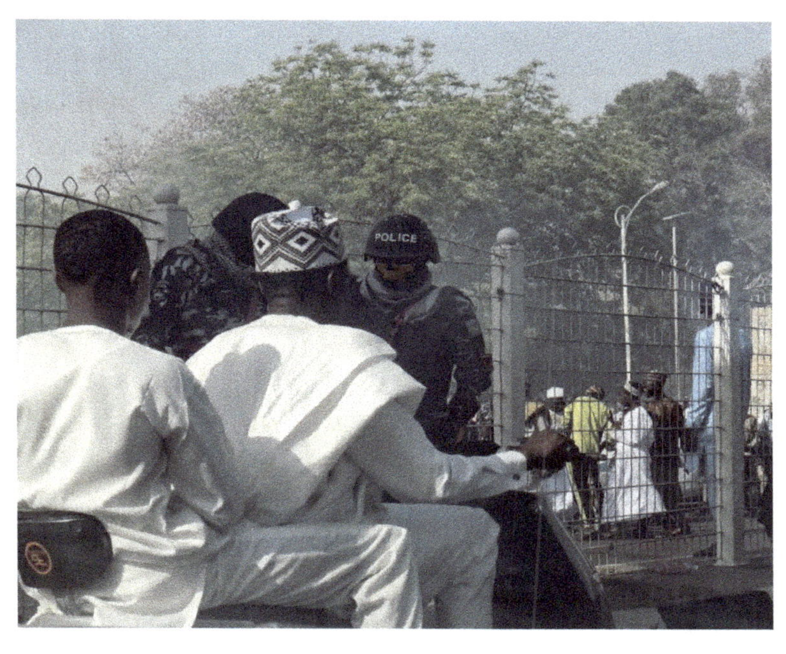

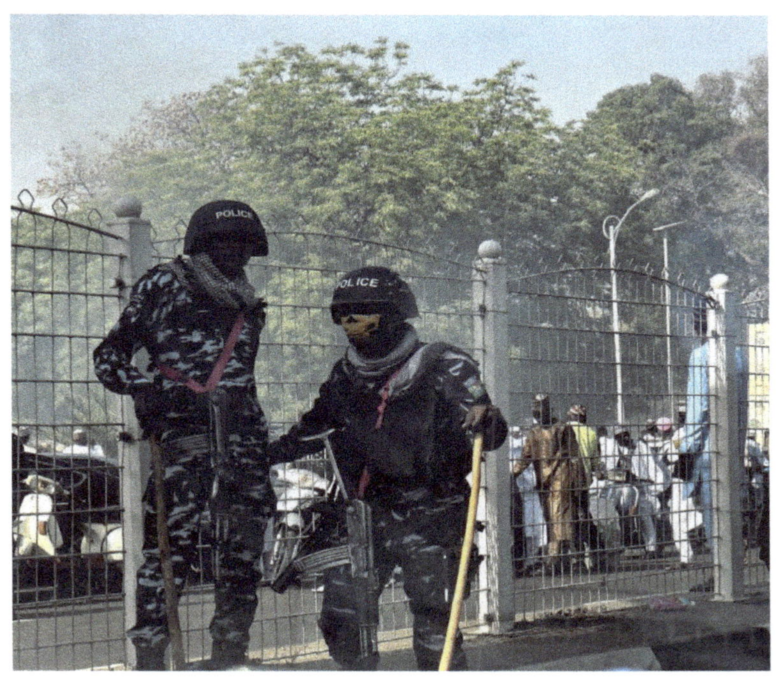

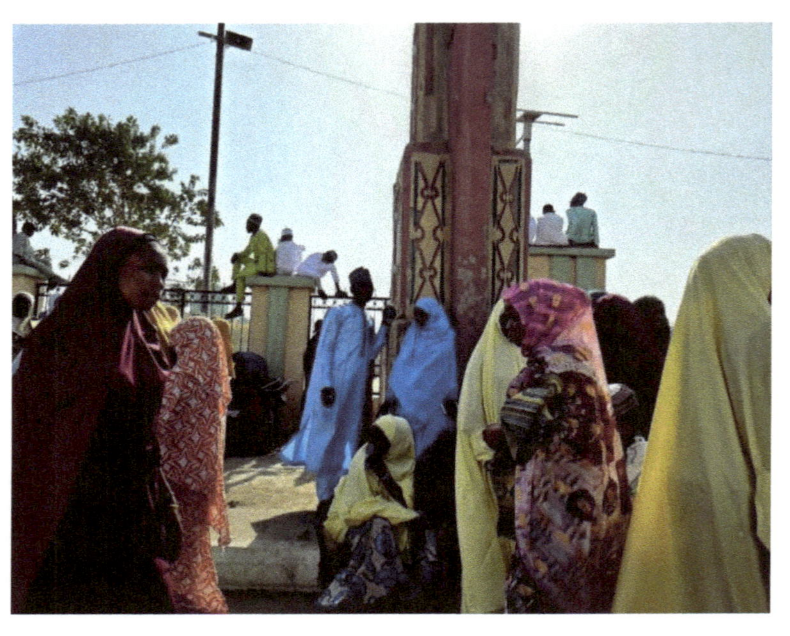

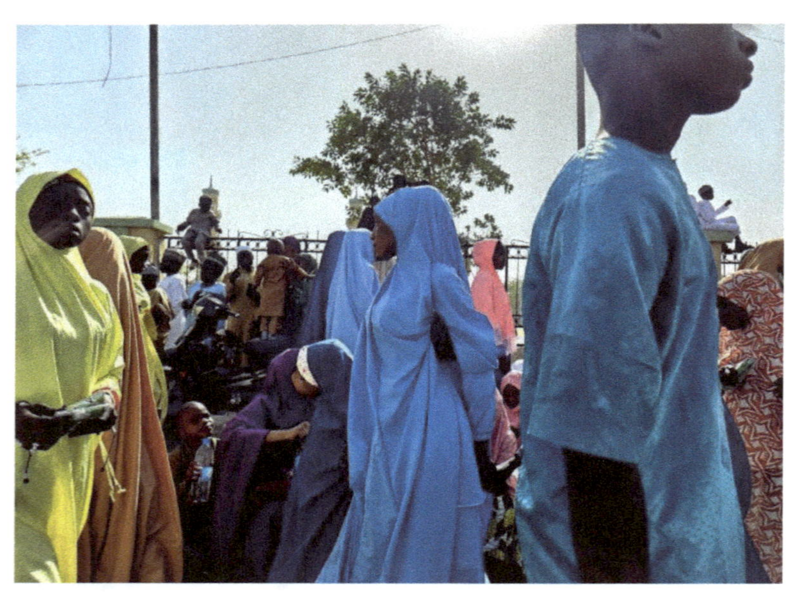

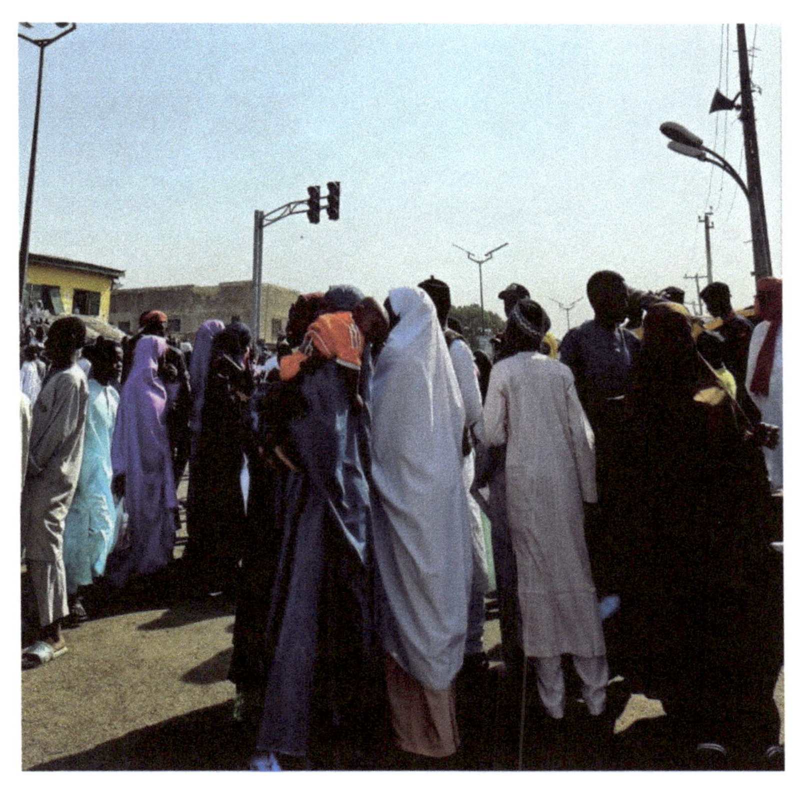

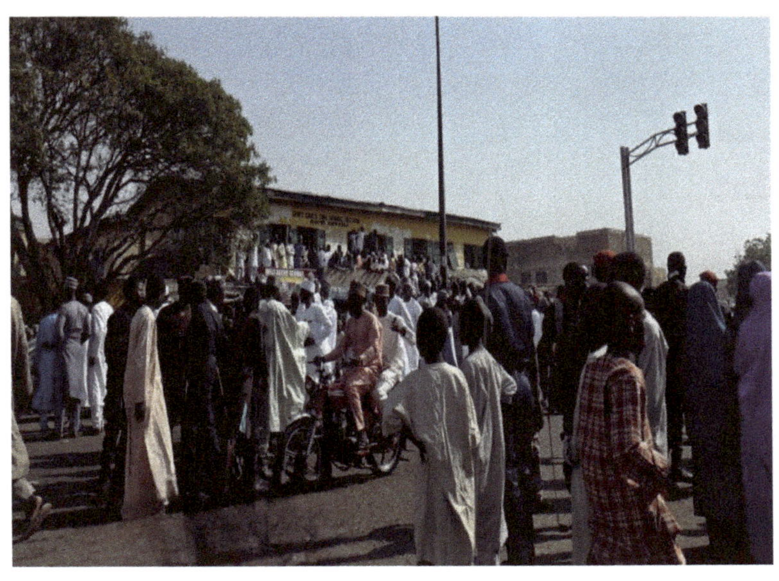

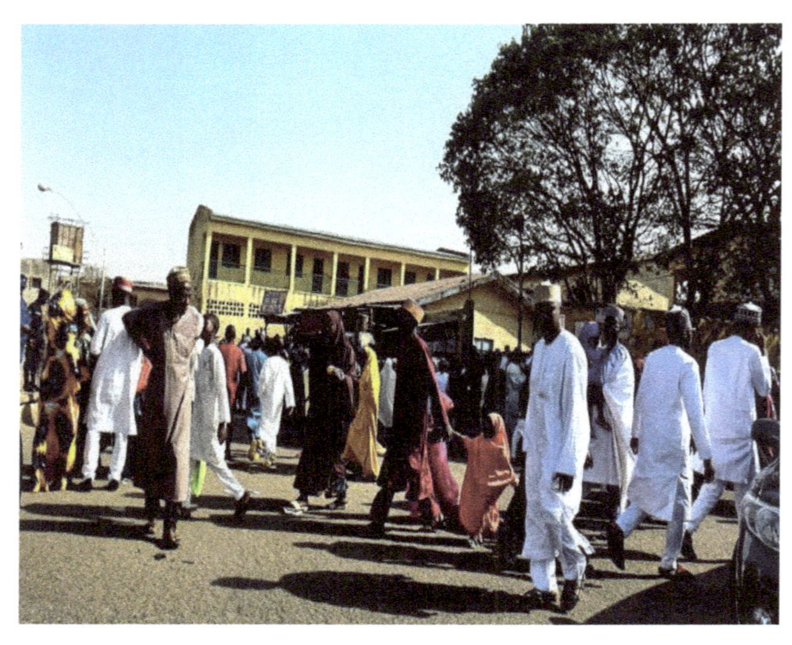

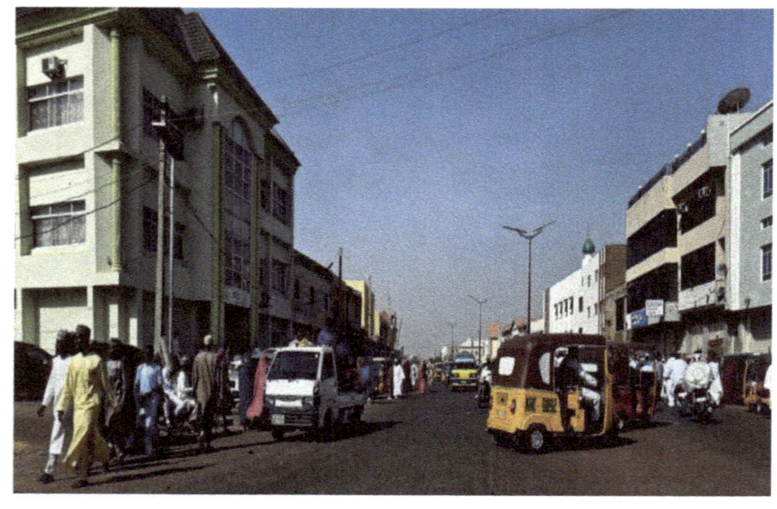

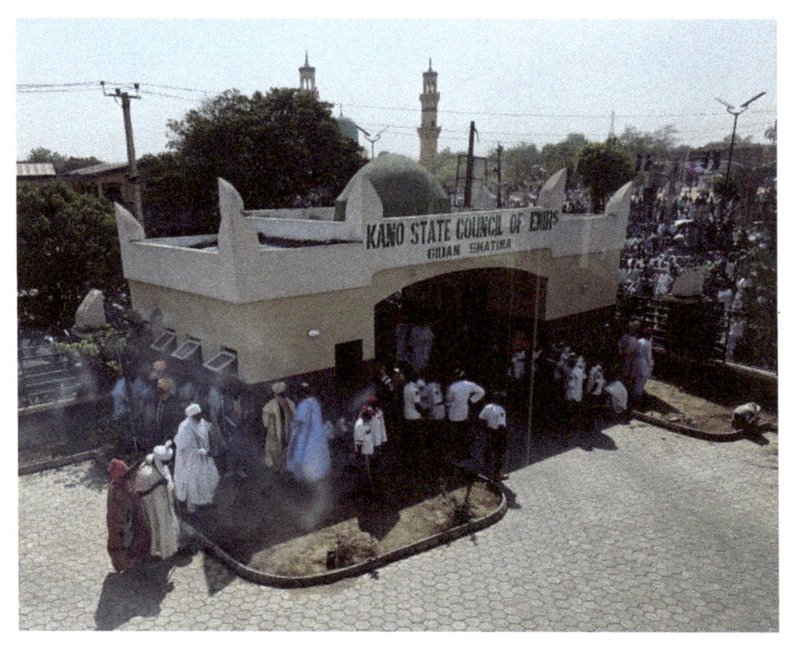
KANO STATE COUNCIL OF EMIRS
GIDAN SHATIMA

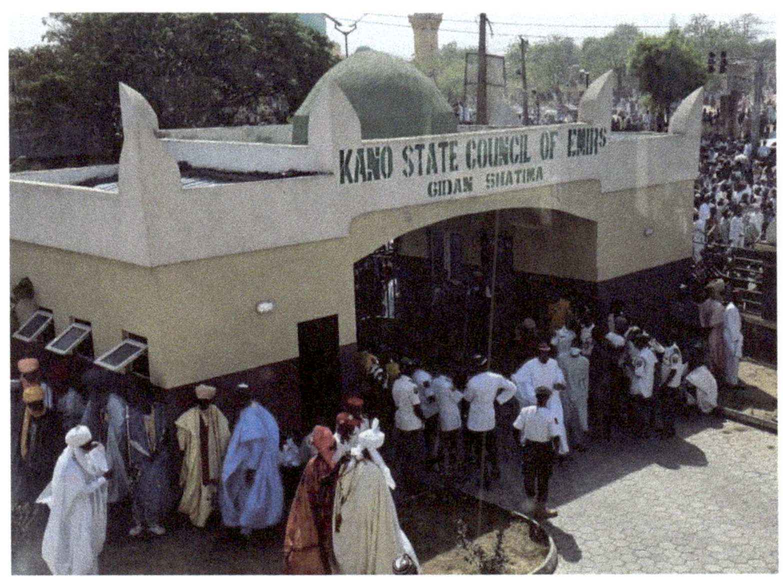
KANO STATE COUNCIL OF EMIRS
GIDAN SHATIMA

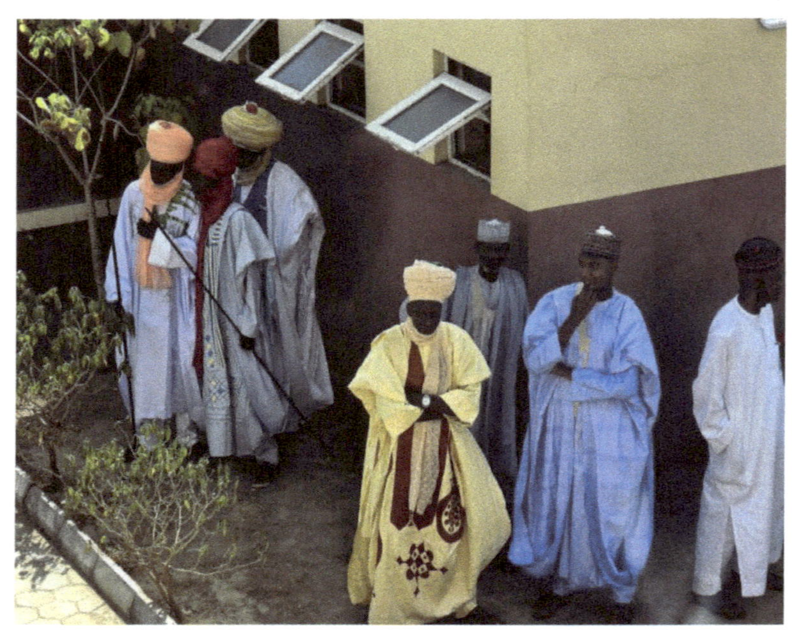

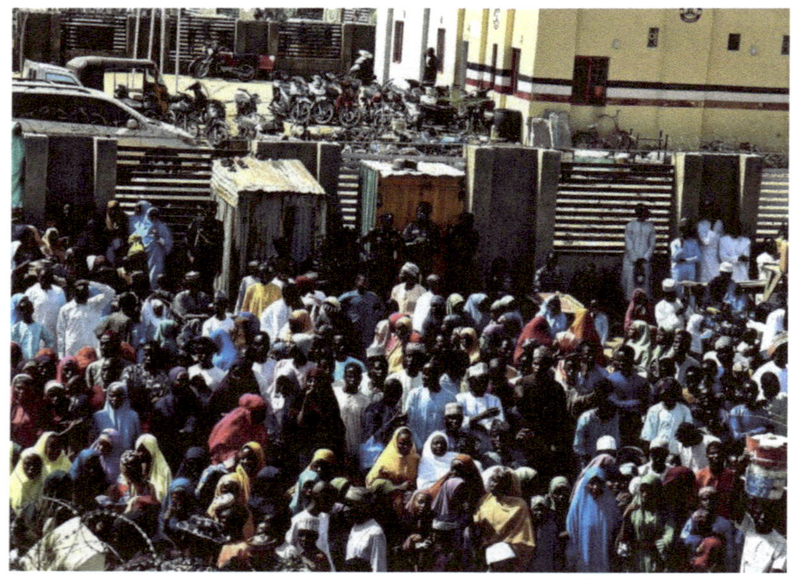

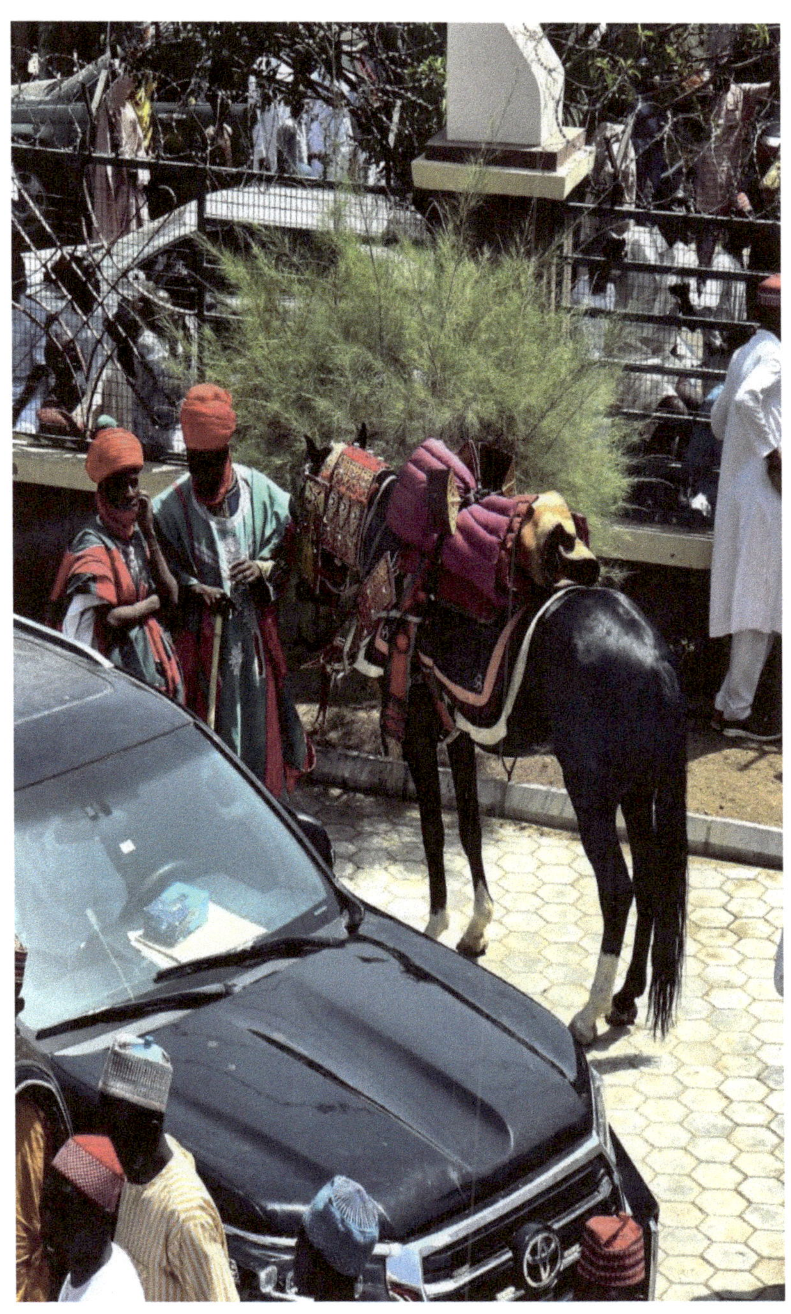

DAY 2

Gaisuwar Sallah, or Sallah Greetings, is a day of celebration when important individuals from across Kano come to the Emir's Palace to greet him and receive his blessings. The Emir arrives at the palace on horseback with his entourage, then proceeds inside to meet those who have come to greet him. The pictures depict people arriving at the palace and bowing before the Emir upon entering Majalisar Waje, (the outer palace court). The men on the left side of the Emir are princes, while other men of rank are positioned across the room. In the images, men surround the Emir with their arms raised whenever he needs to adjust his garments.

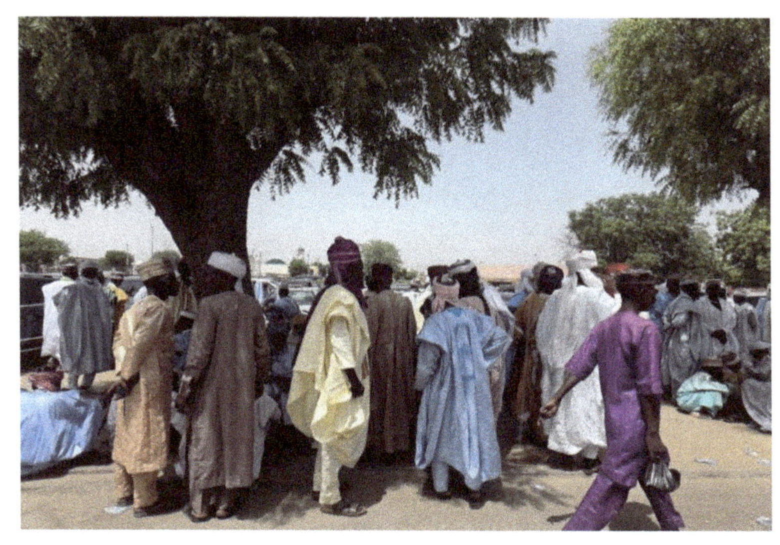

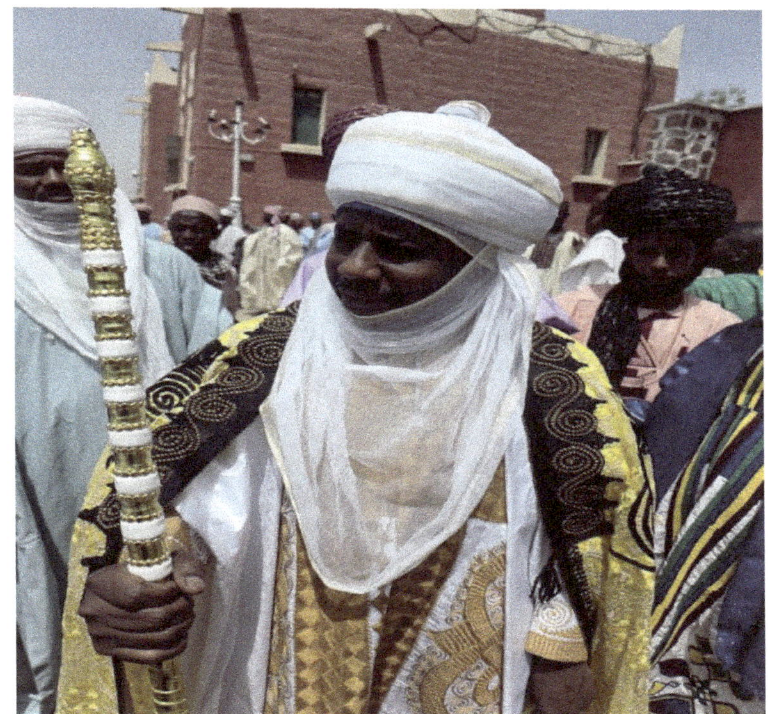

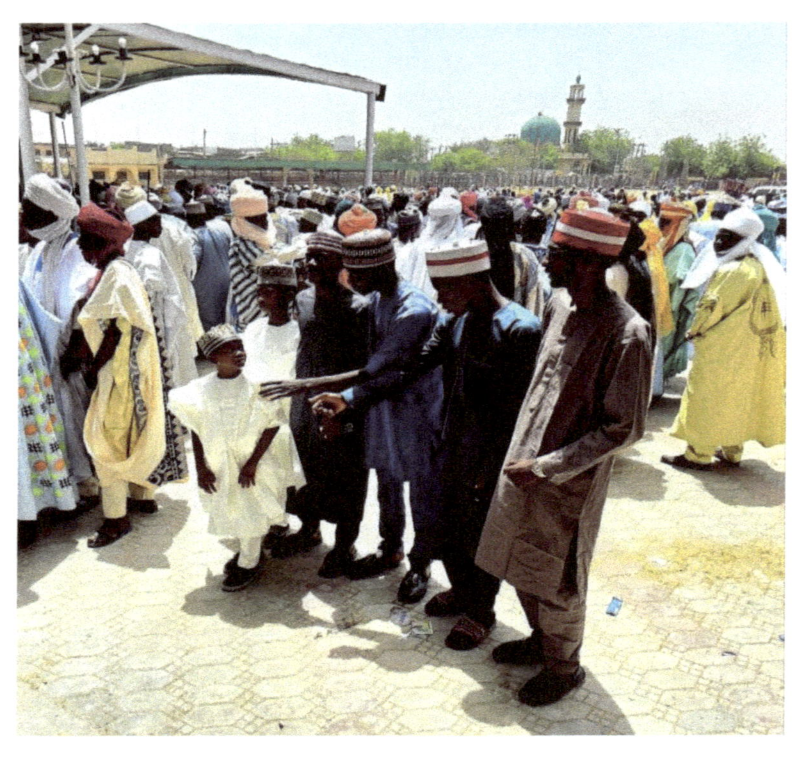

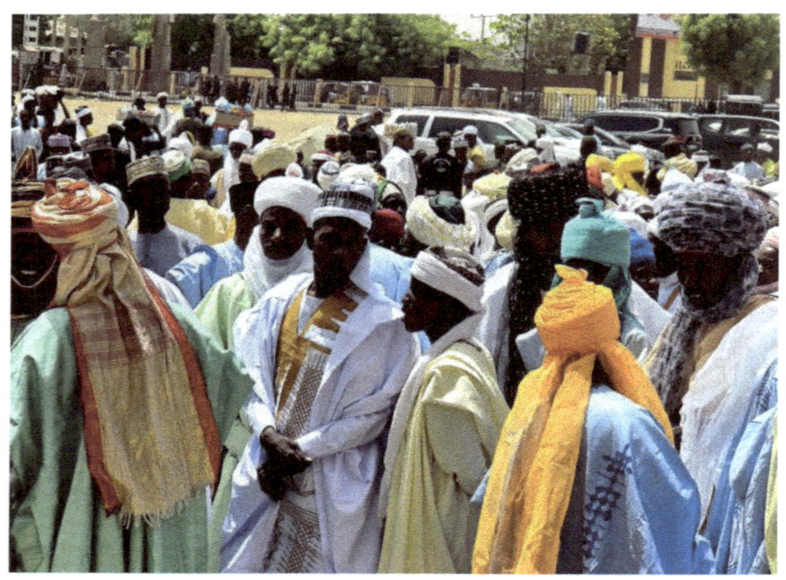

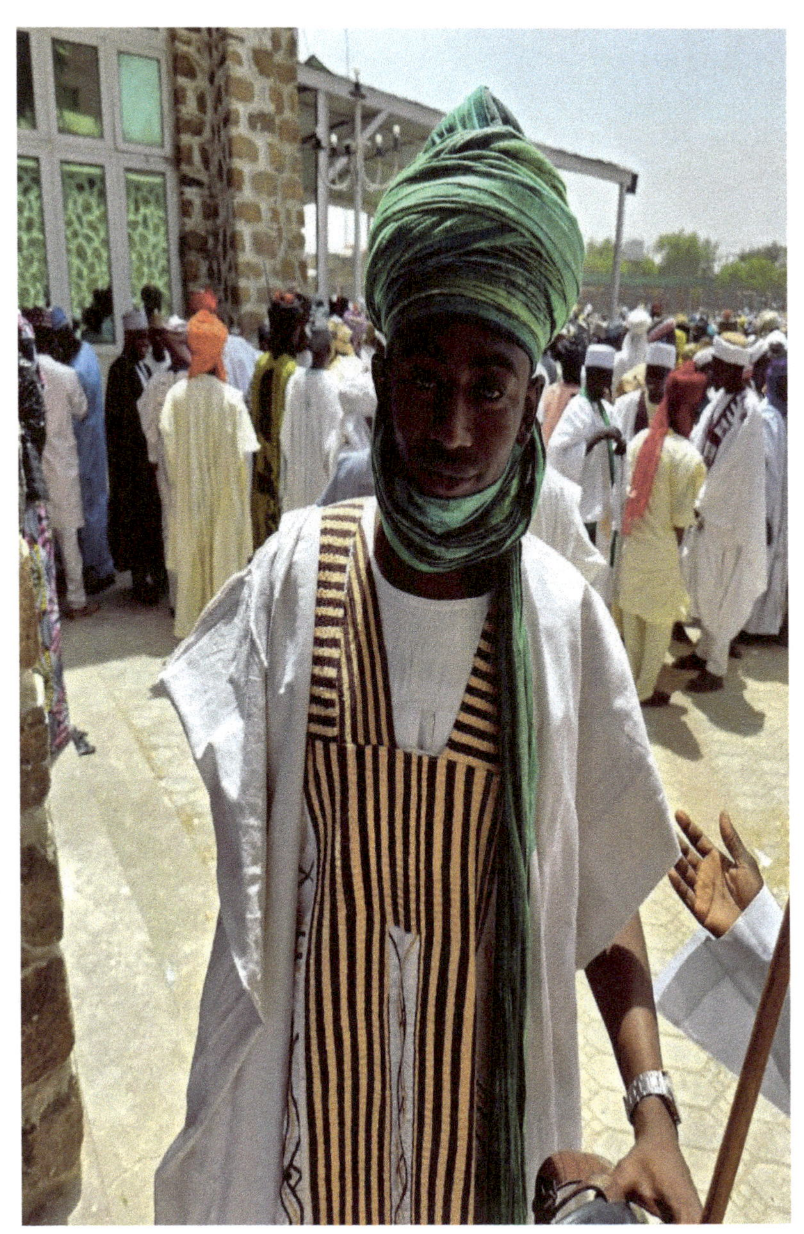

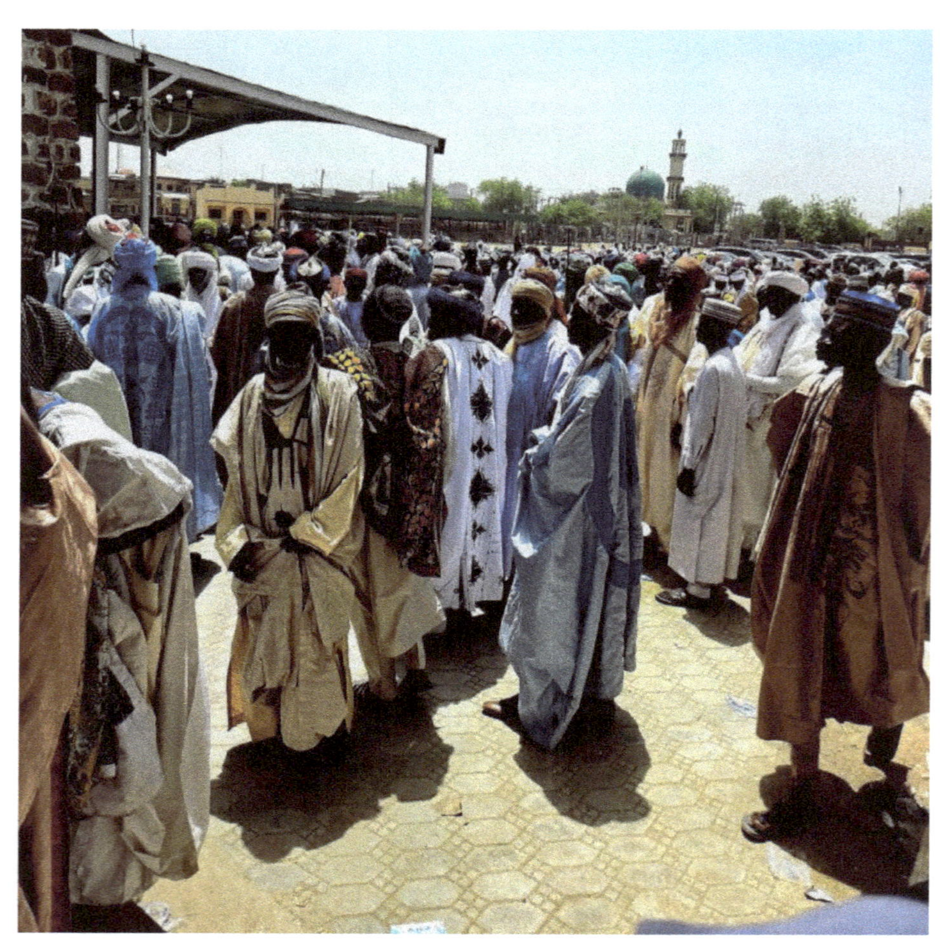

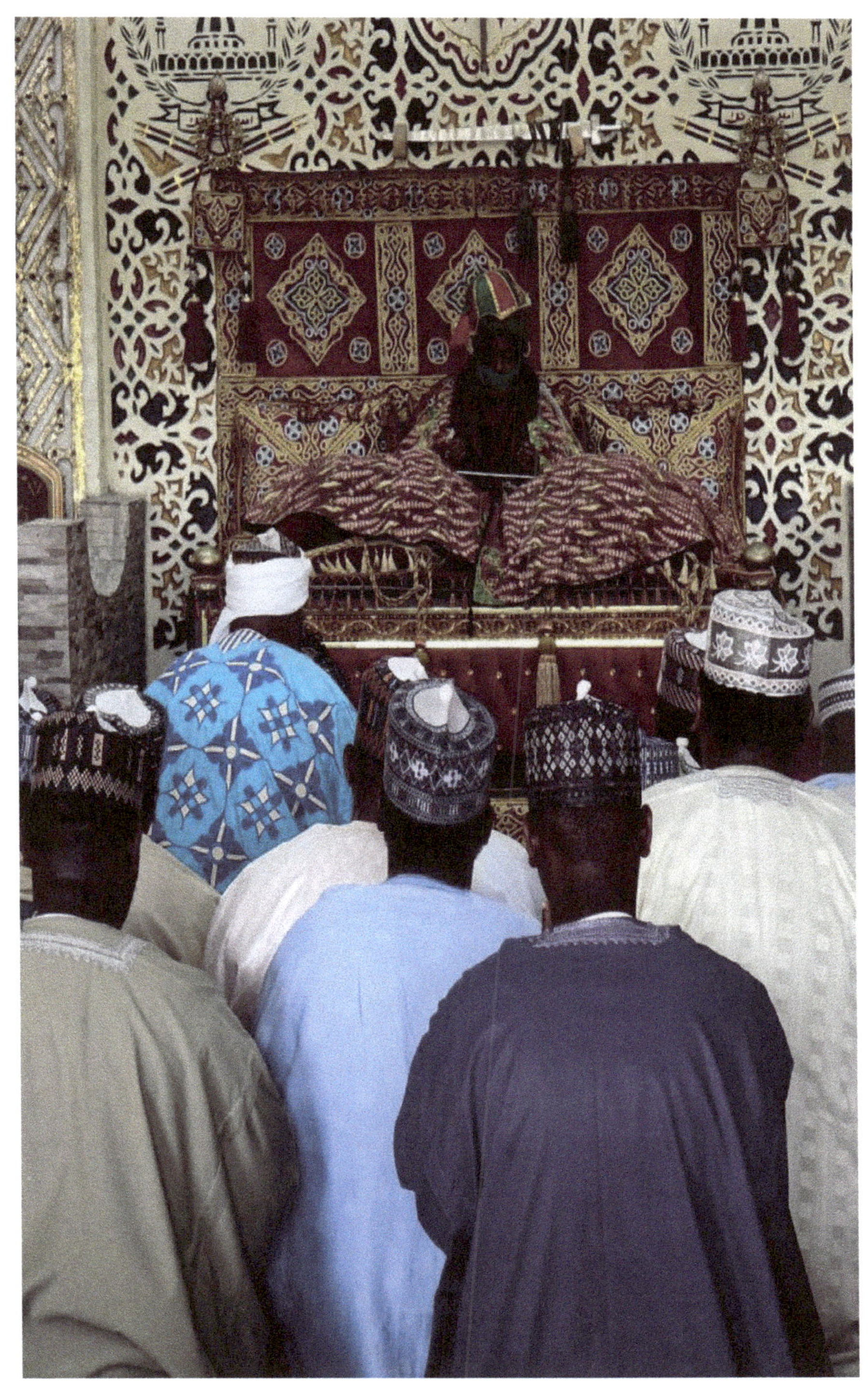

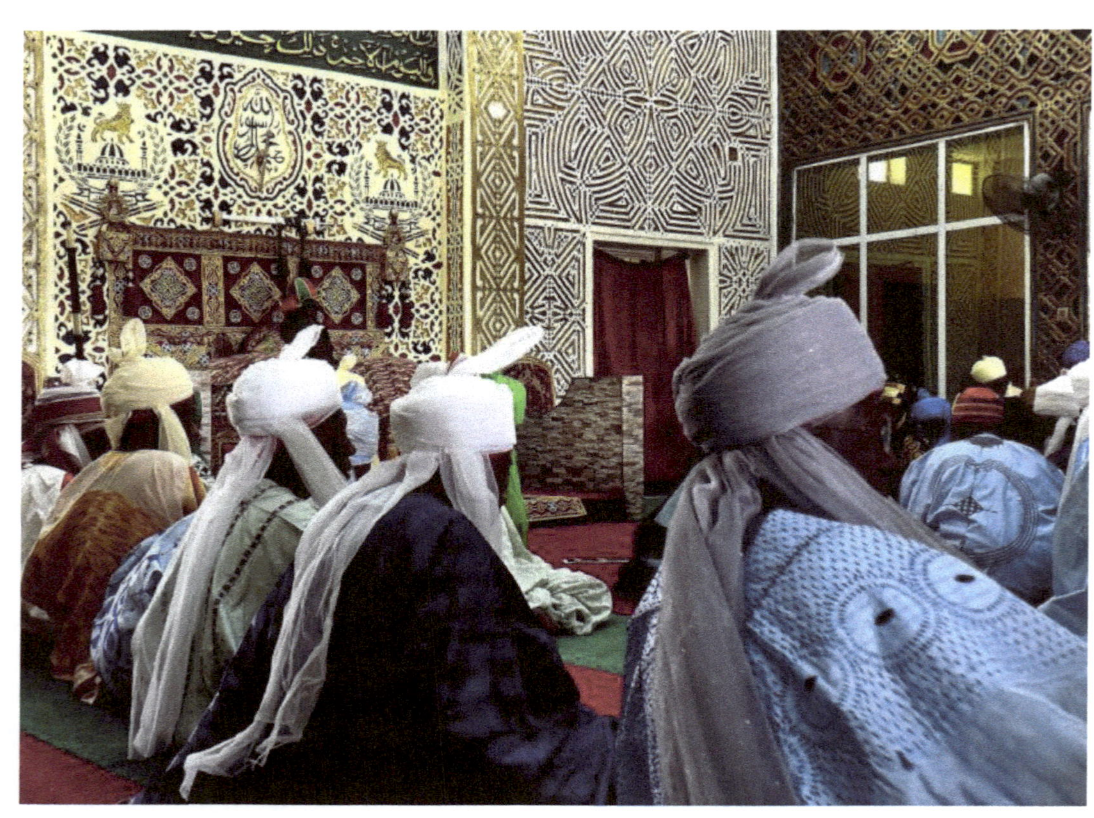

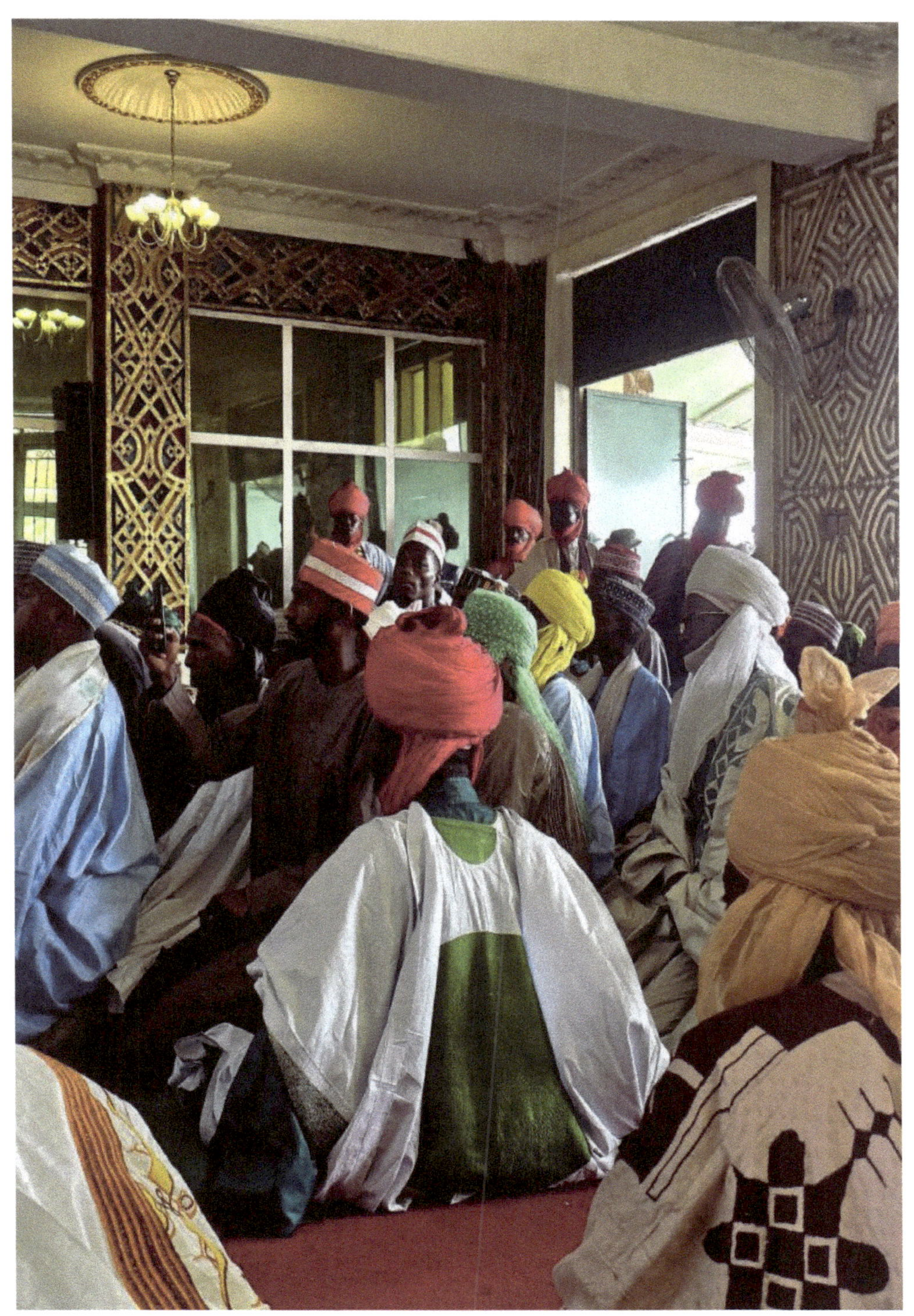

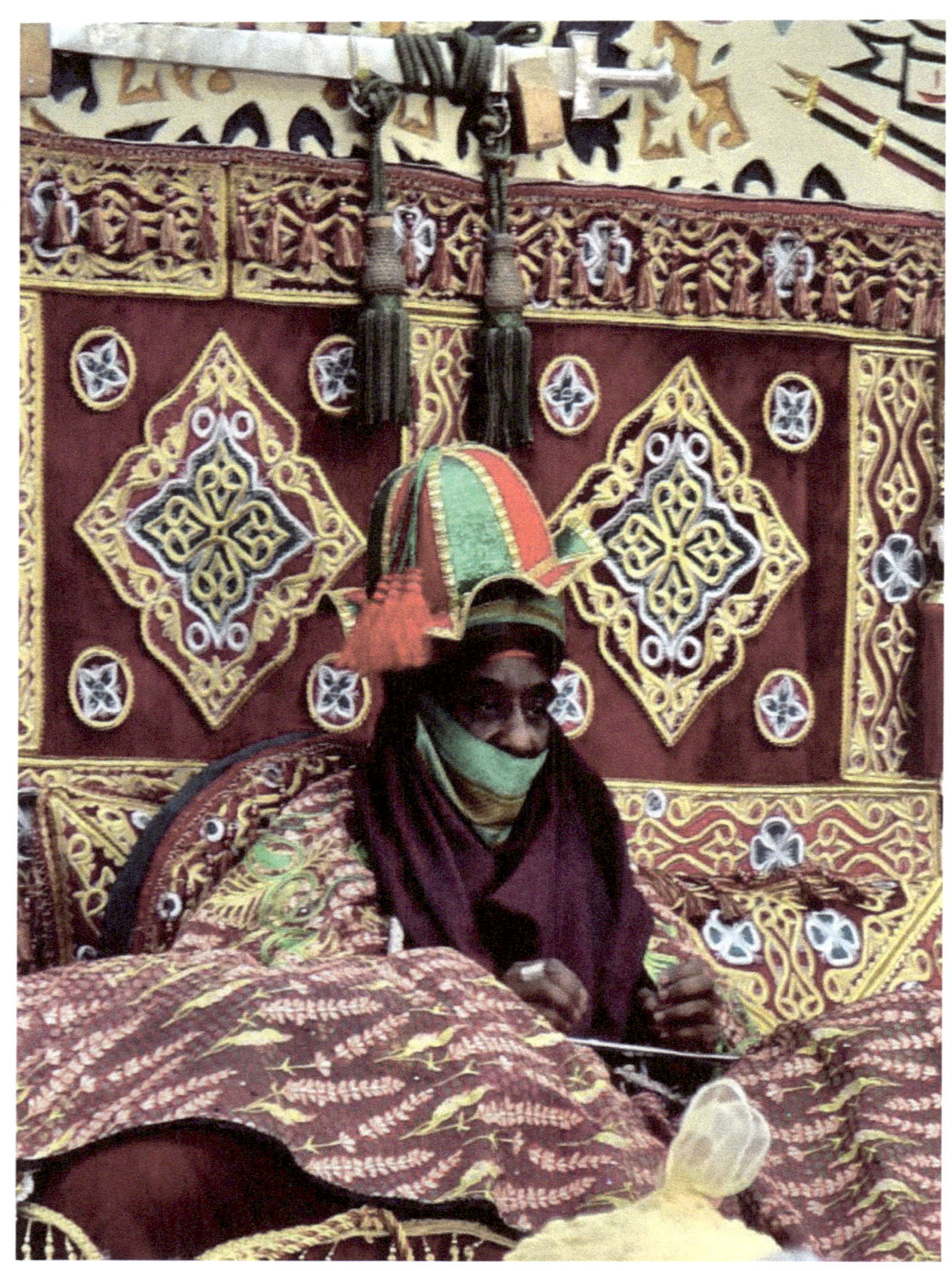

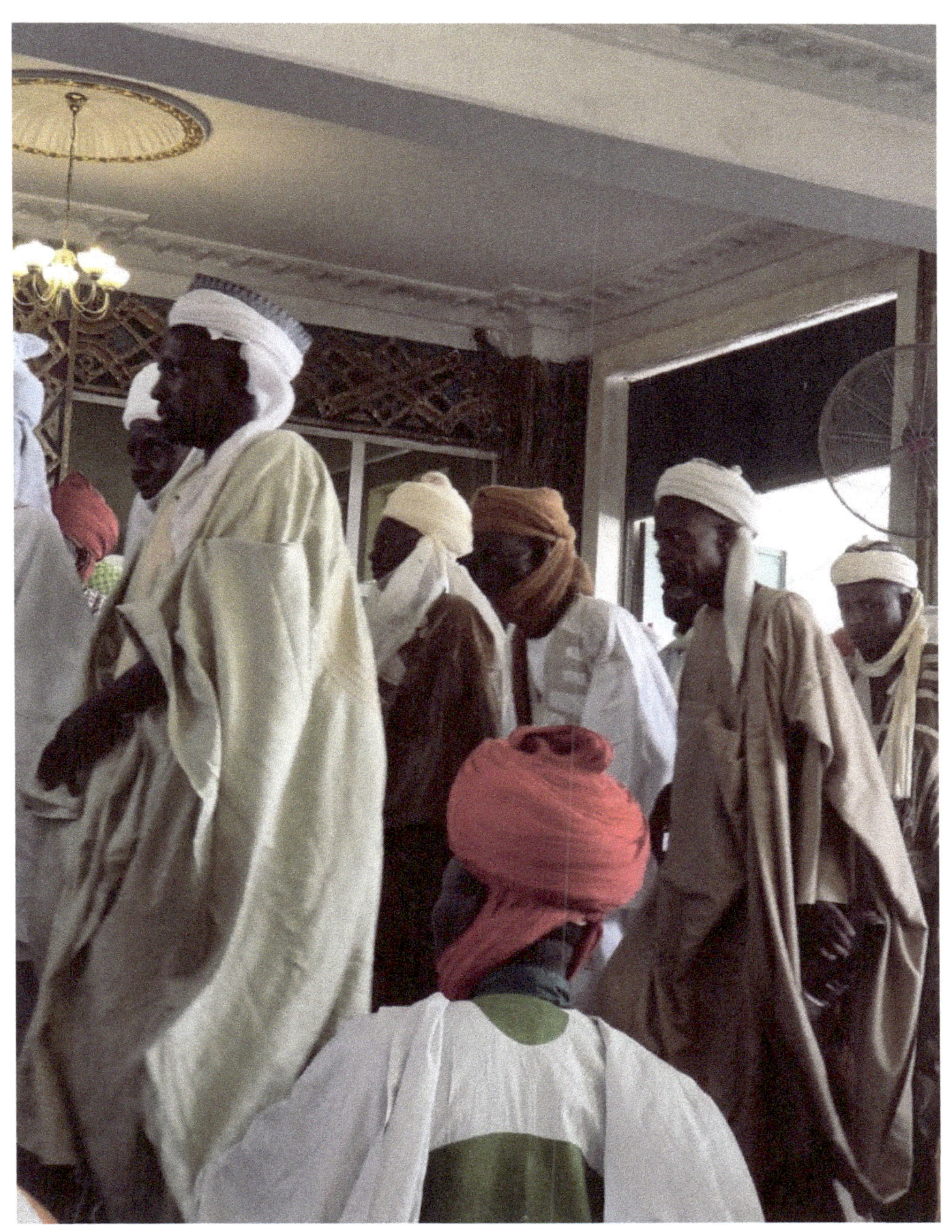

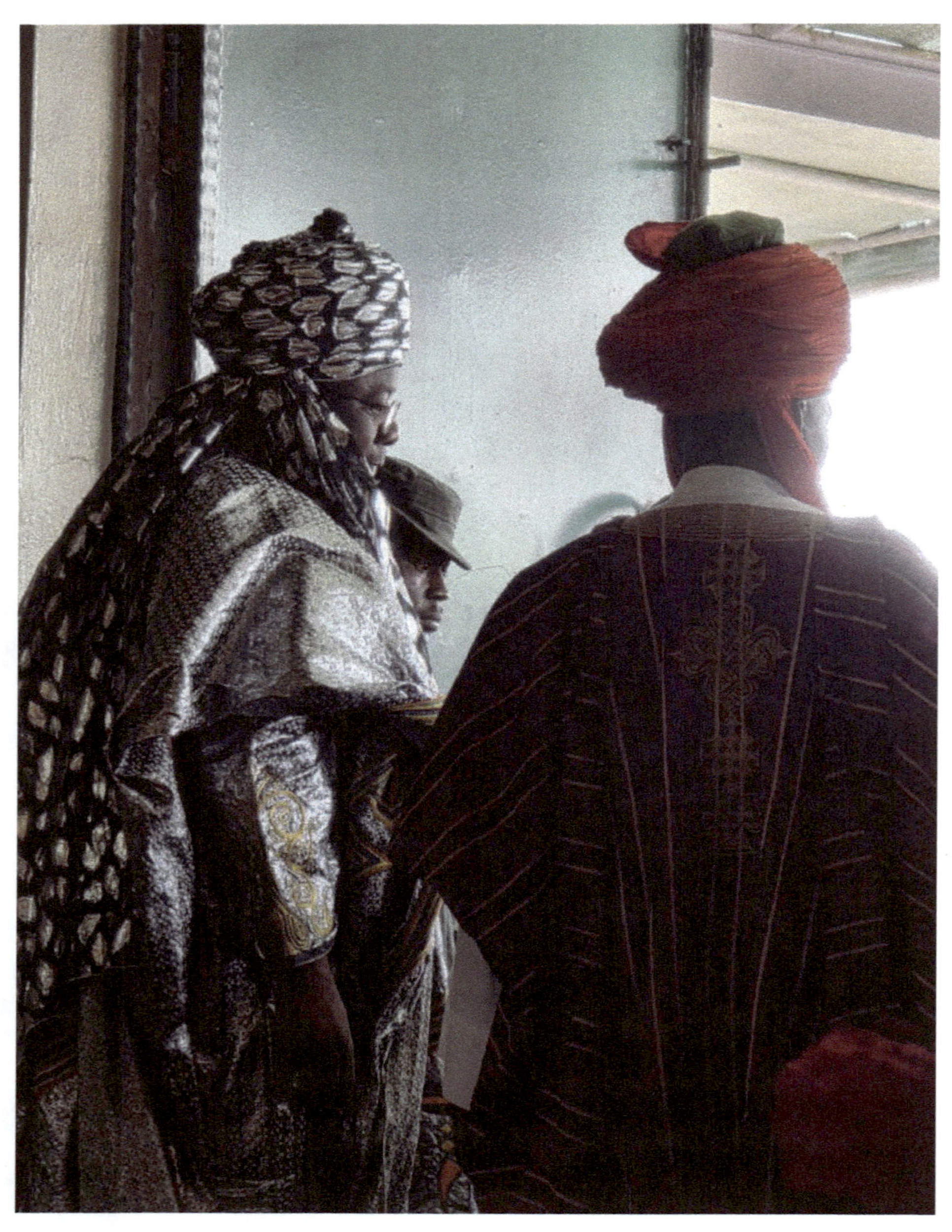

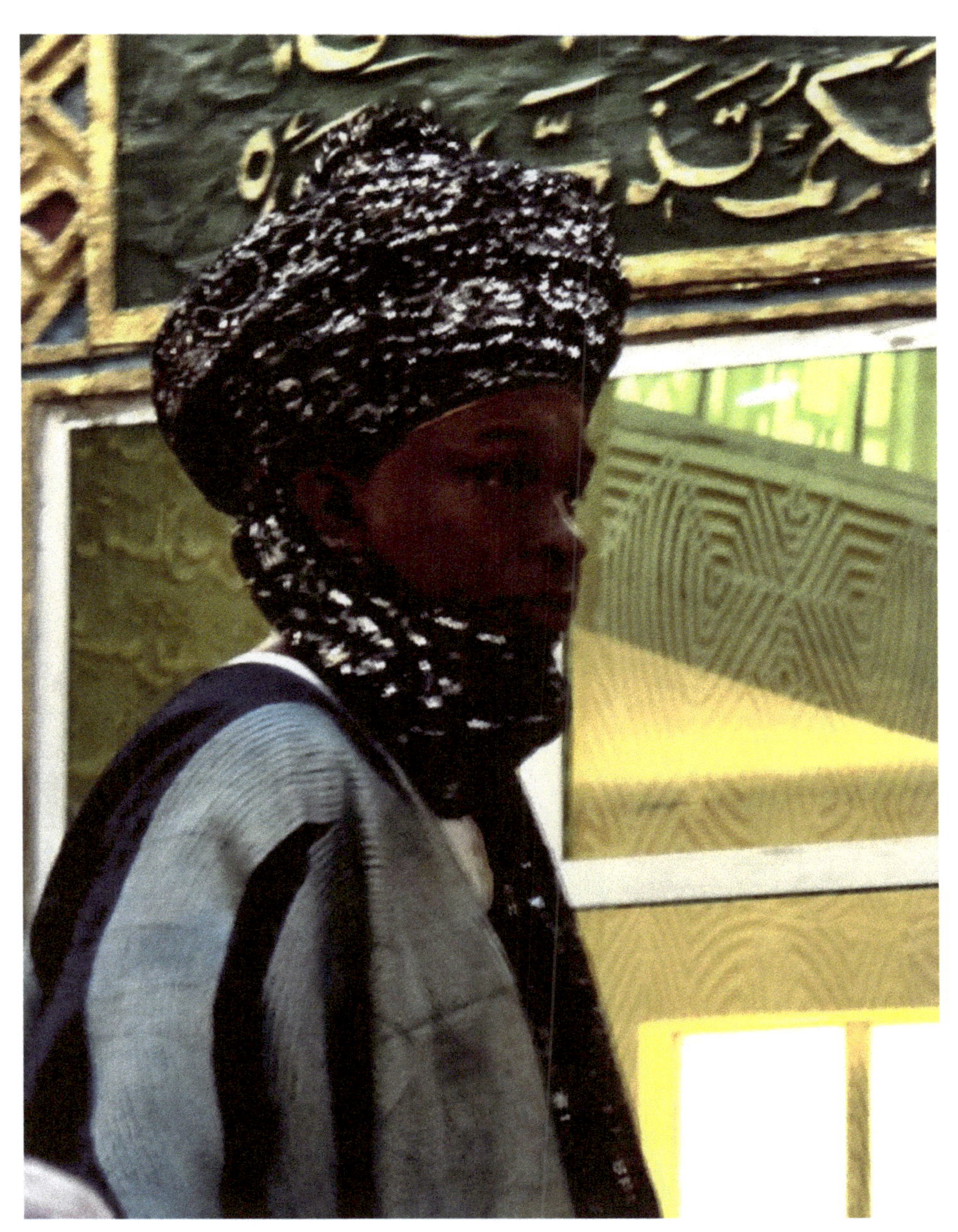

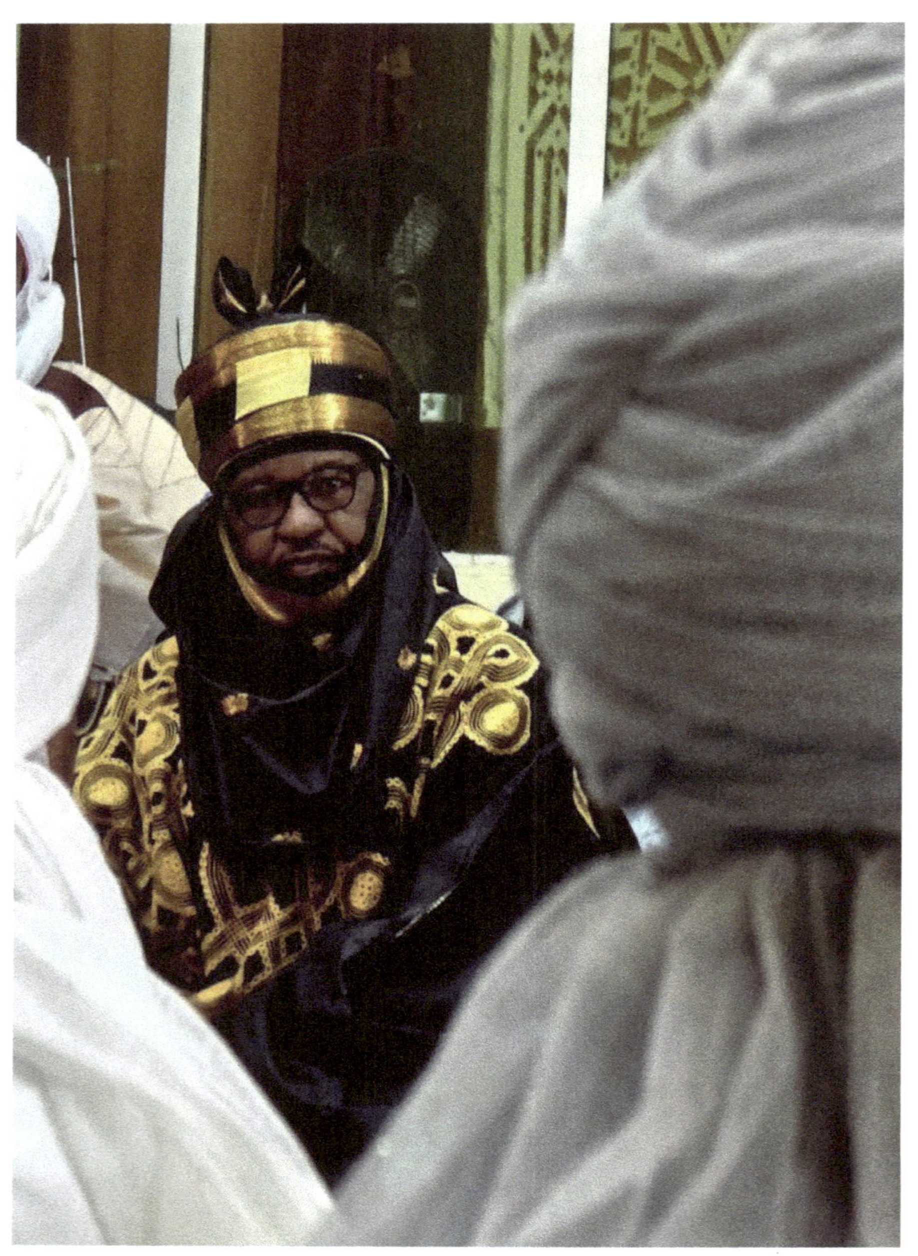

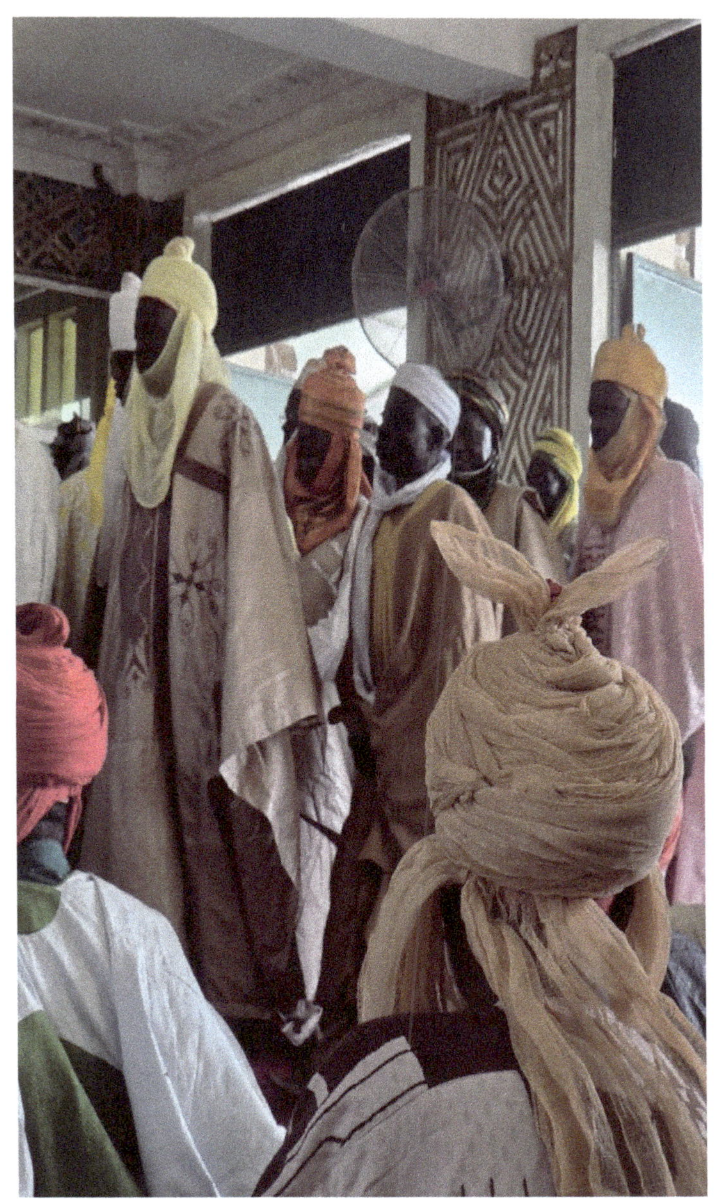

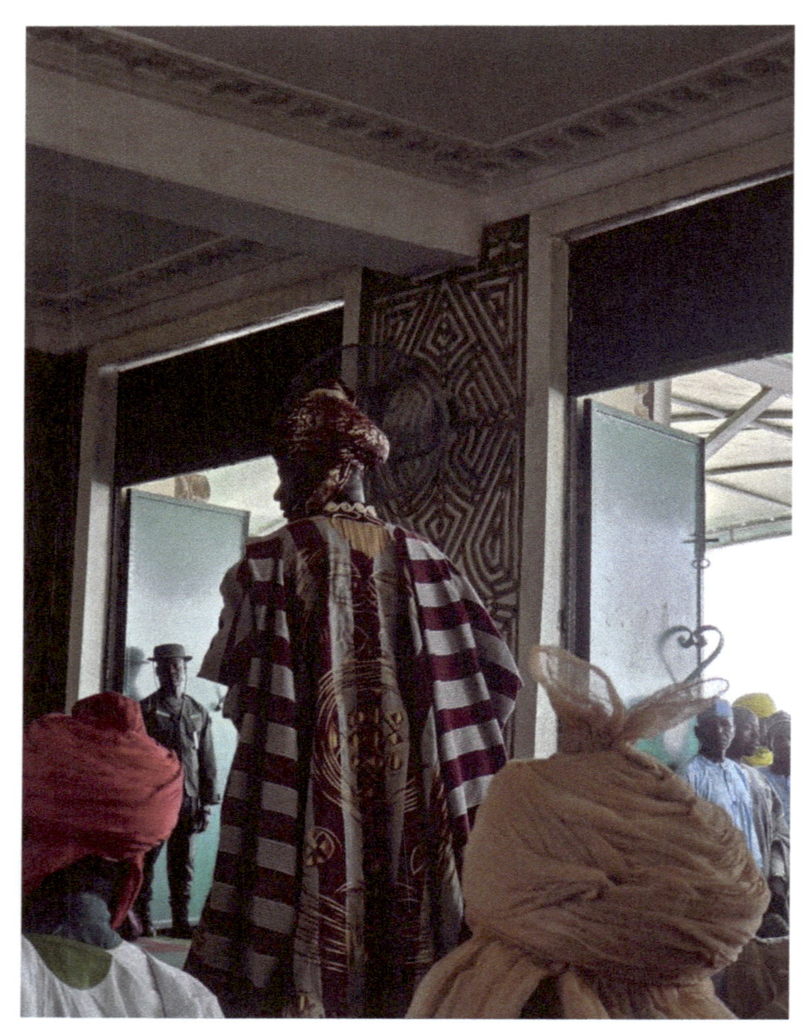

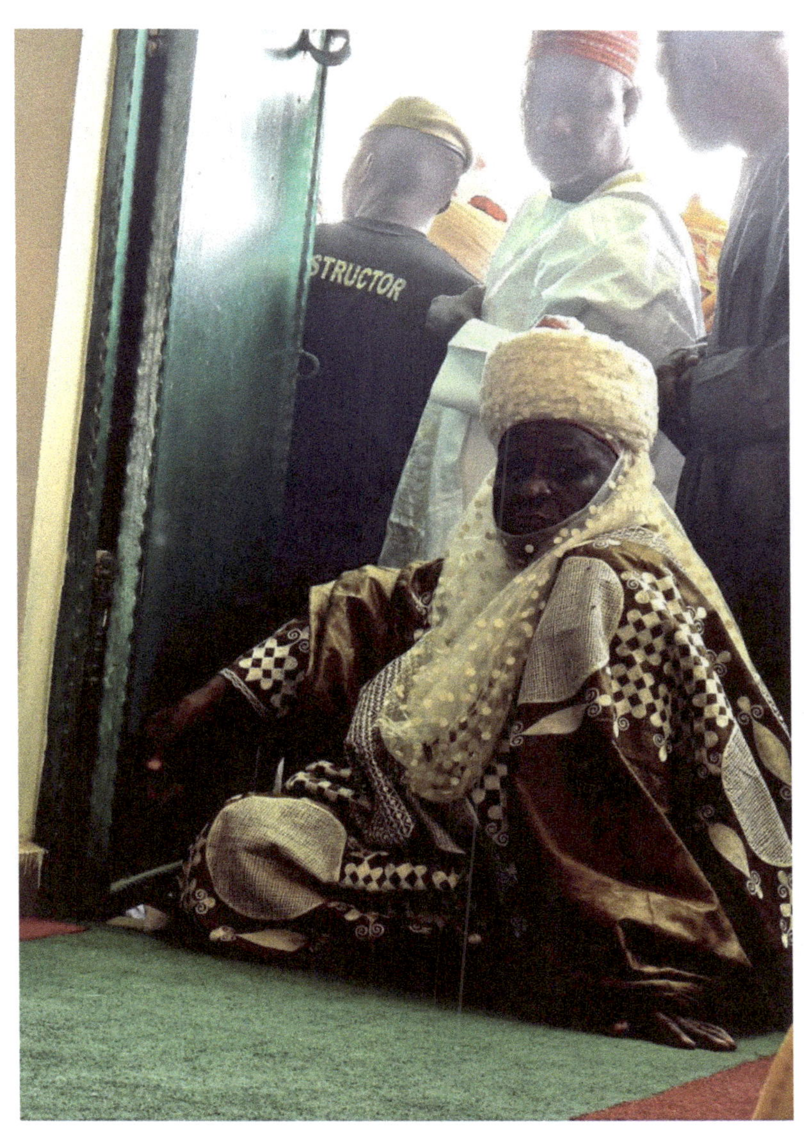

STRUCTOR

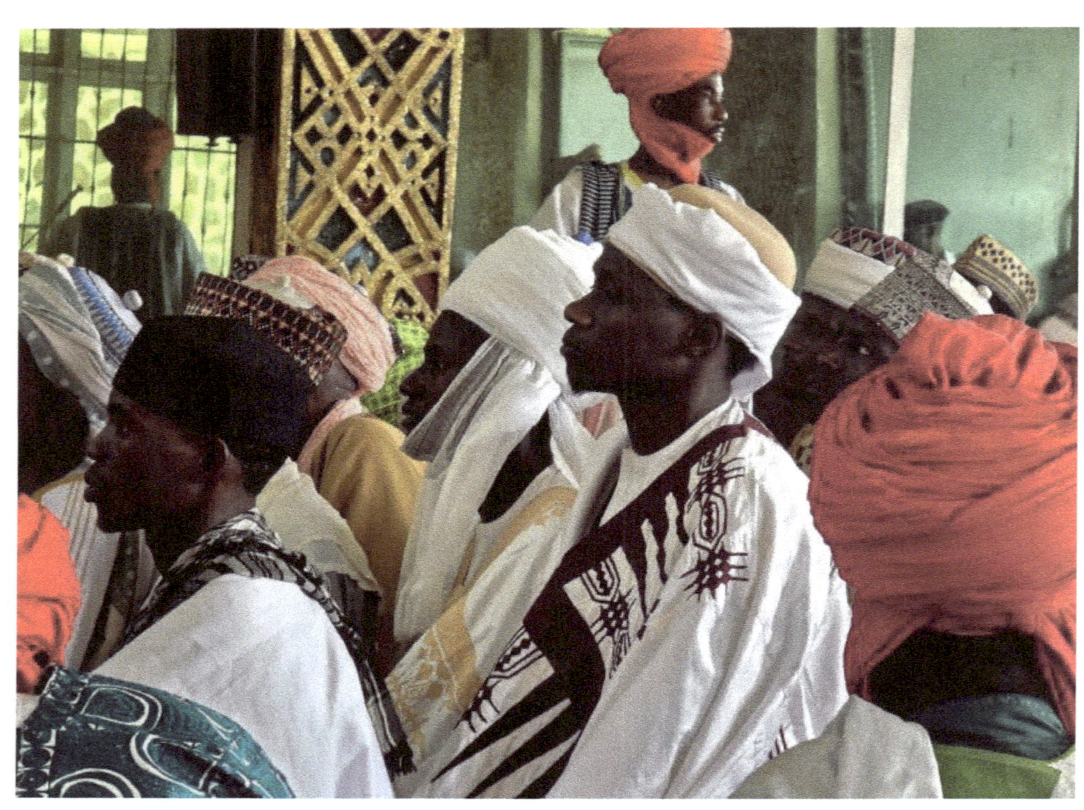

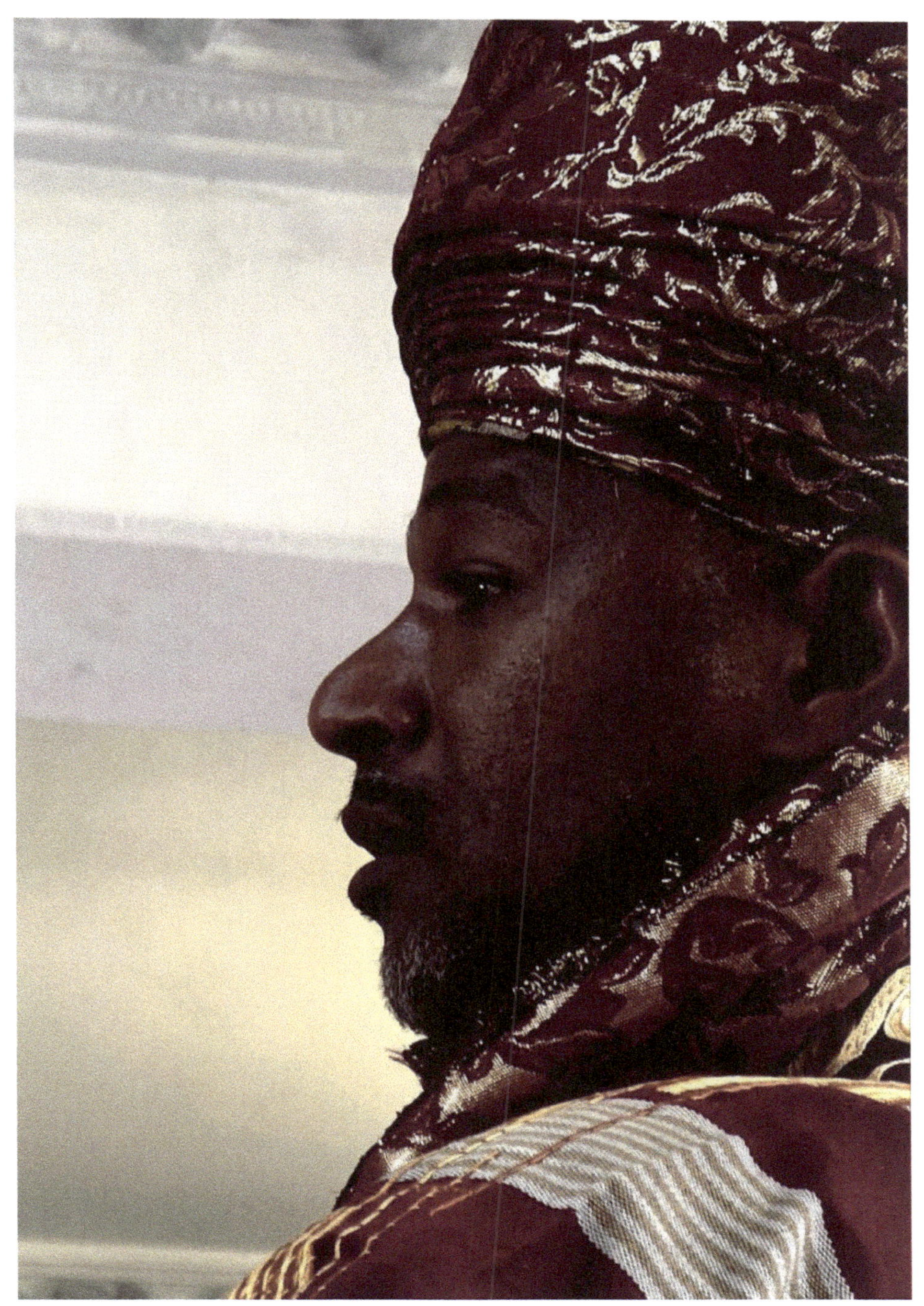

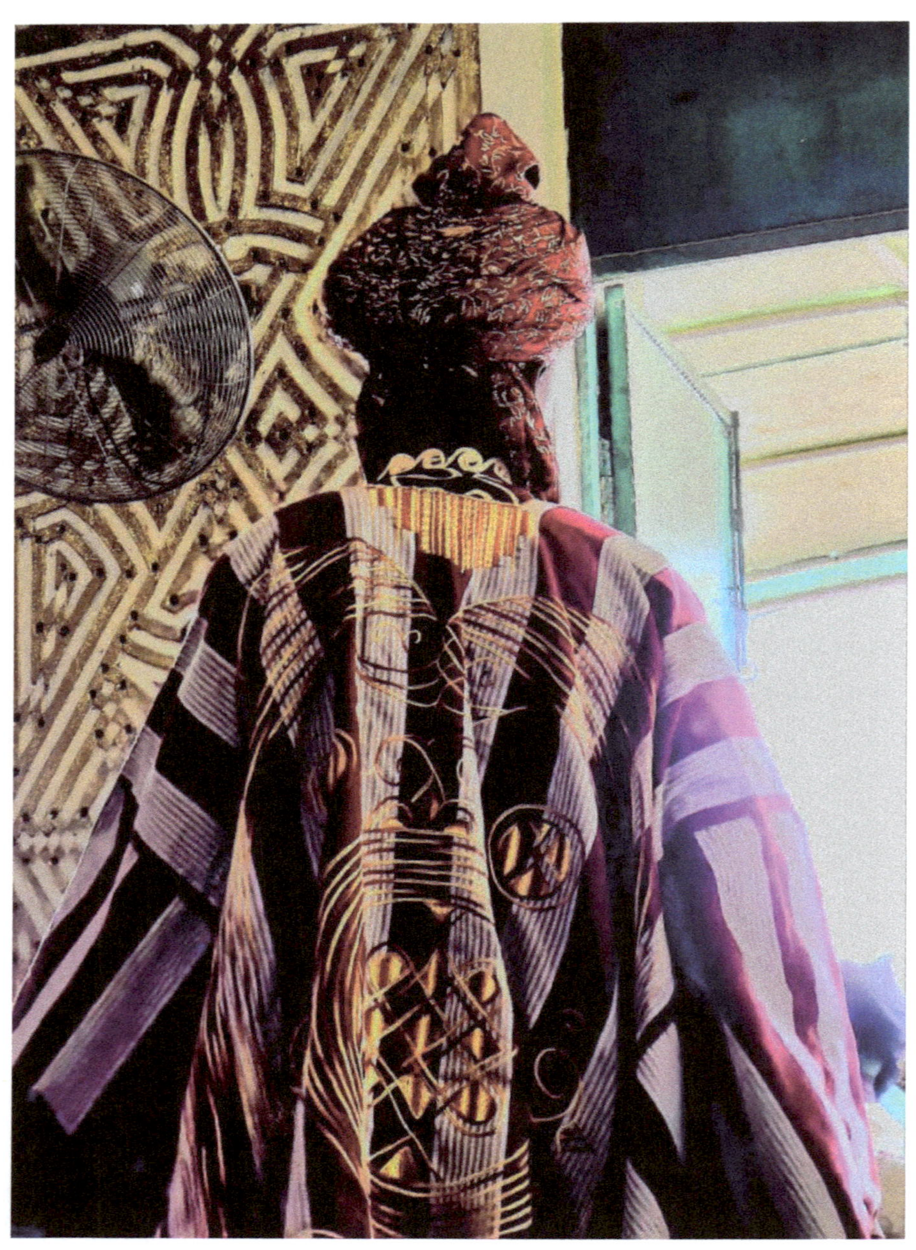

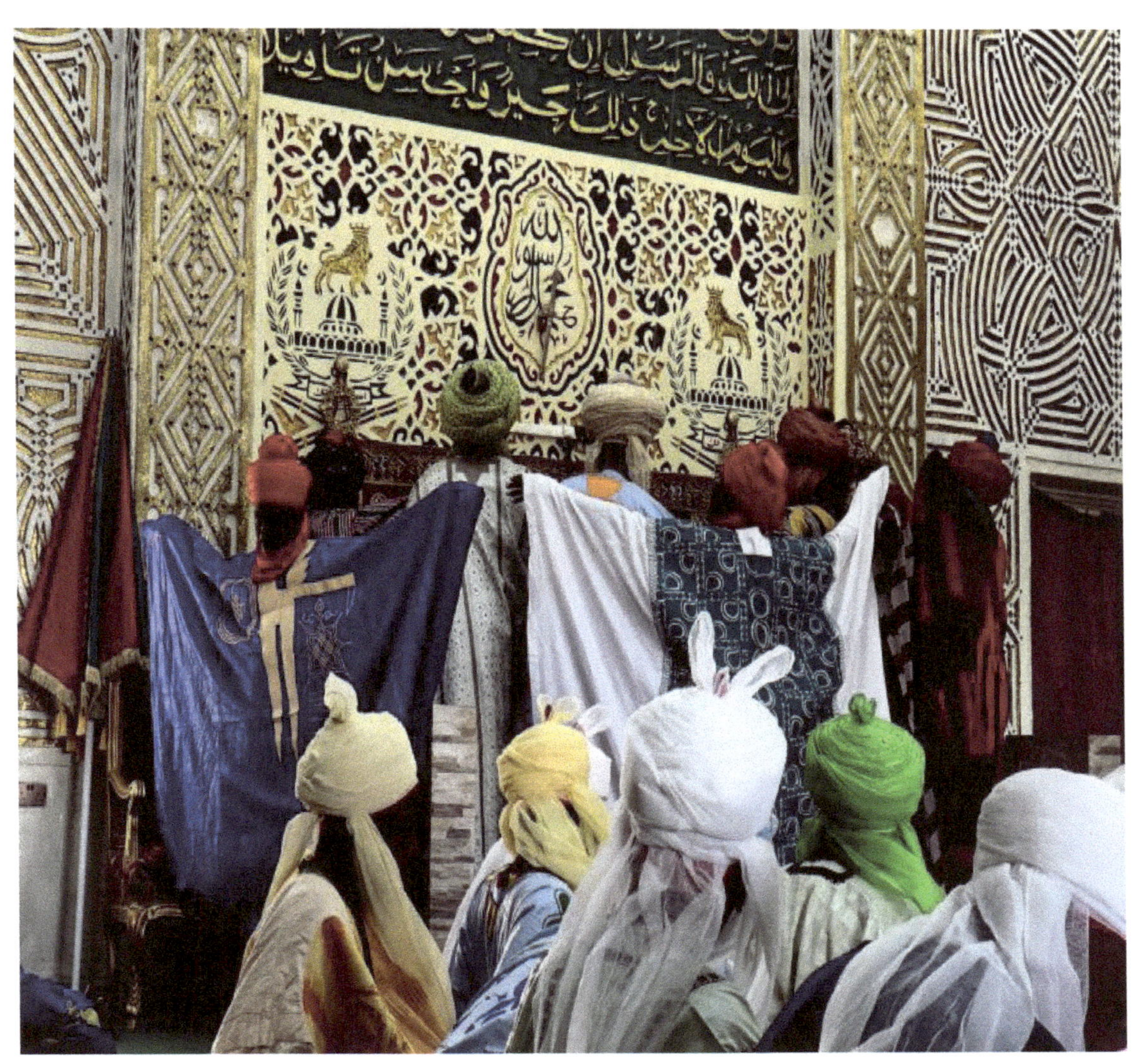

DAY 3

Hawan Nassarawa was held on the third day of Sallah. This traditional event is where the Emir pays homage to the resident of the Government House. In a lavish ceremony held on the grounds of the Government House, His Excellency Alhaji Abba Kabir Yusuf, Governor of Kano, received His Highness Muhammadu Sansui II, Emir of Kano.

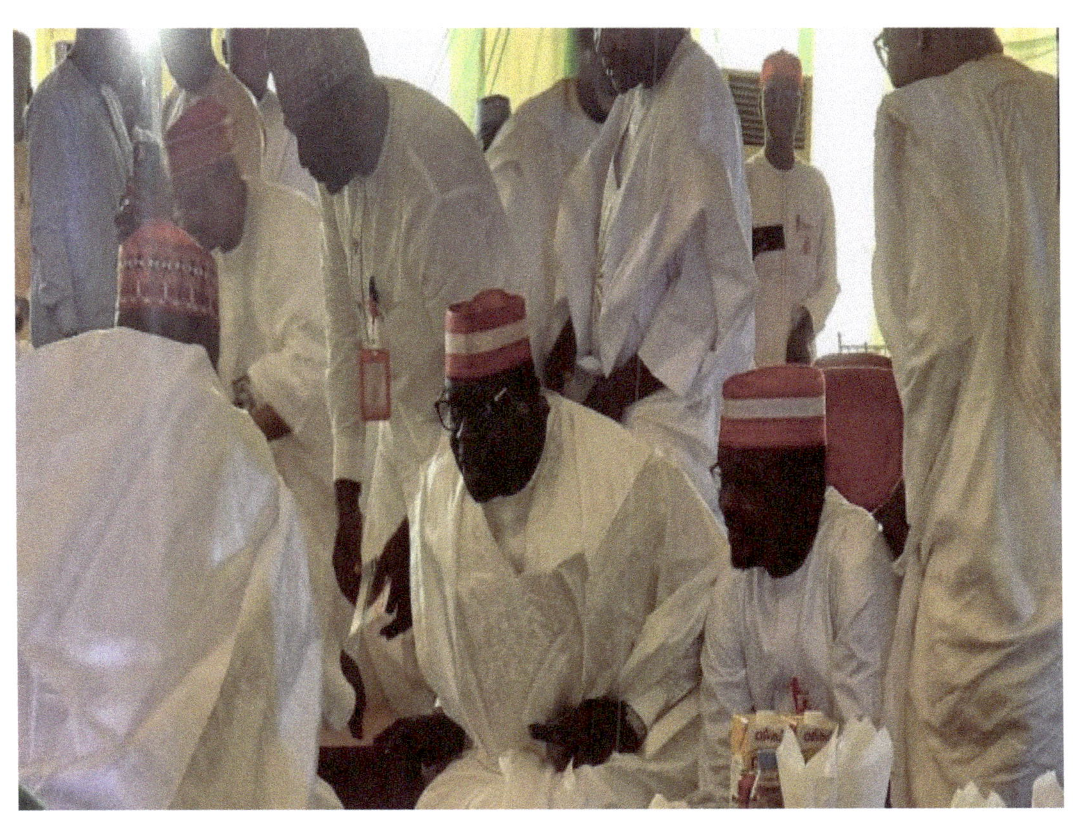

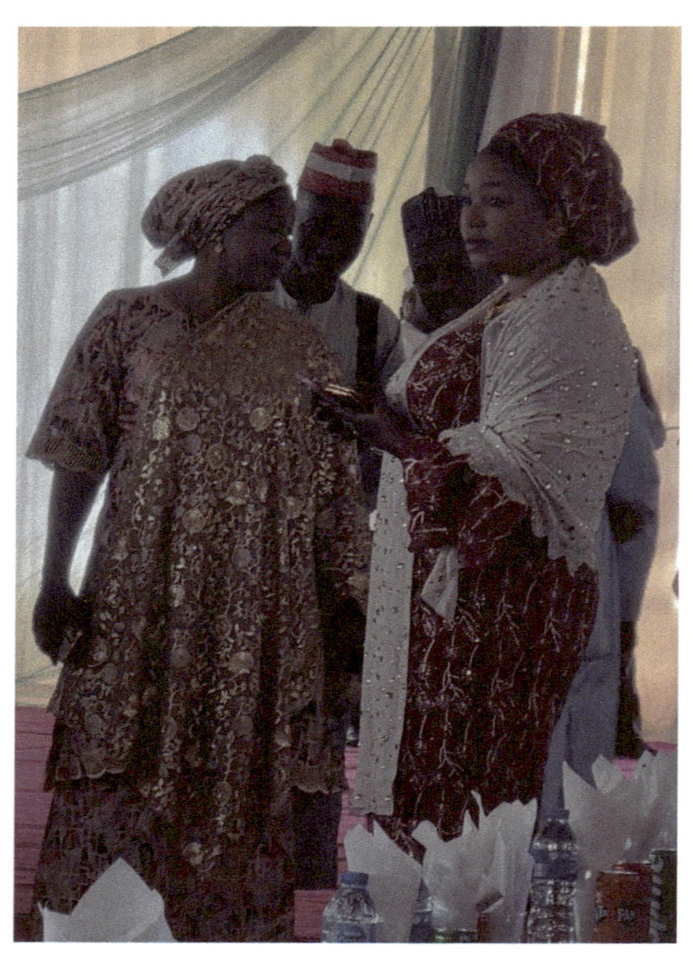

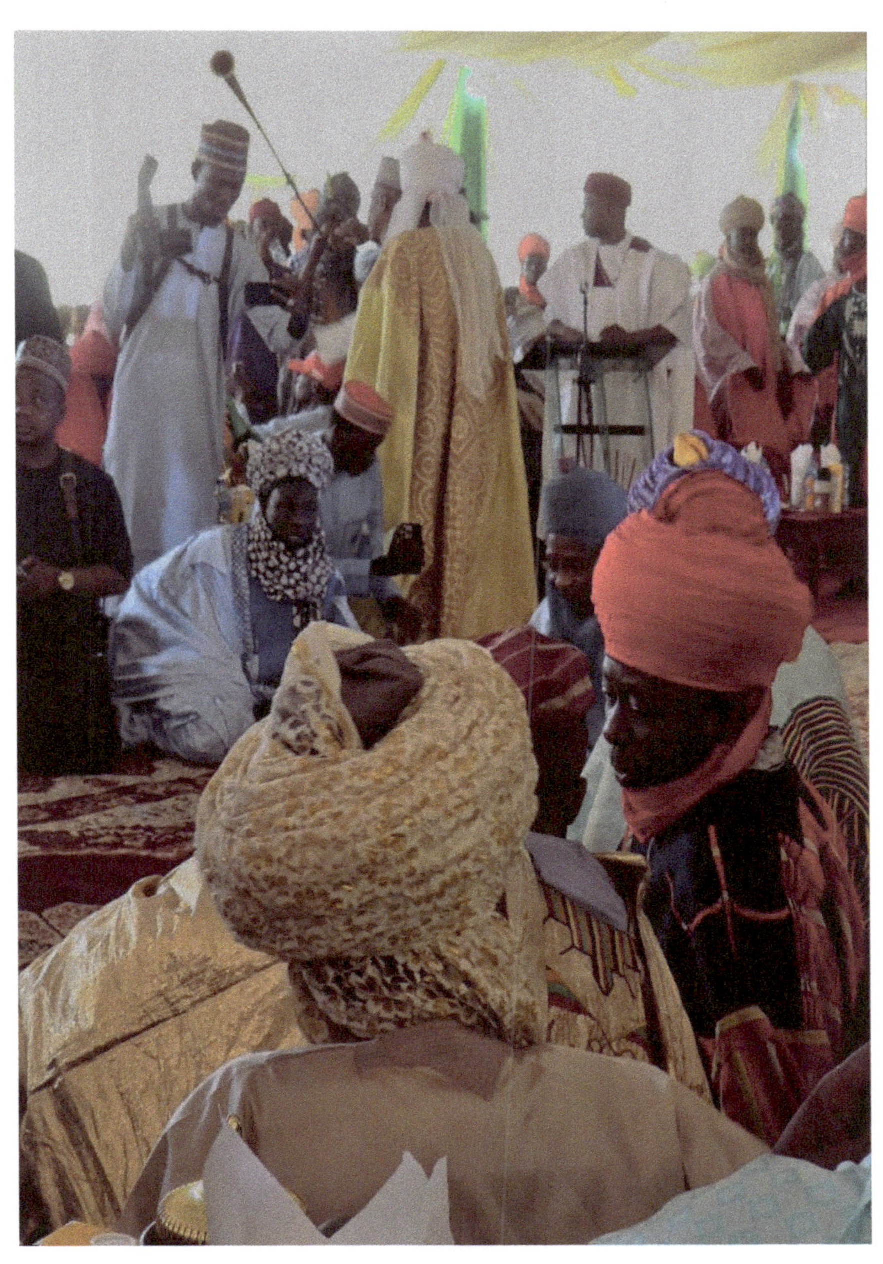

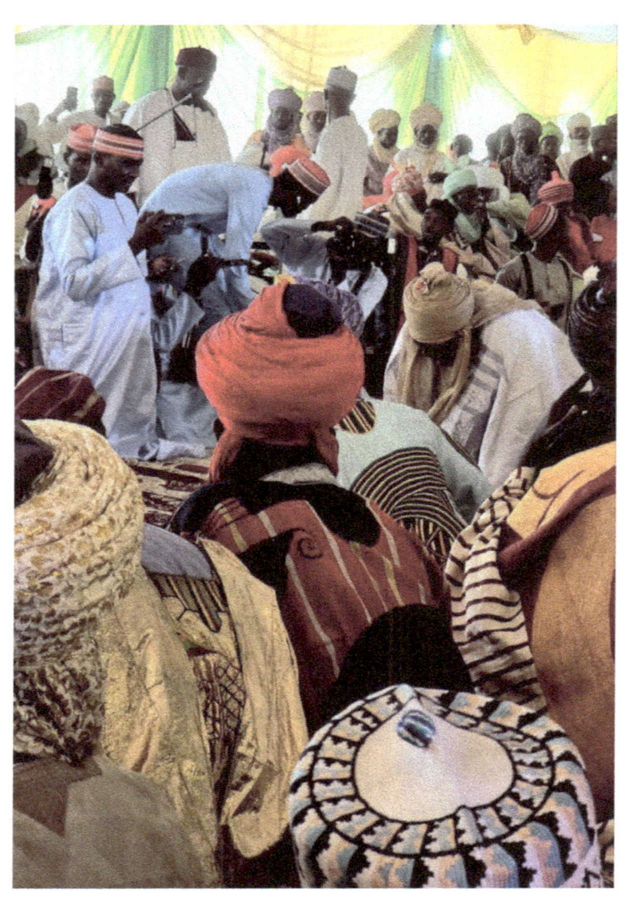

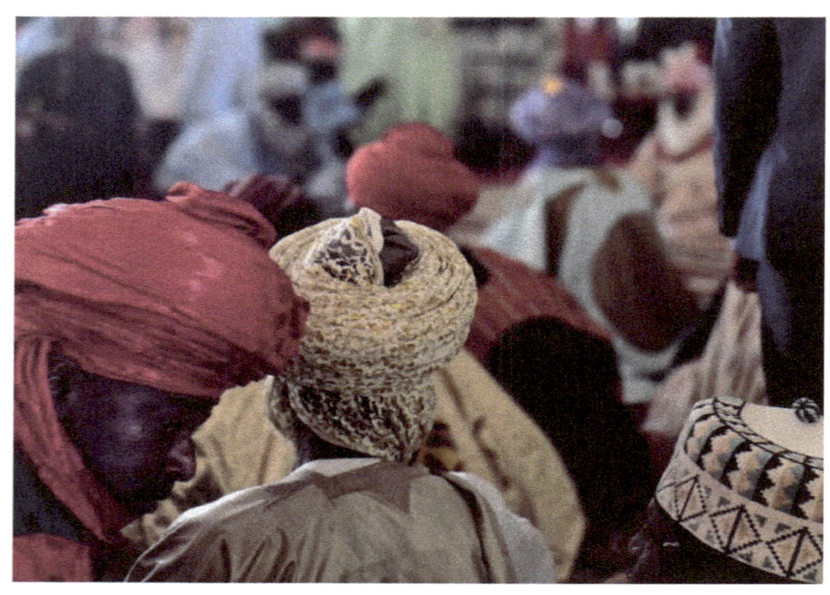

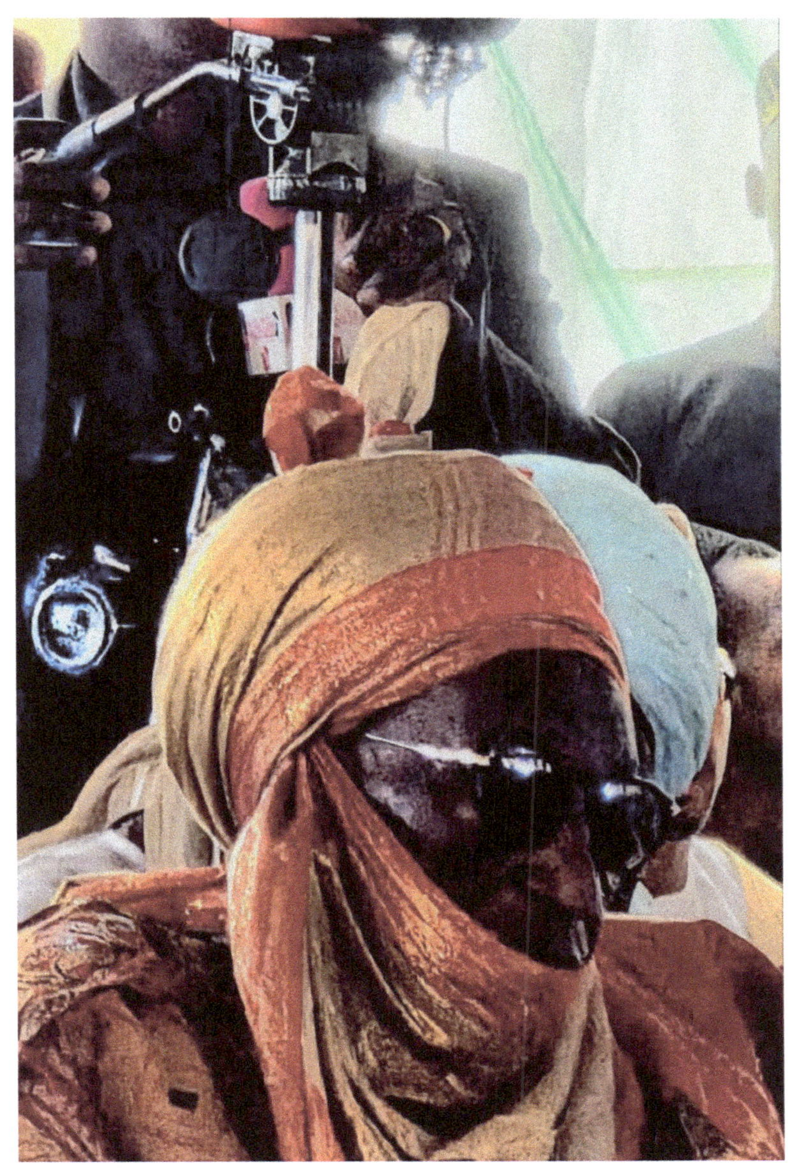

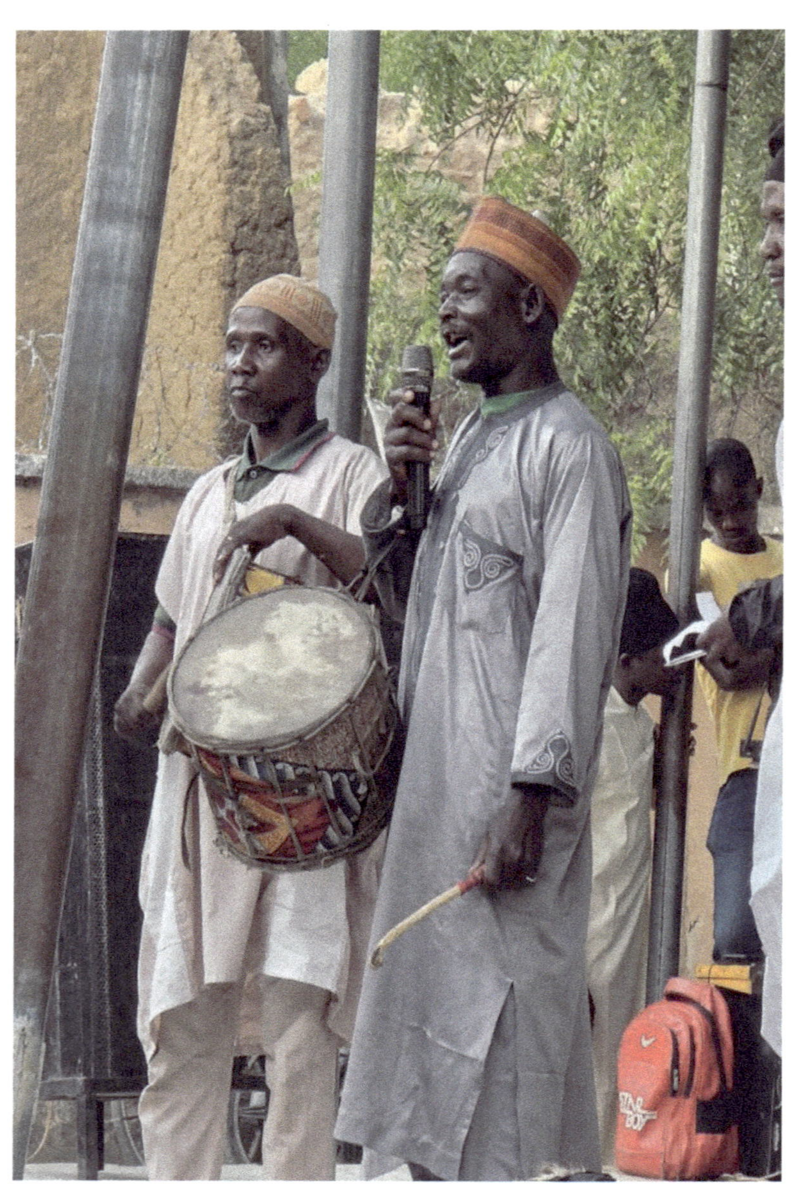

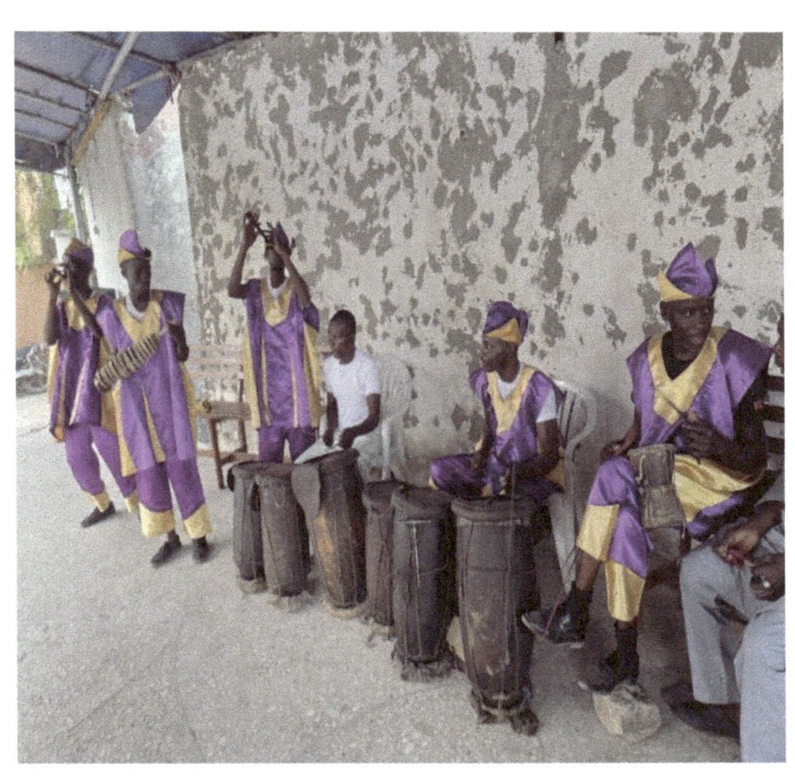

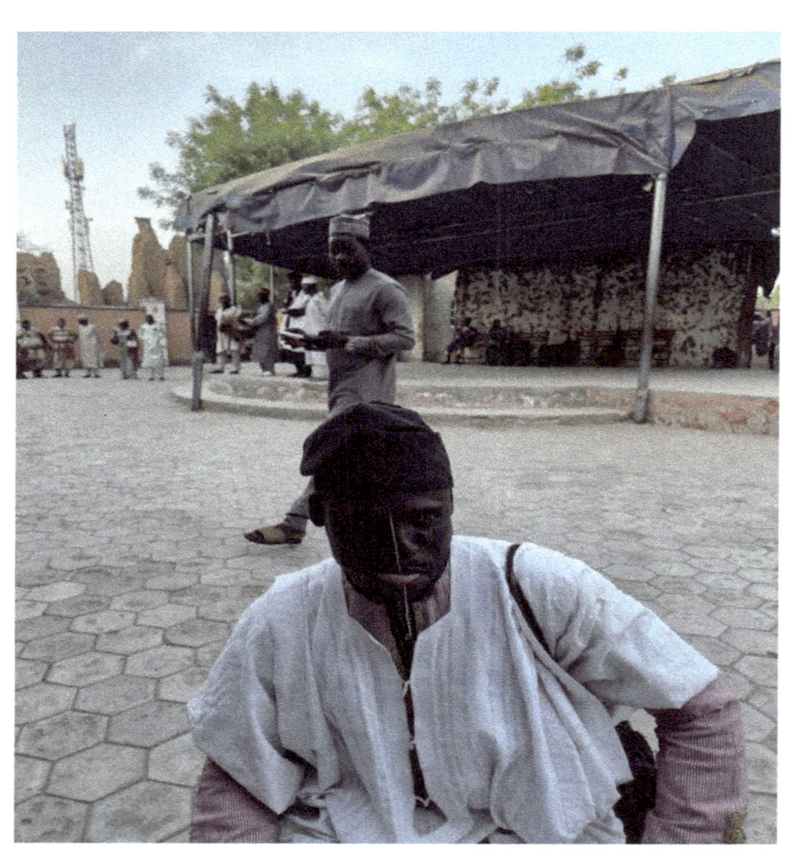

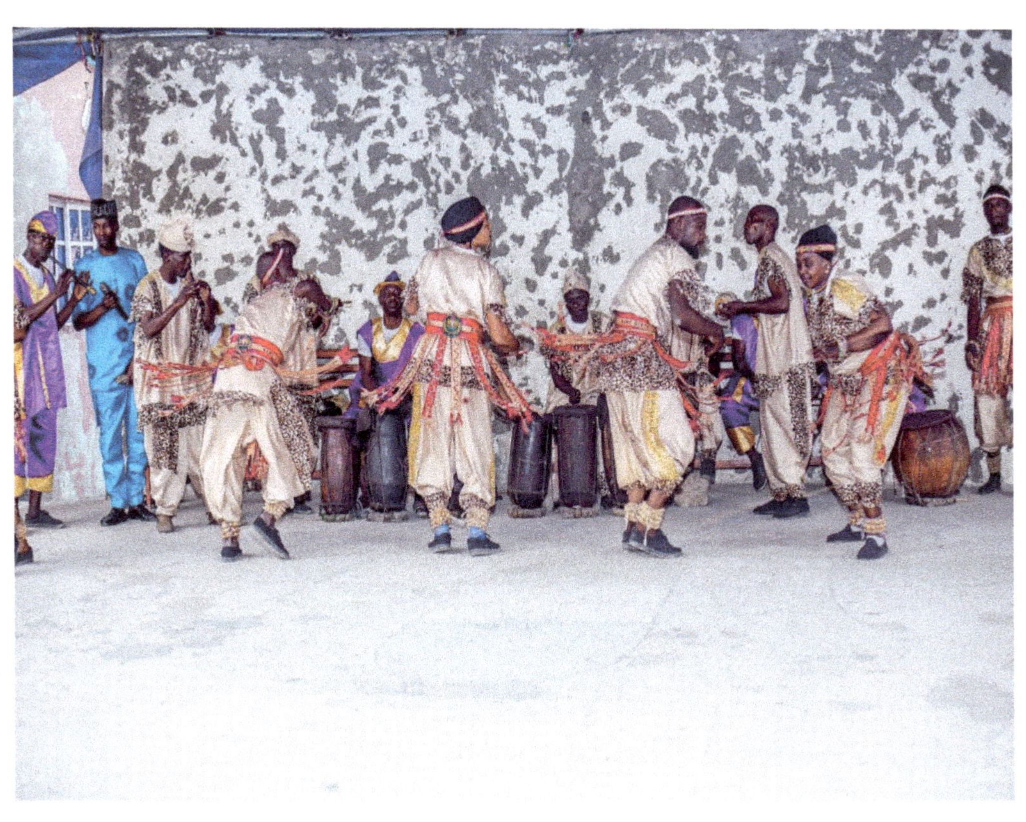

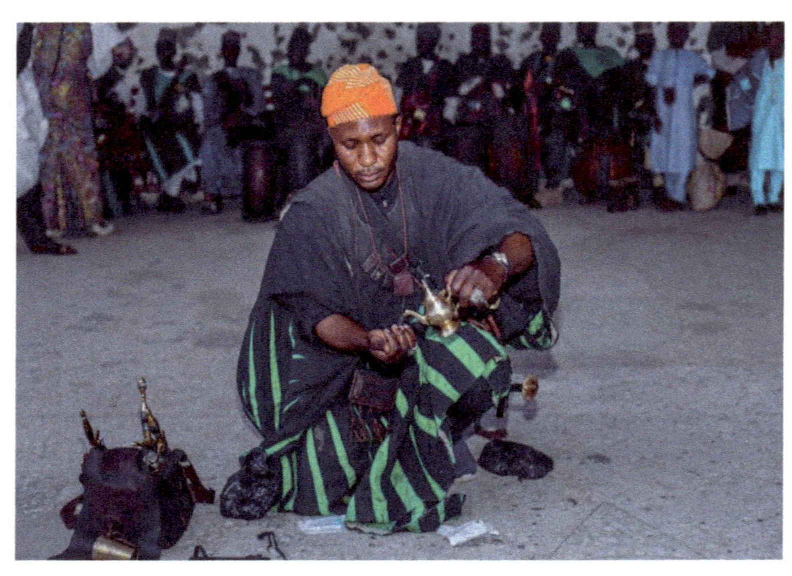

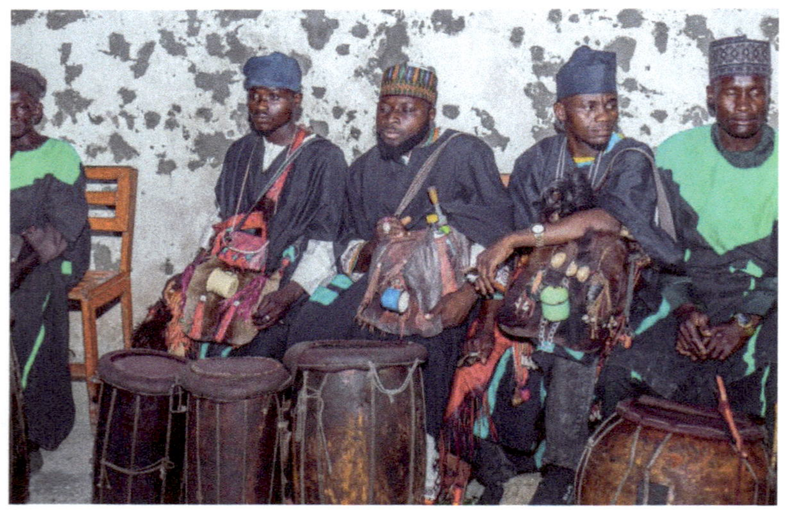

DAY 4

During my visit to the Kano State History and Culture Bureau, which is currently undergoing reconstruction, I was captivated by the old architecture.

The restoration uses traditional mud techniques to return the buildings to their original state. I had the privilege of examining many rare antique and historic documents, including a five-hundred-year-old Koran, reportedly transcribed by an individual who had committed the sacred text to memory.

Additionally, various antique artifacts are housed in a prominent building at the center of the grounds, many of which are set to be displayed in the upcoming museum.

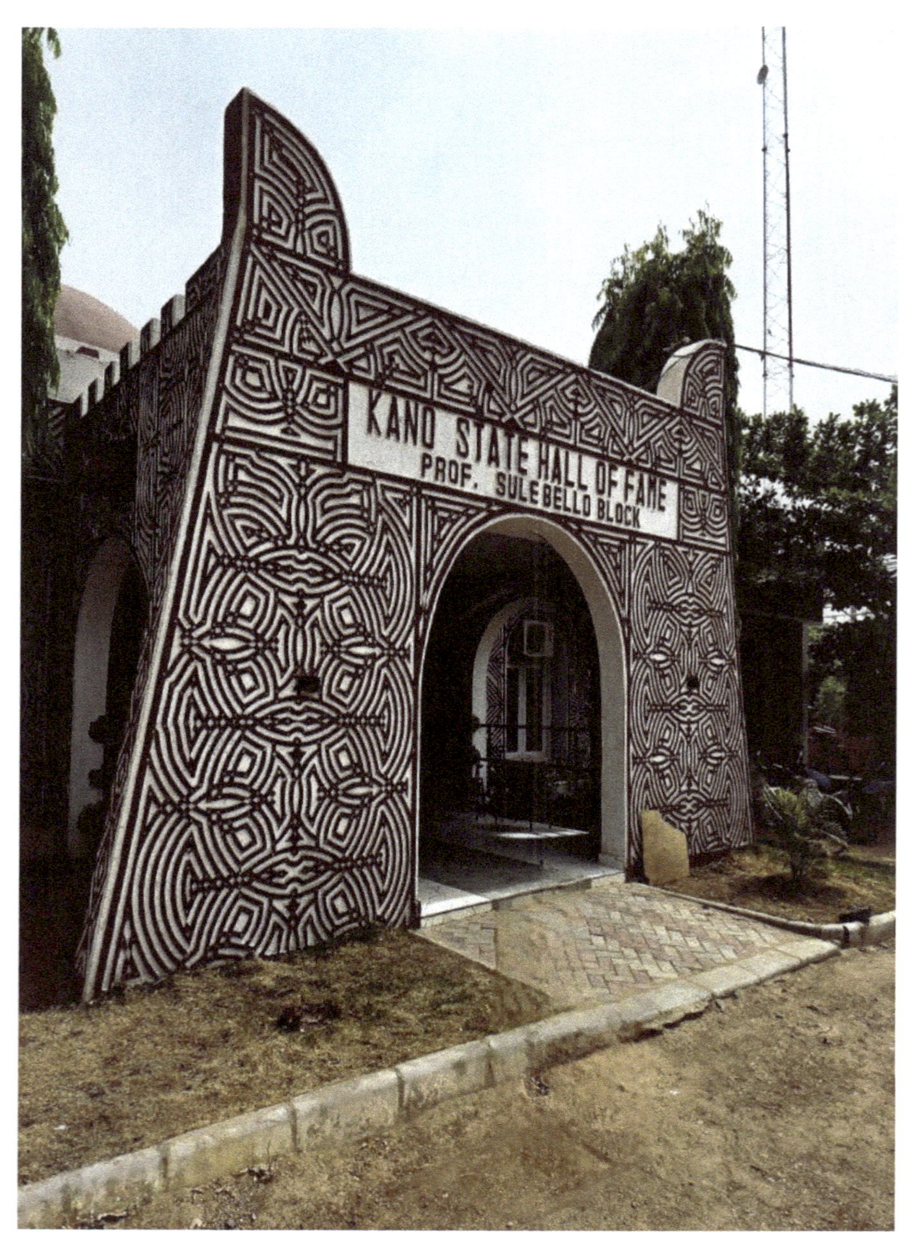
KANO STATE HALL OF FAME
PROF. SULE BELLO BLOCK

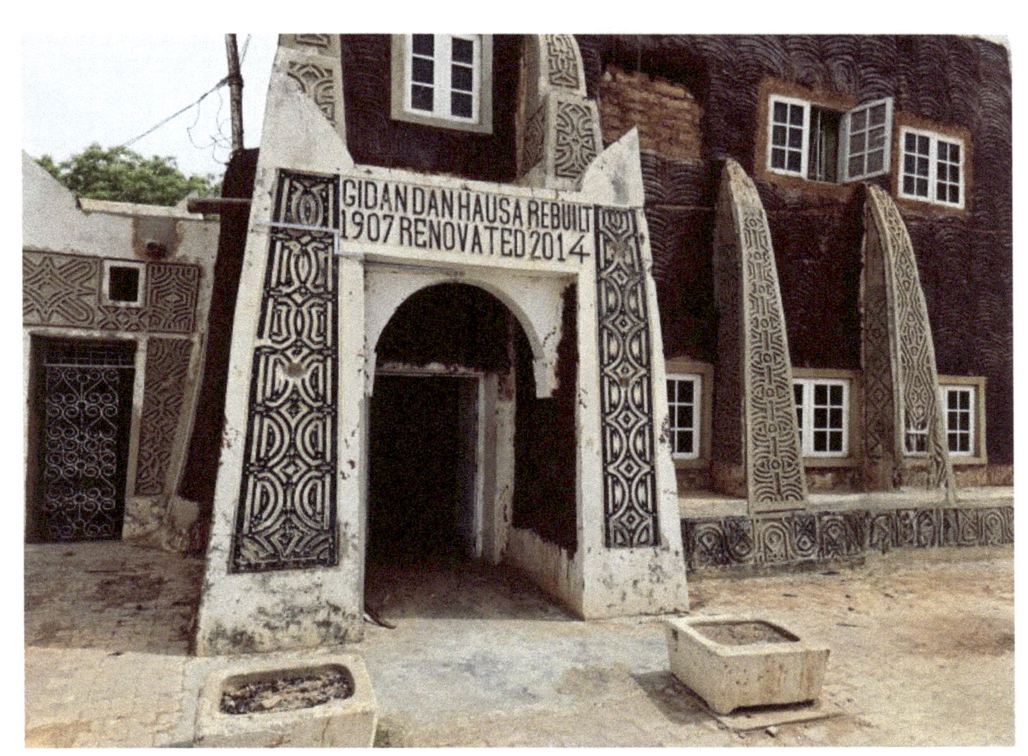

GIDAN DAN HAUSA REBUILT
1907 RENOVATED 2014

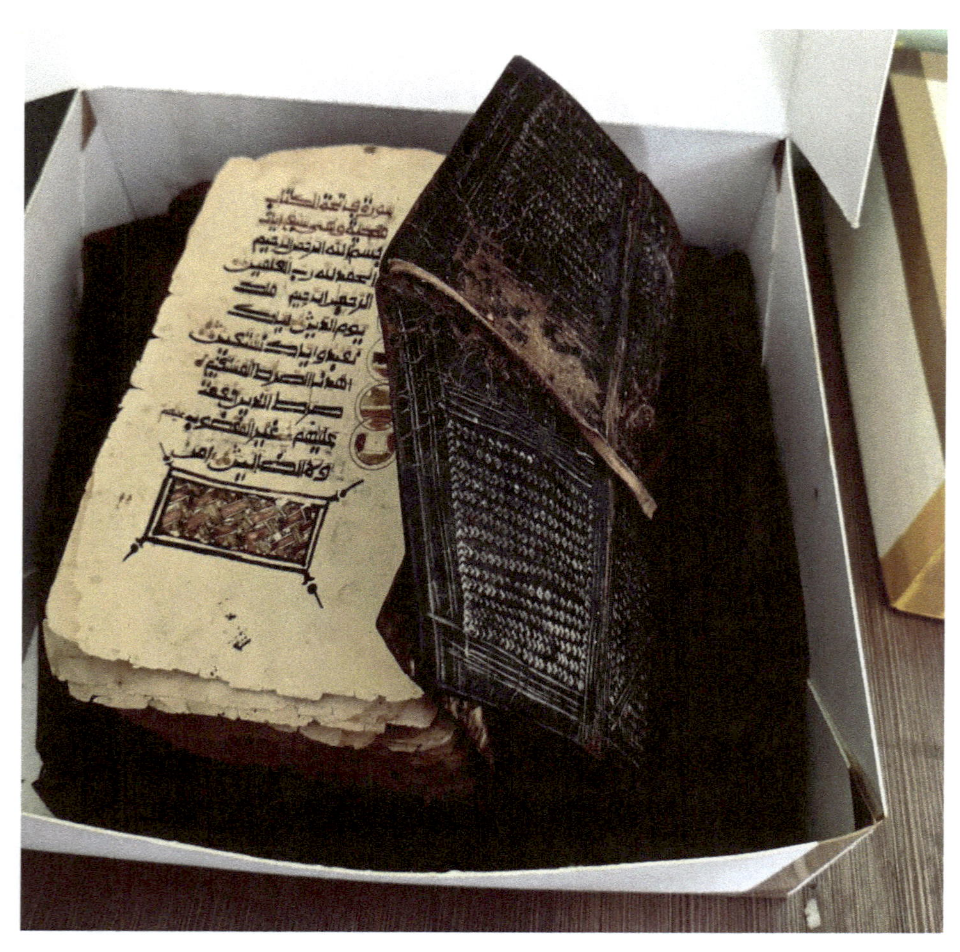

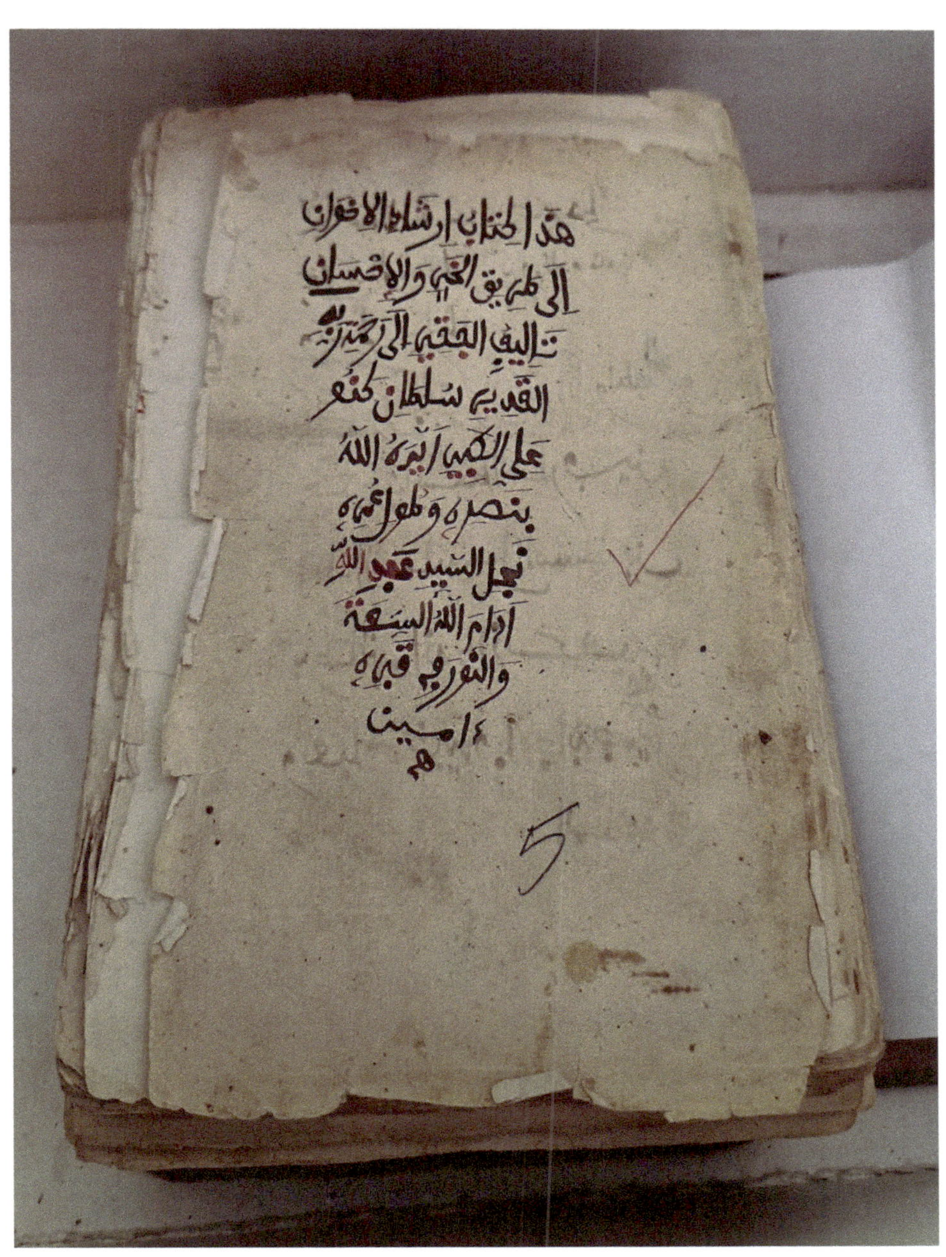

هذا الكتاب ارشاد الاخوان
الى طريق الغنى والاحسان
تأليف الحقير الى رحمته
القديم سلطان كنو
على الكبير ايده الله
بنصره وطول عمره
نجل السيد عبد الله
ادام الله السعة
والنور في قبره
امين
٥

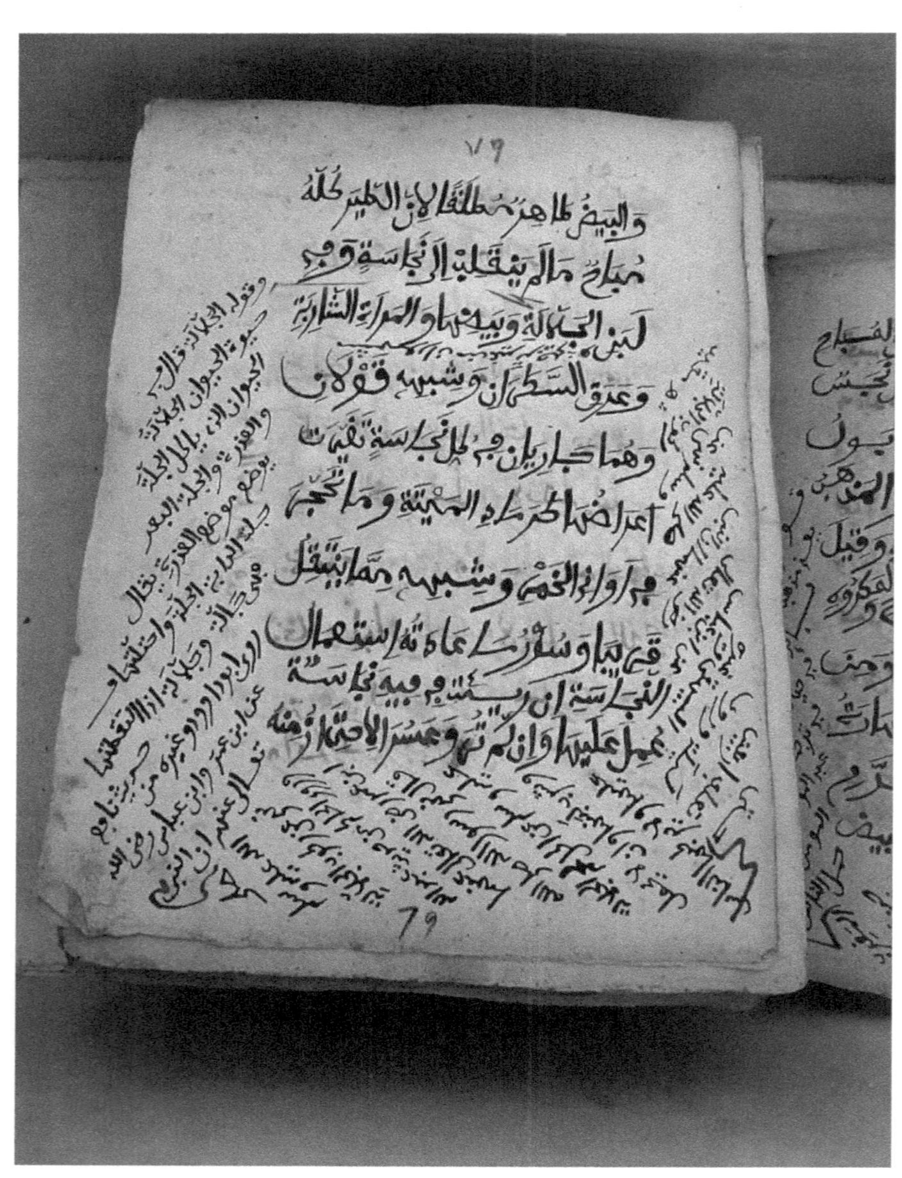

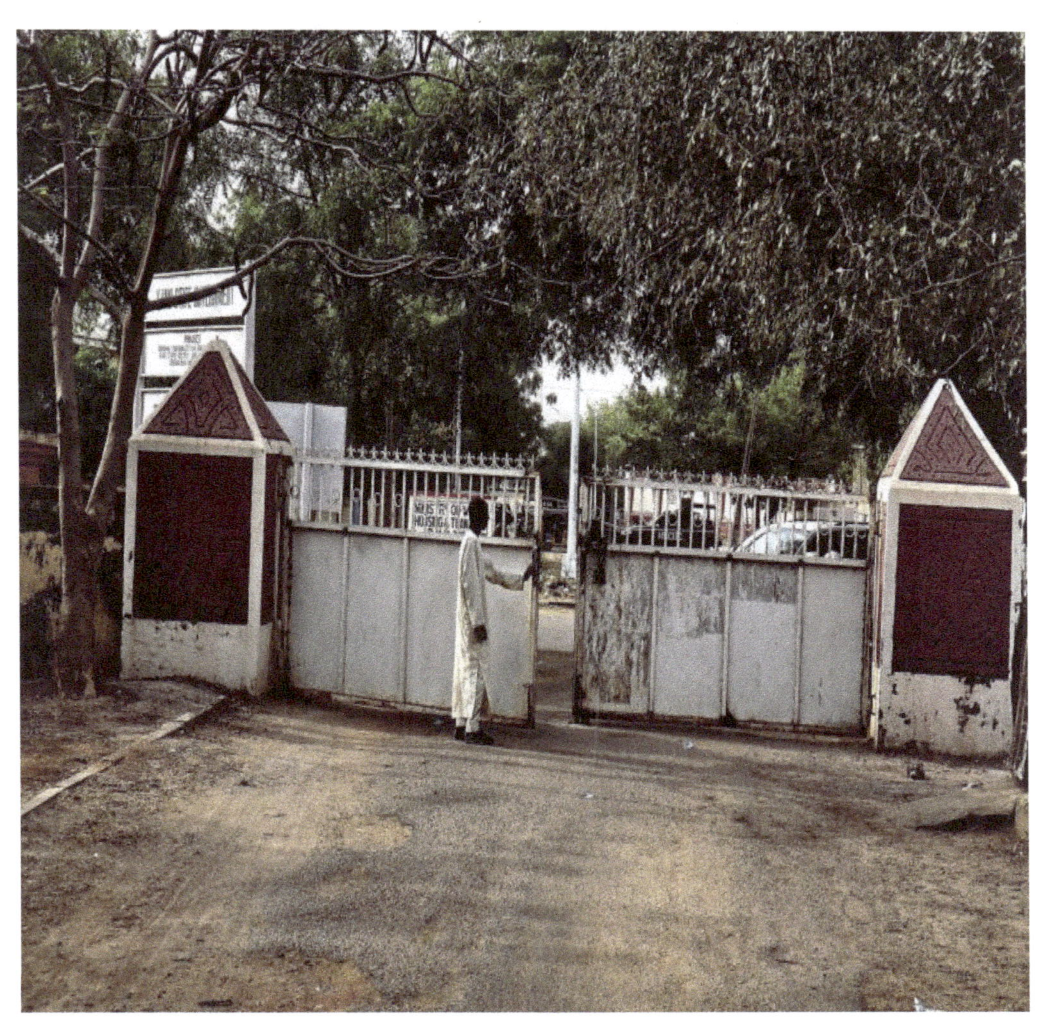

DAY 5

On this day, I explored the city, it was captivating to observe farm animals tethered outside homes and along residential streets. In certain areas, animals roamed freely; it was common to encounter chickens, goats, and other livestock on the roads. I was amazed by the variety of farm animals roaming the streets and horses stabled near the Queen Mother's residence and the Emir's Palace. I ended the day with a visit to the Kofar Mata Dye Pits. Established in 1498, the Kofar Mata Dye Pits are recognized as the oldest in Africa and the last of their kind.

The indigo-dyed cotton gained fame during the Trans-Saharan Trade Period. To this day, the dyers steadfastly refuse to utilize artificial dyes; their commitment to honoring their medieval dyeing process renders each item produced unique. The dye master displayed the materials employed to create a range of indigo-colored garments, from deep blue-black to a very light blue. I was fascinated to learn that the dyeing technique known as tie-dye, which became popular in youth culture in the West during the 1960s and 1970s, originated in the Kofar Mata Dye Pits centuries ago.

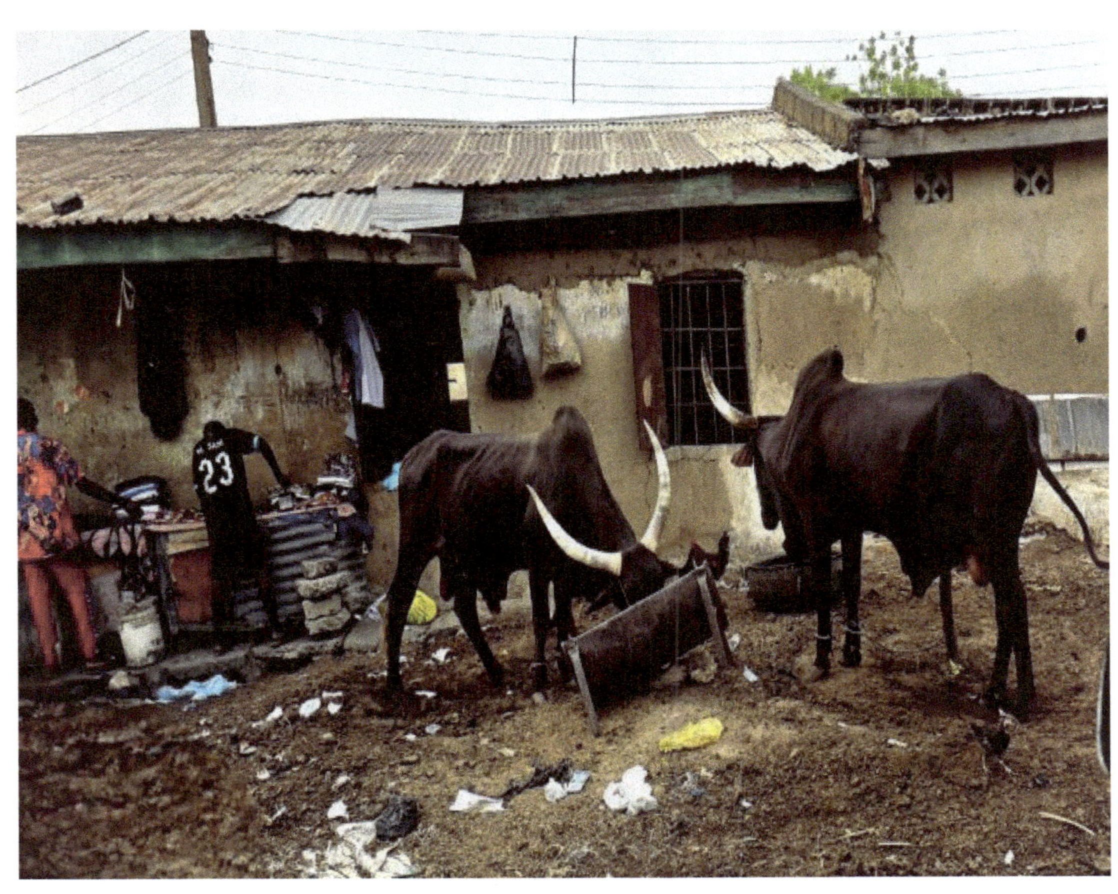

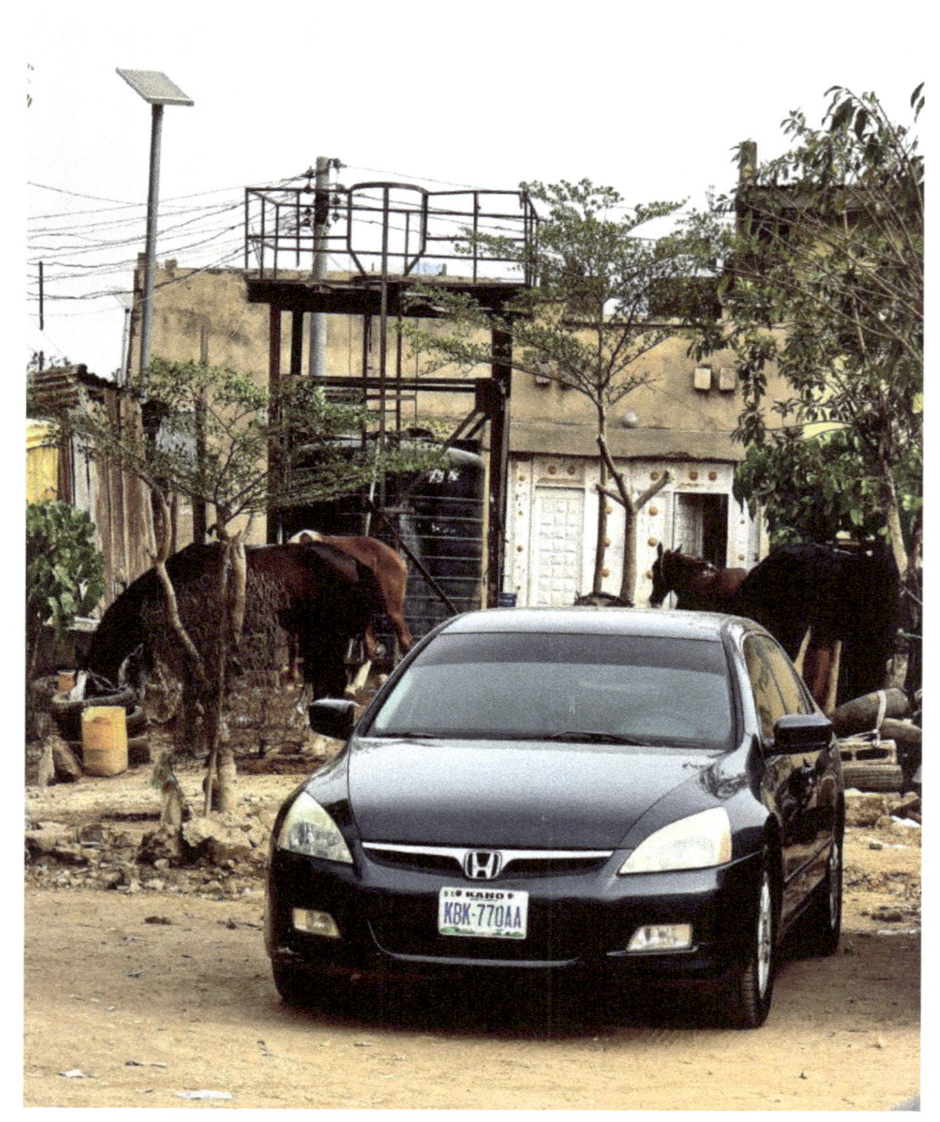

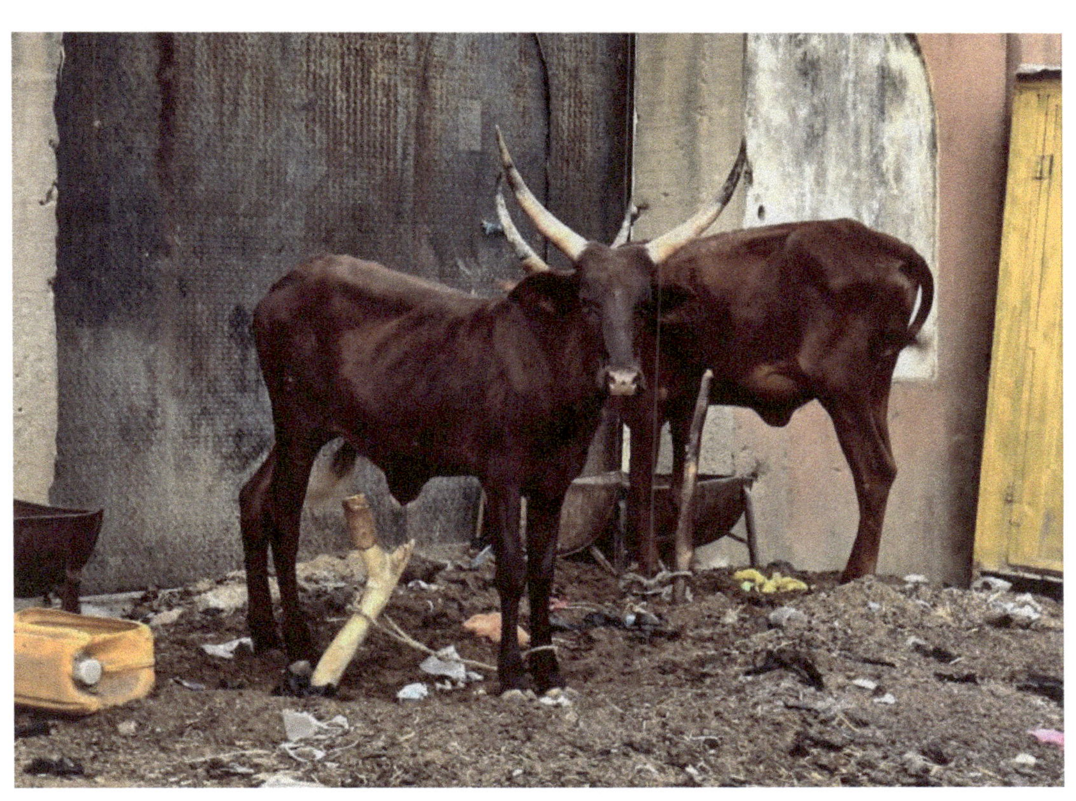

Kofar Mata Dye Pits

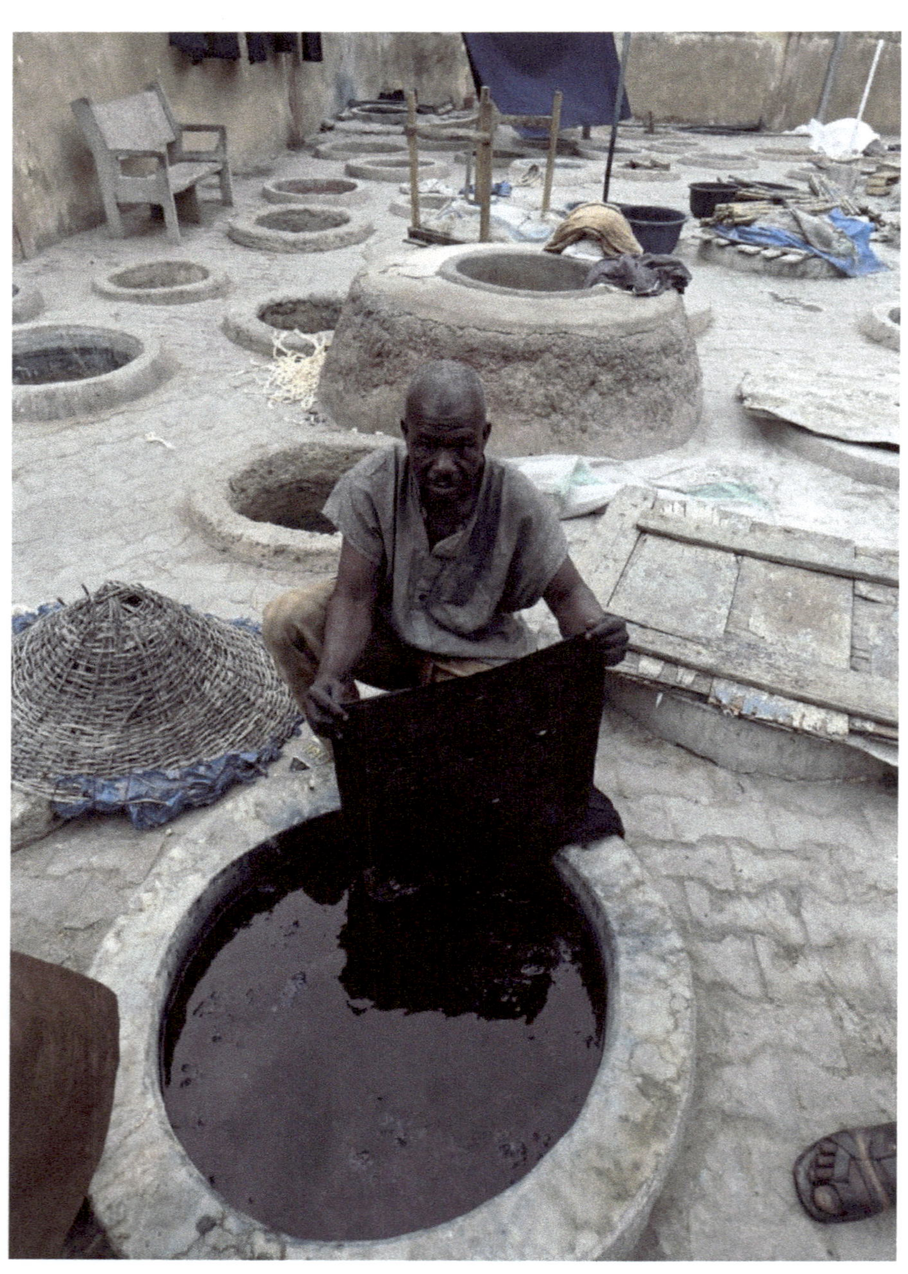

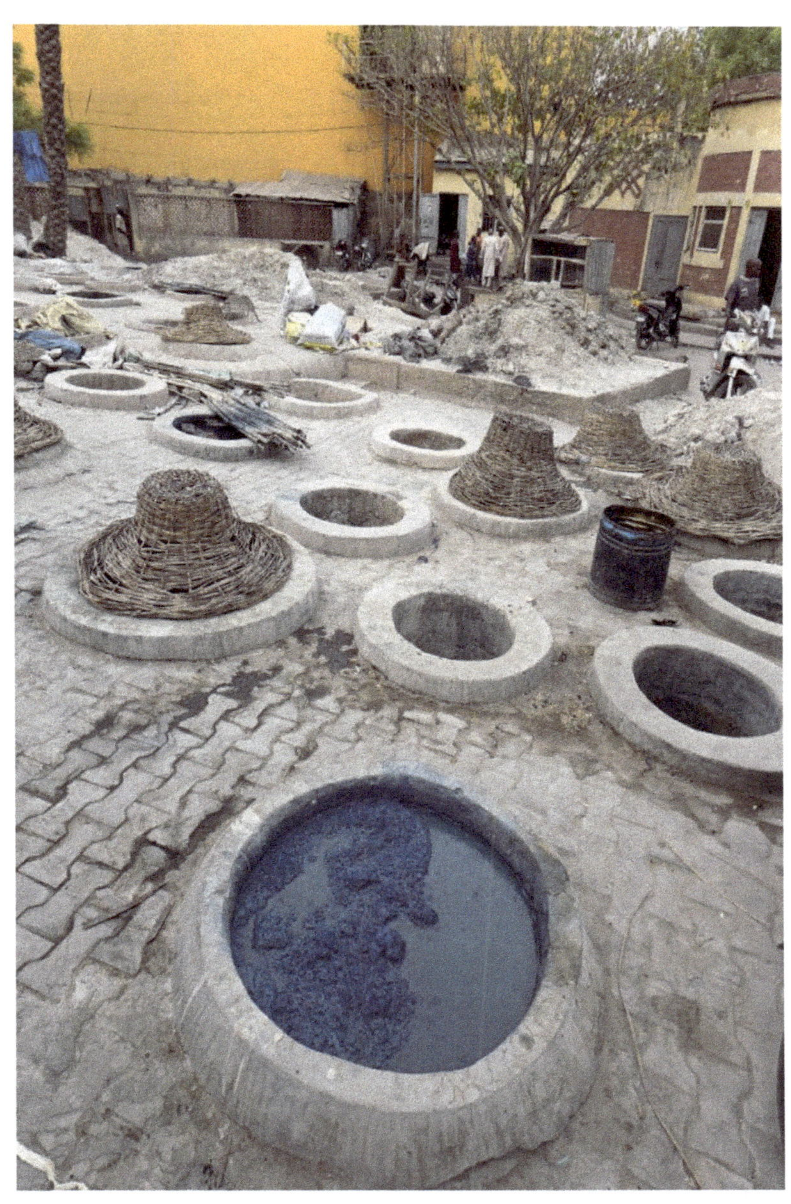

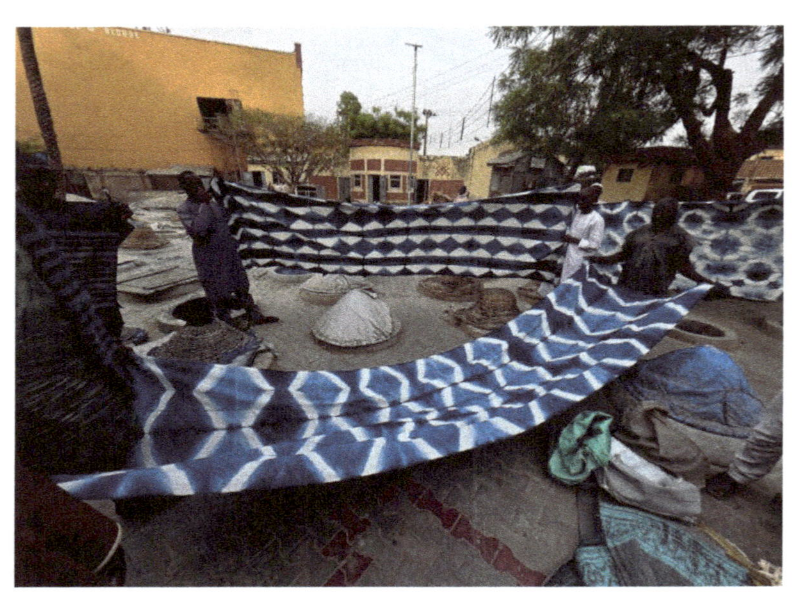

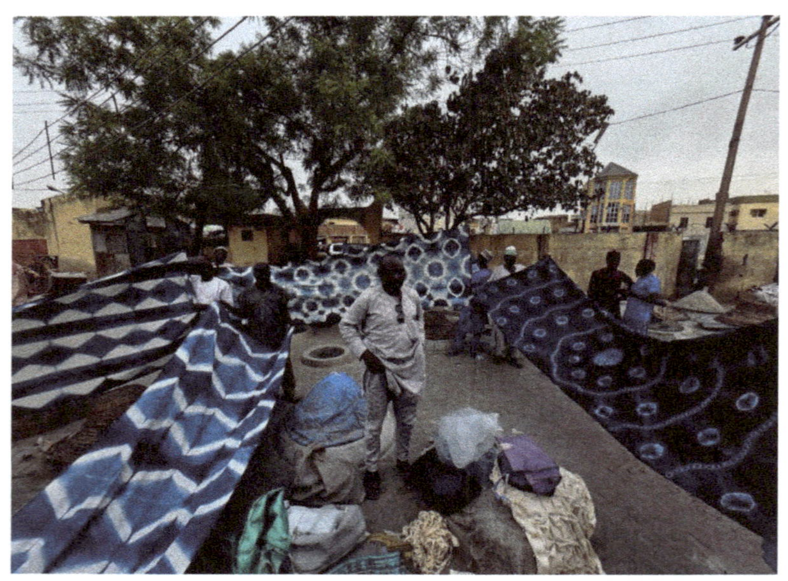

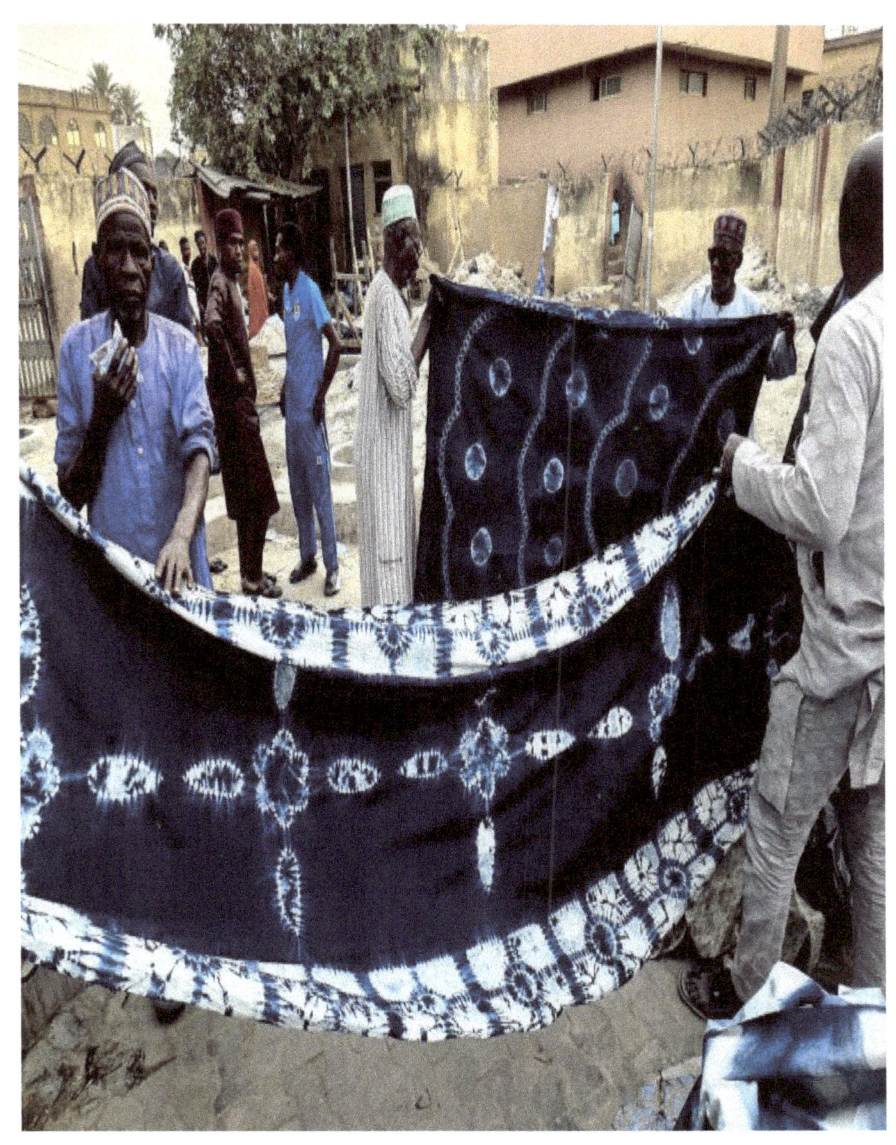

DAY 6

The Kurmi Market, established in the fifteenth century by Muhammad Rumfa, a king of Kano, holds rich historical significance. Initially serving as a prominent slave market, it later transformed into a vital warehousing and trading center during the Trans-Saharan trade period. Today, the market spans over 16 hectares and houses over 1,000 shops. Navigating the narrow ancient streets was challenging, and the variety of items available was overwhelming. I could have easily spent hours exploring the shops; however, the intense heat and the sun beating down through the open-air market limited the time I wished to spend there. I briefly visited the nearby tannery, but the strong odor from the tanning pits, animal skins, and extreme heat curtailed my stay. Furthermore, my visit coincided with the Sallah celebrations, which reduced activity at the tannery, as explained by my guide.

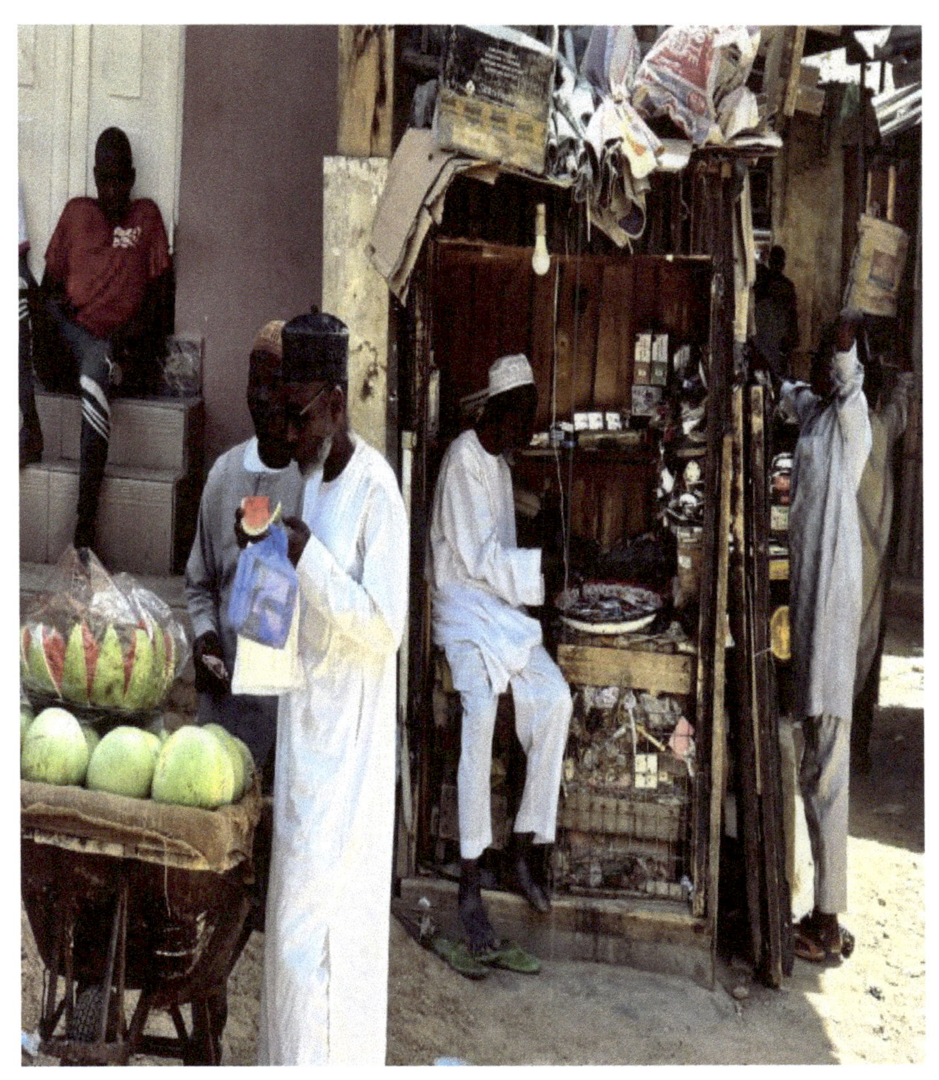

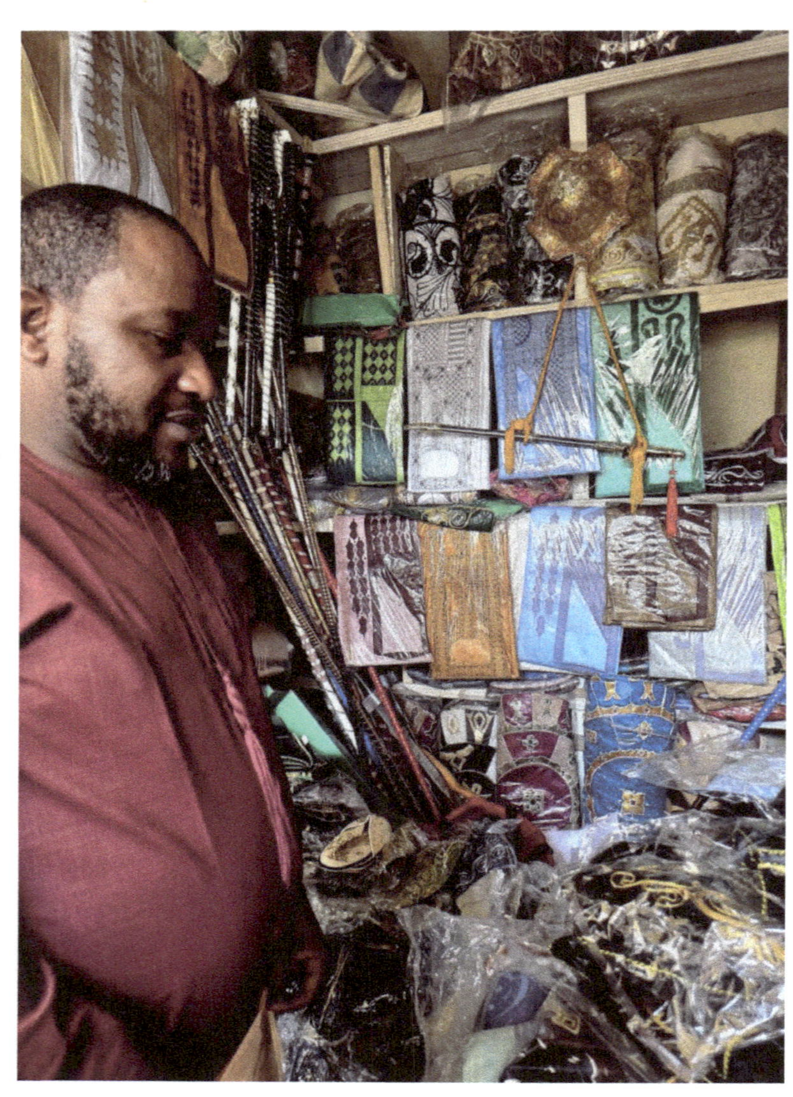

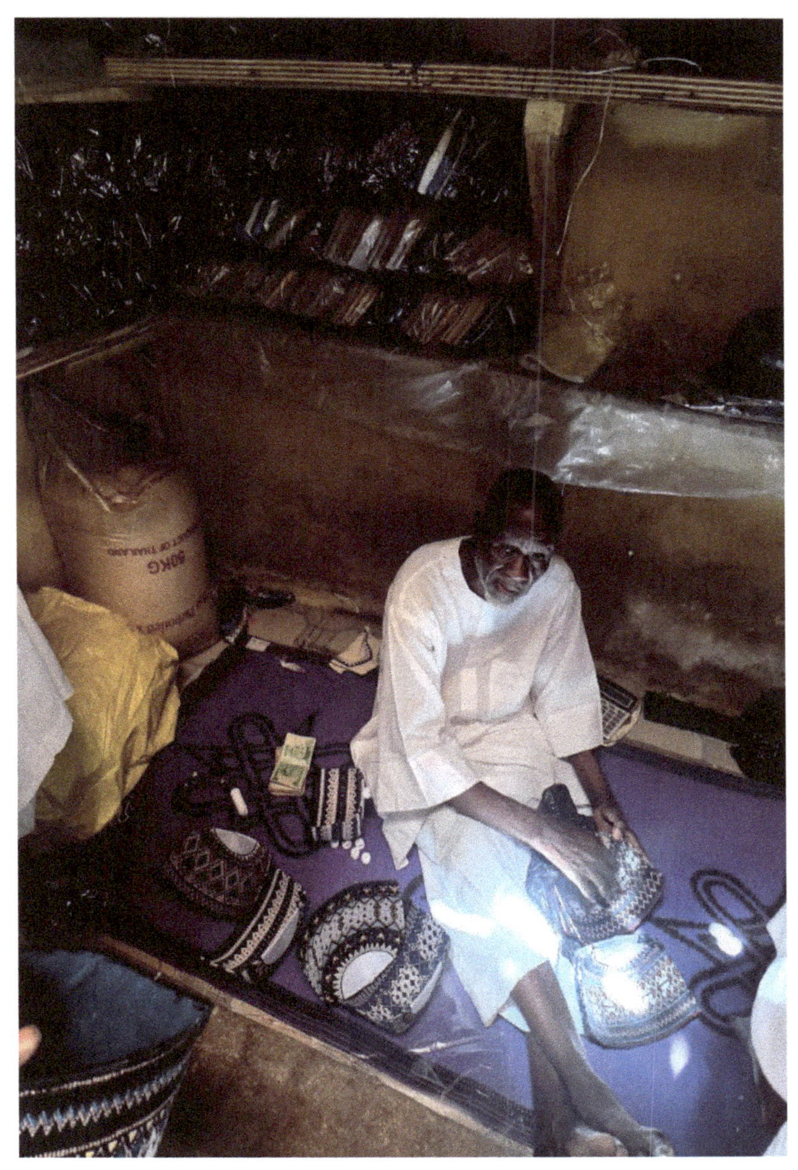

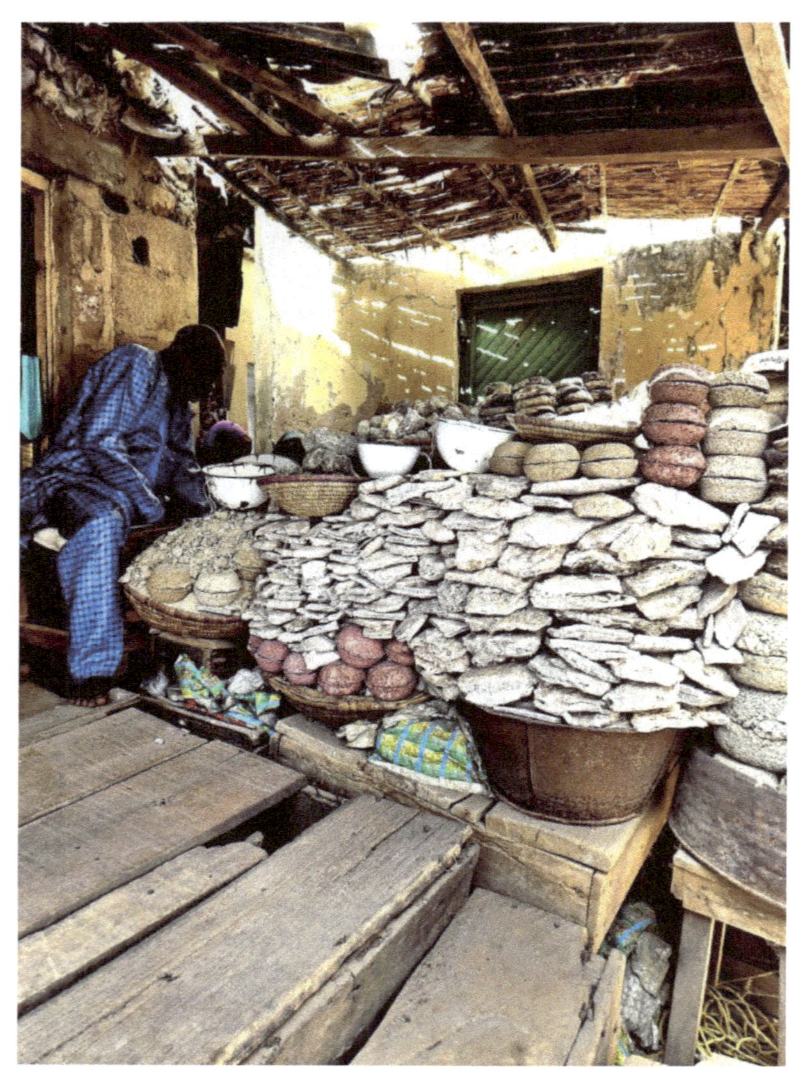

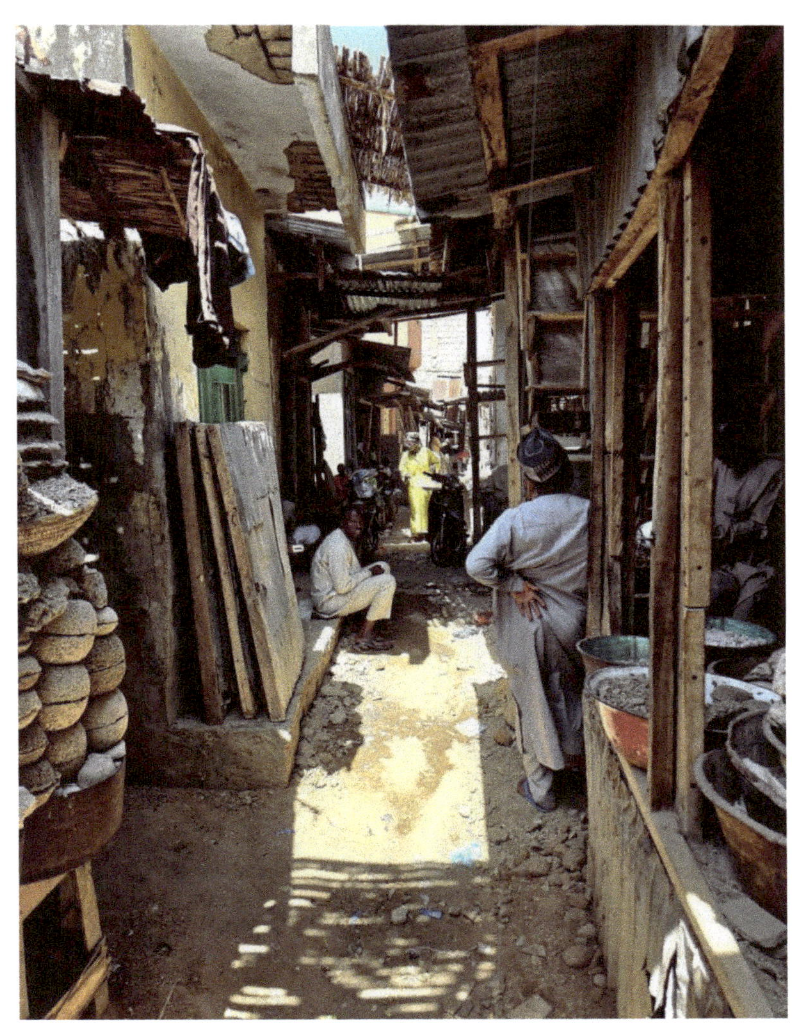

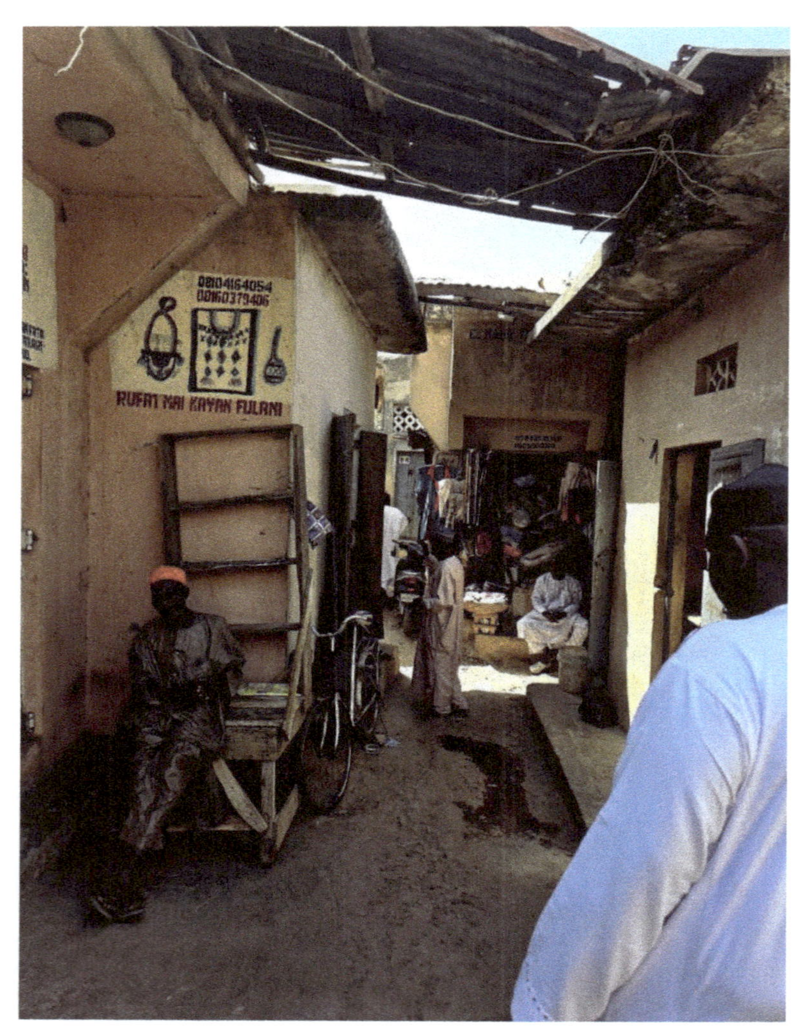

08104164054
08160379406
RUFAI MAI KAYAN FULANI

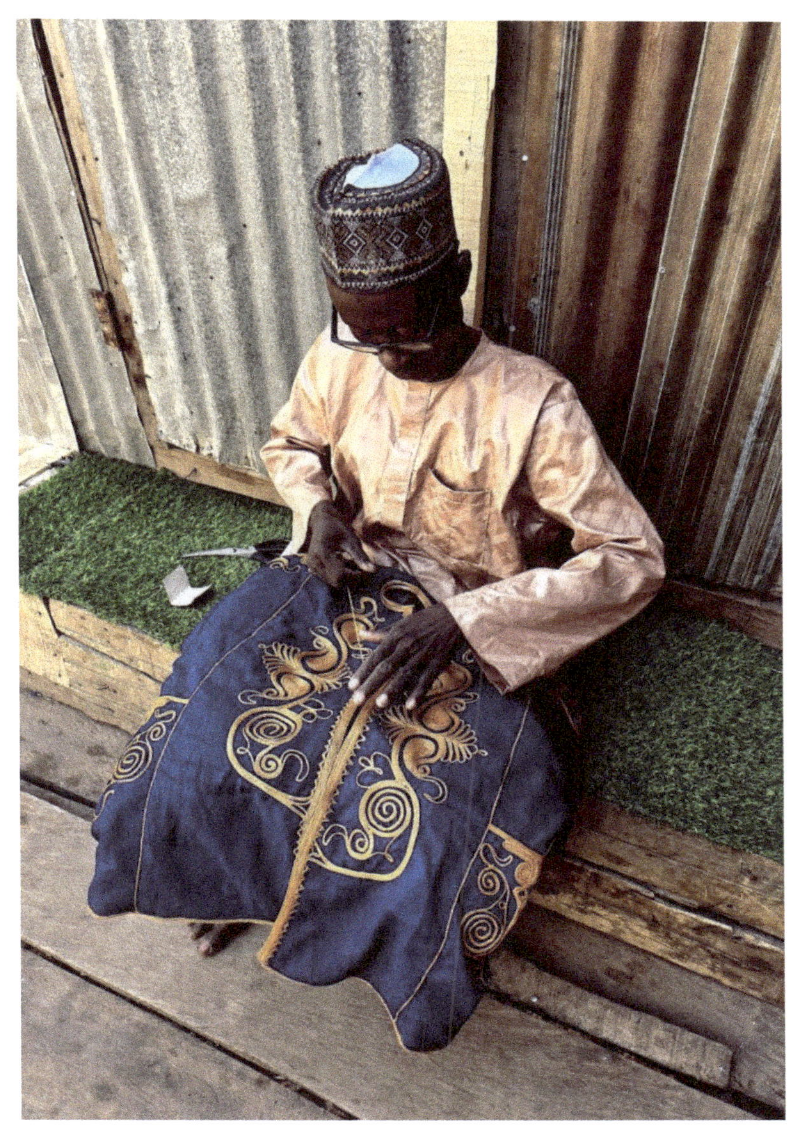

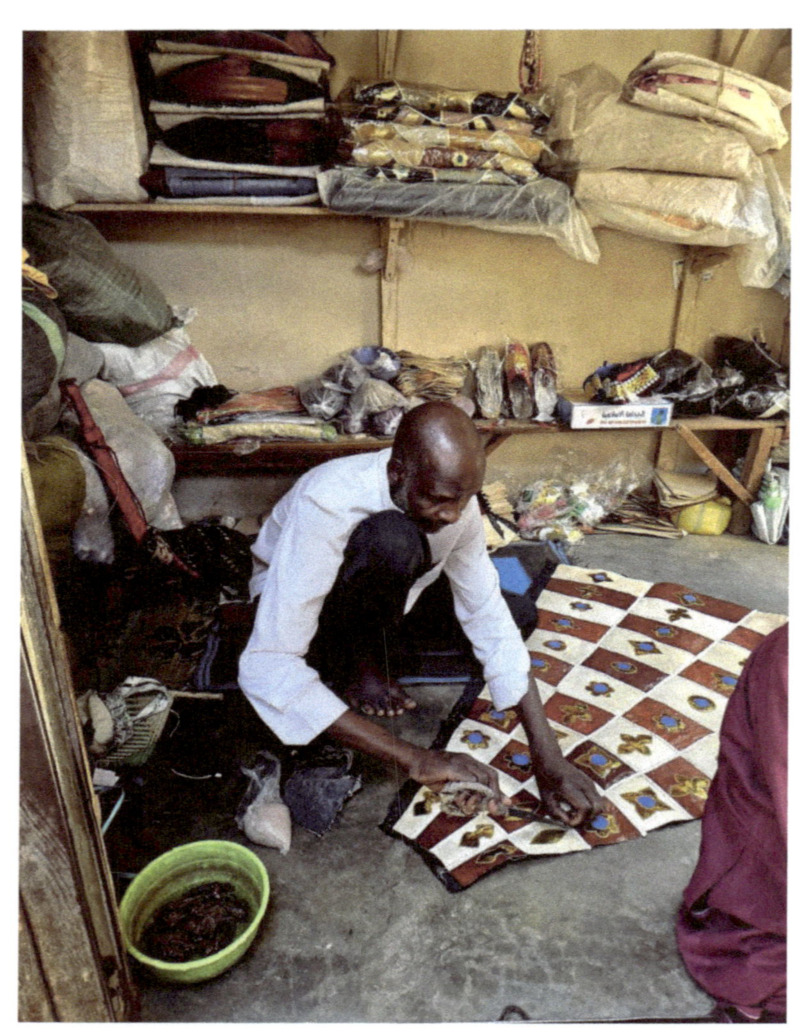

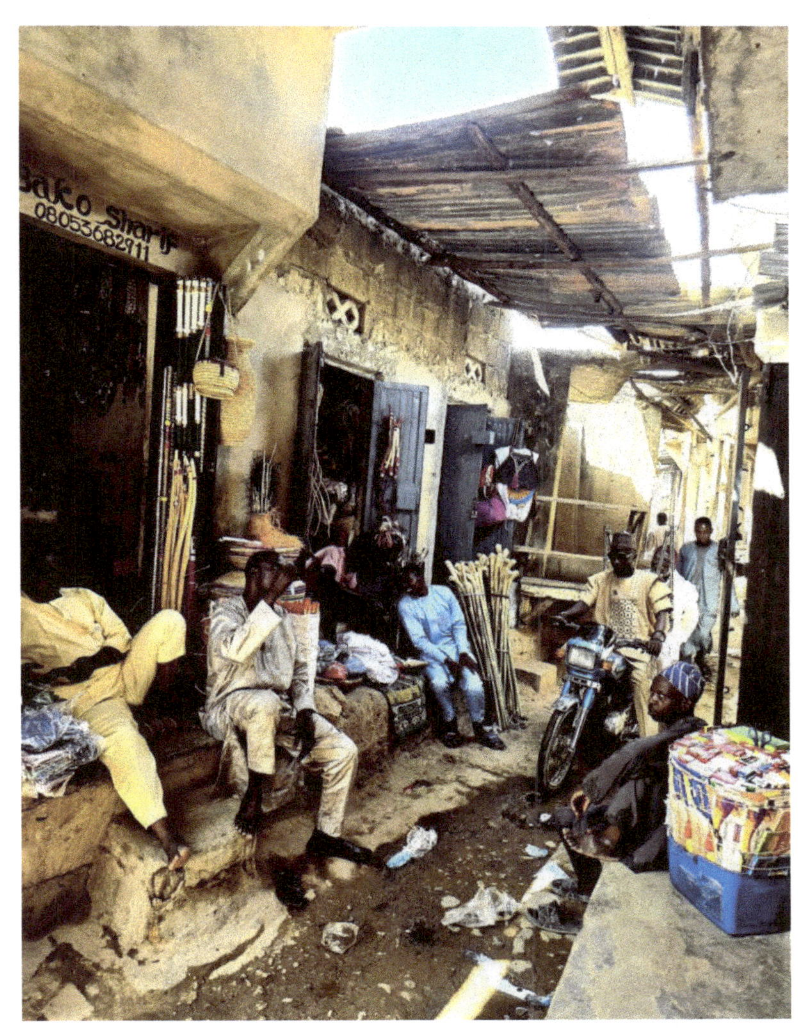

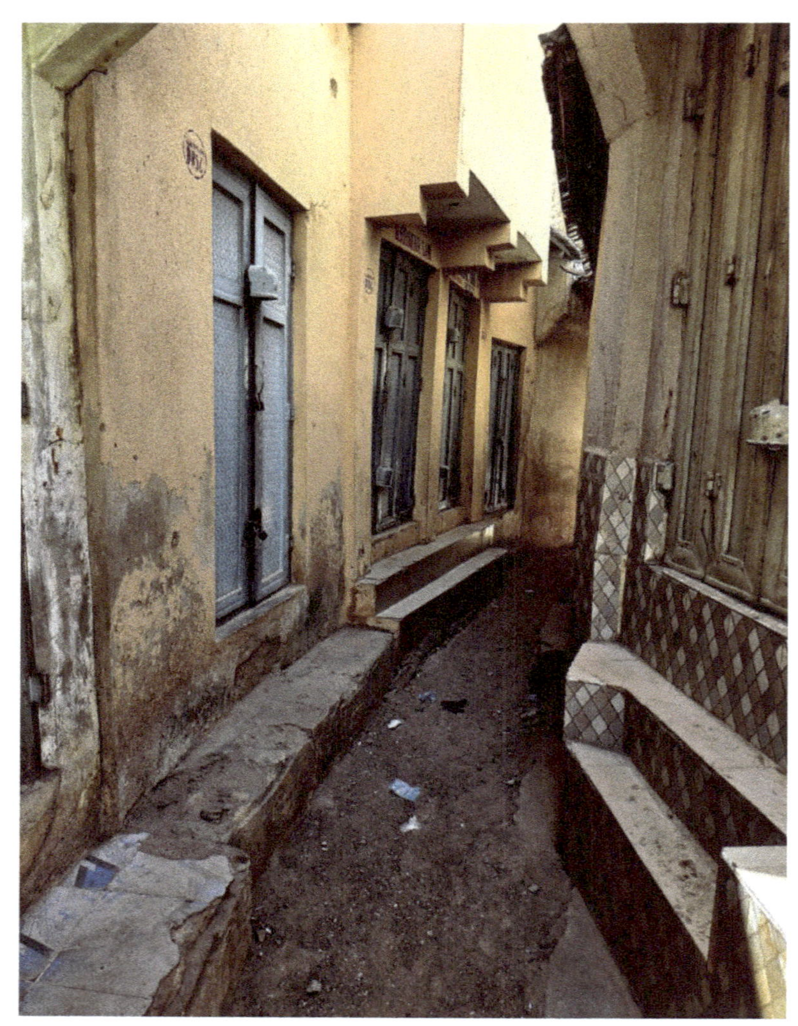

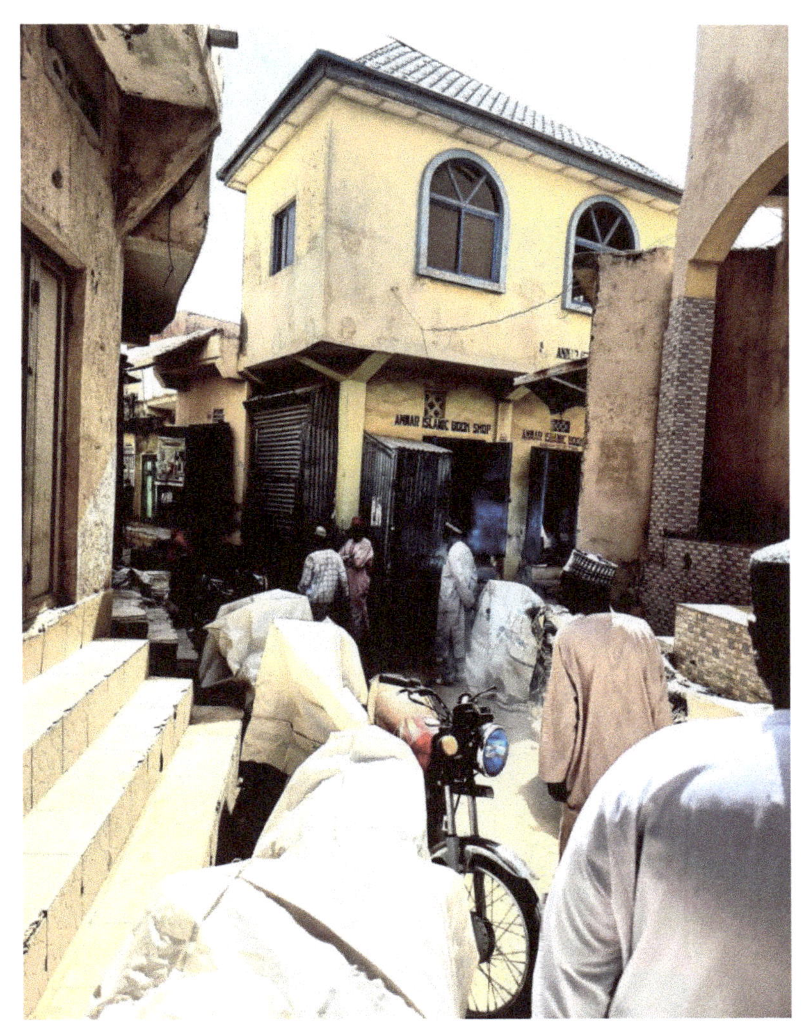

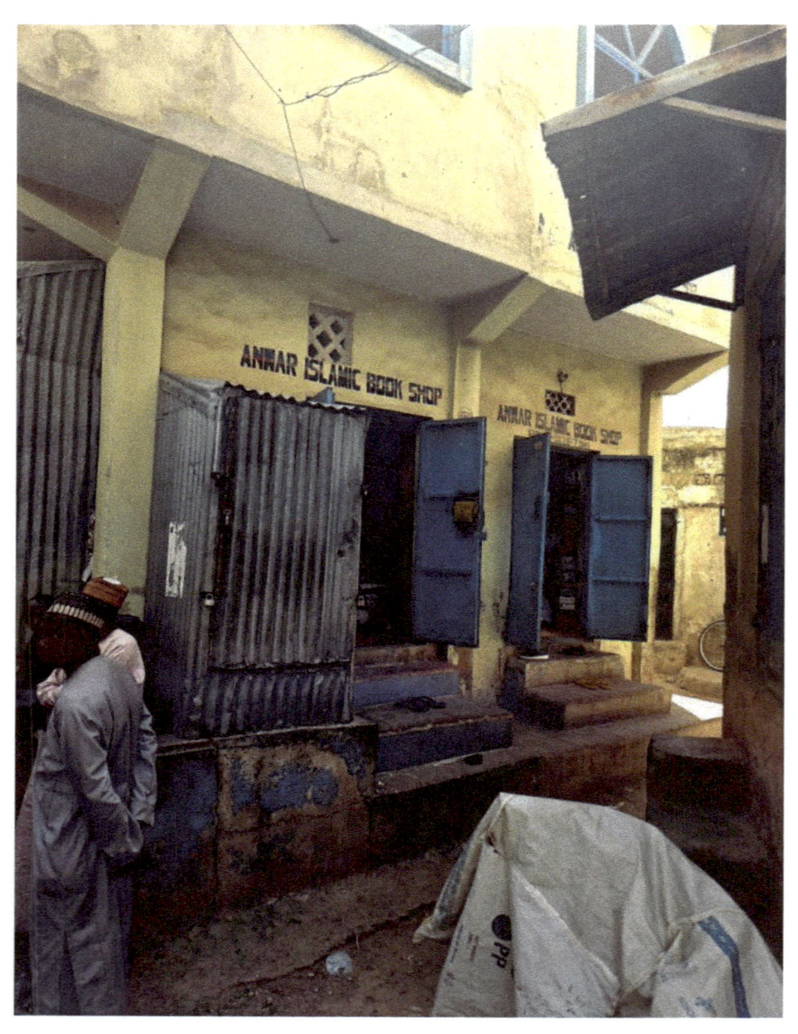

ANWAR ISLAMIC BOOK SHOP
ANWAR ISLAMIC BOOK SHOP

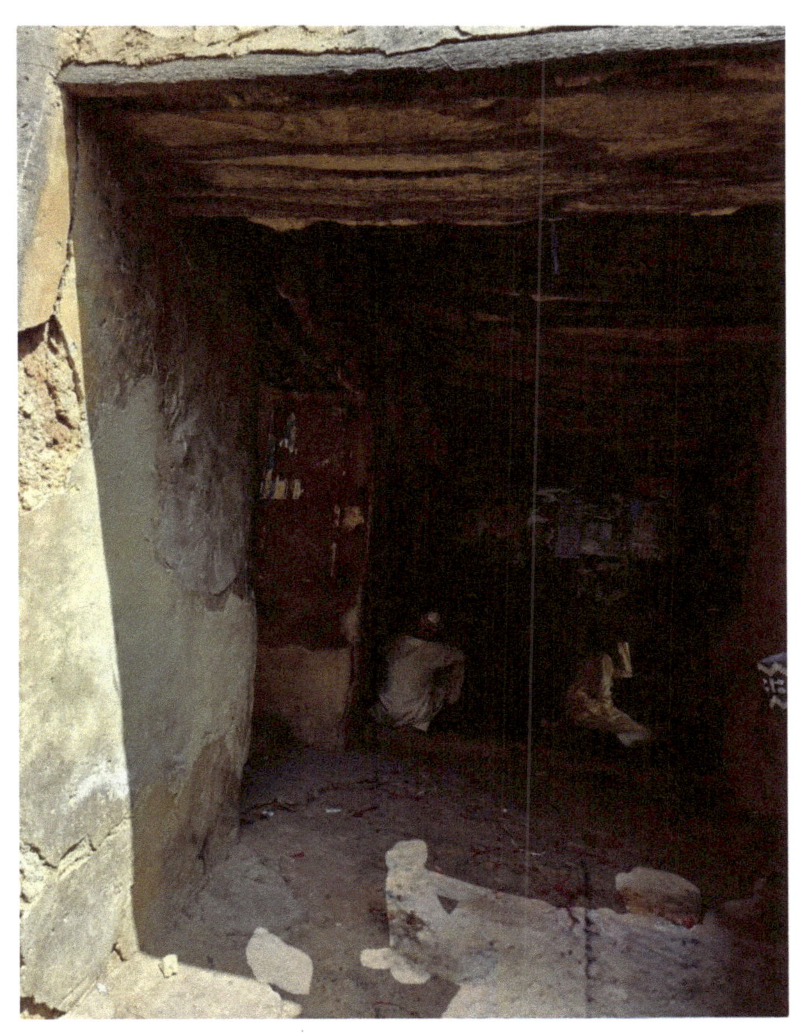

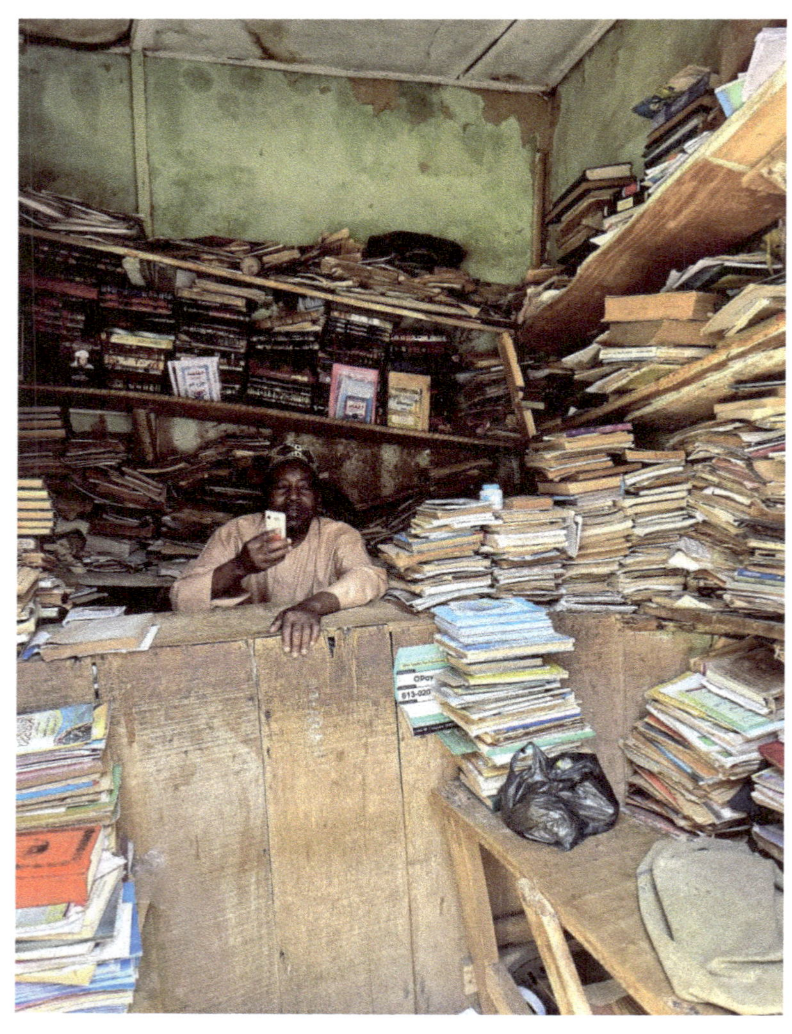

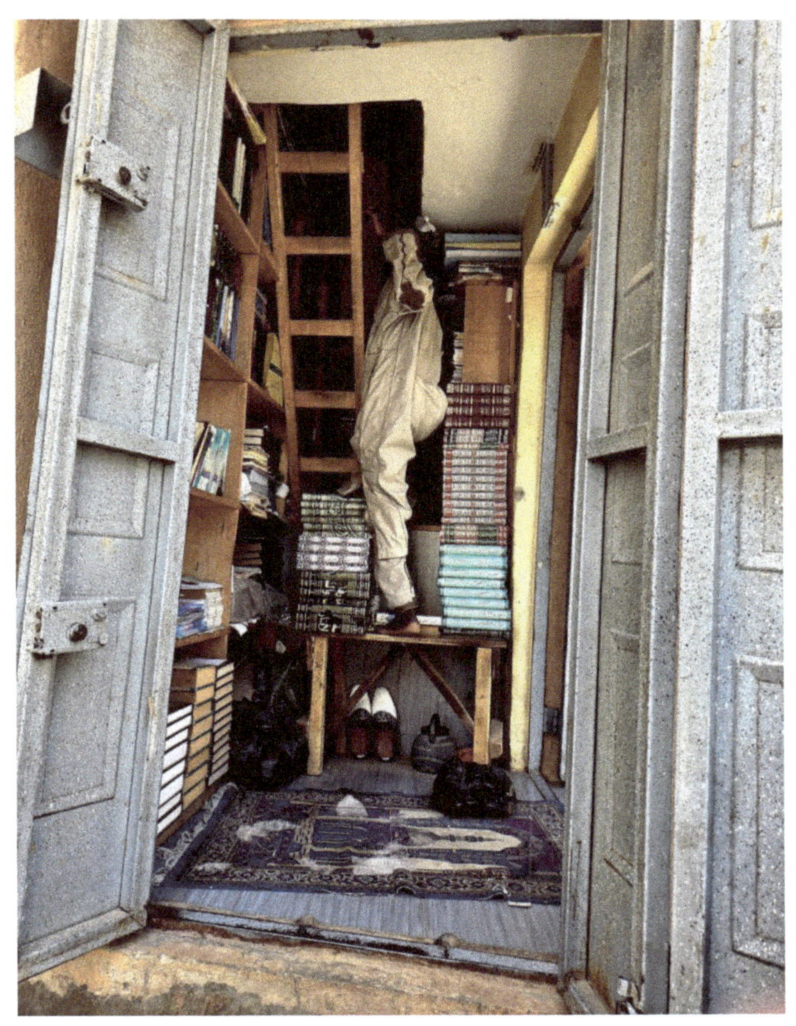

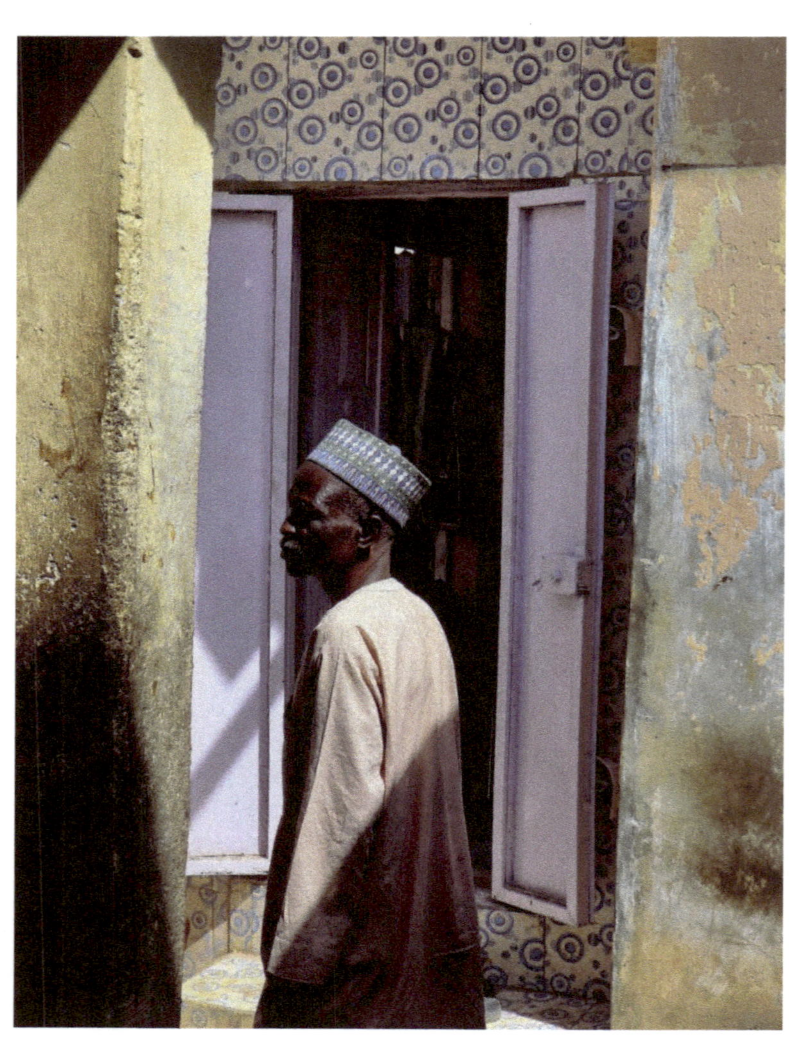

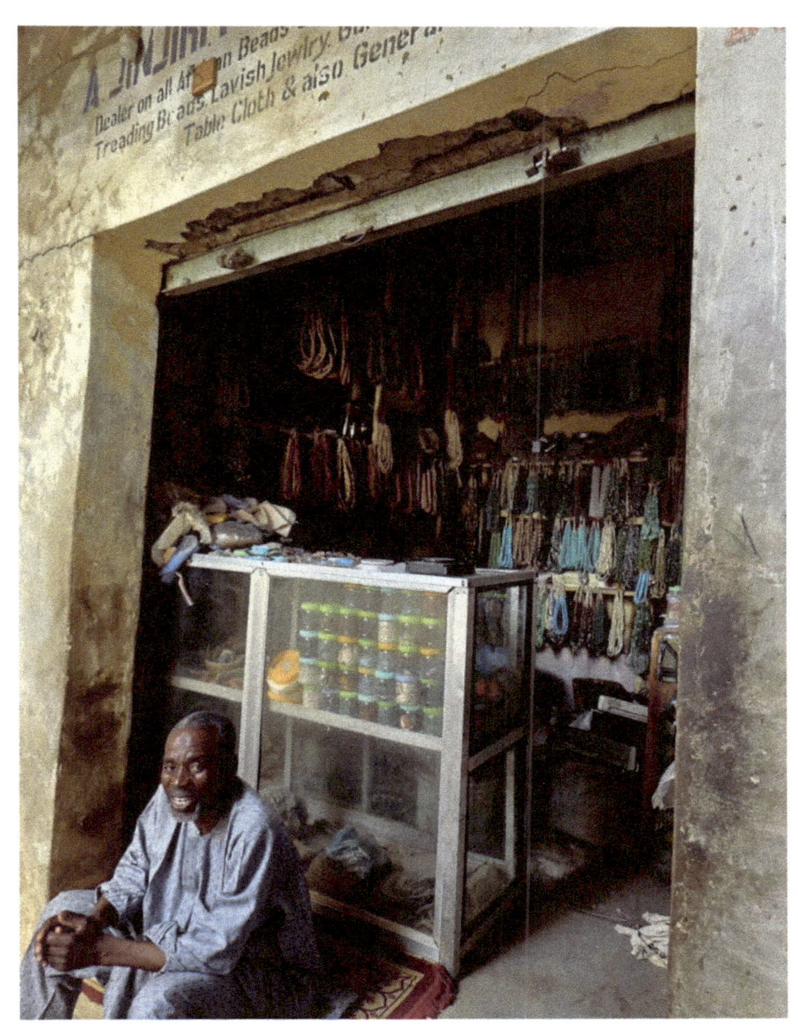

A. JINJIRI
Dealer on all African Beads
Treading Beads, Lavish Jewlry,
Table Cloth & also General

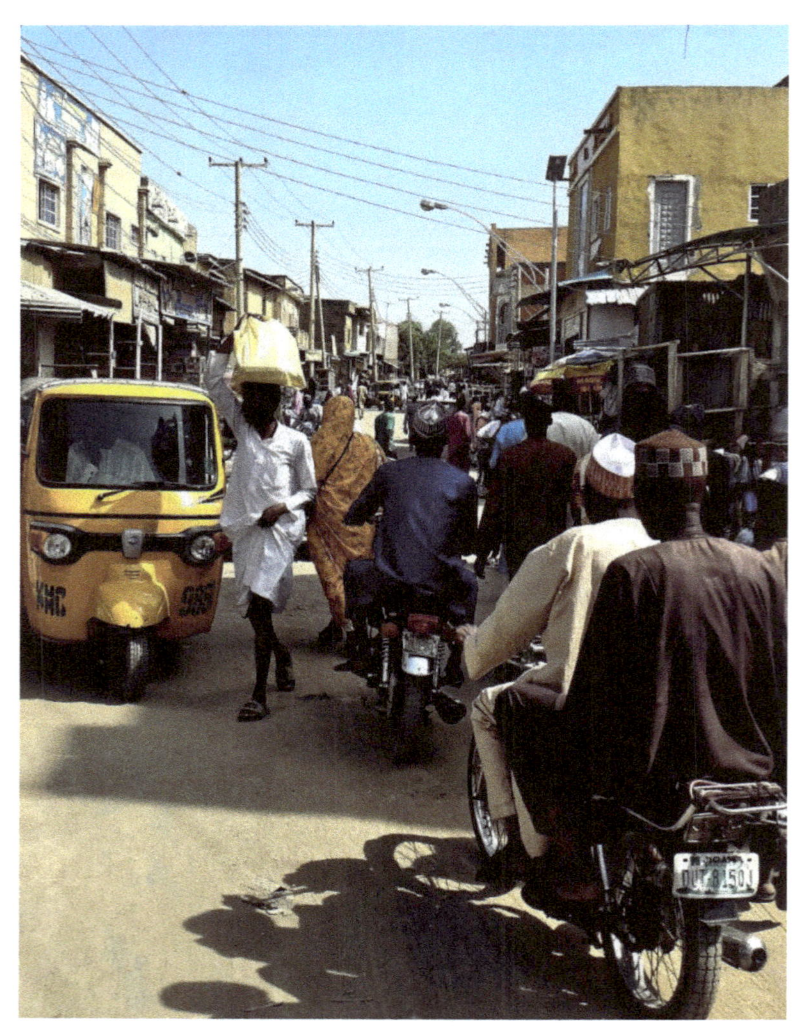

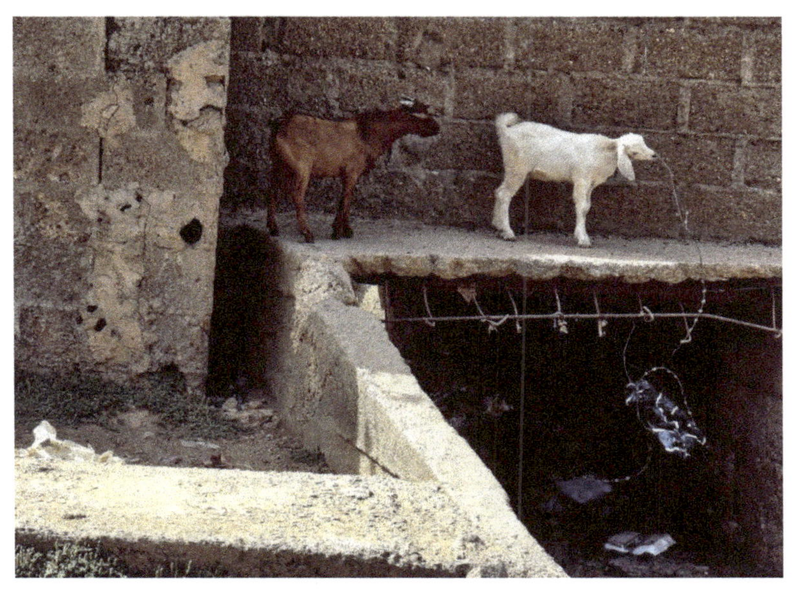

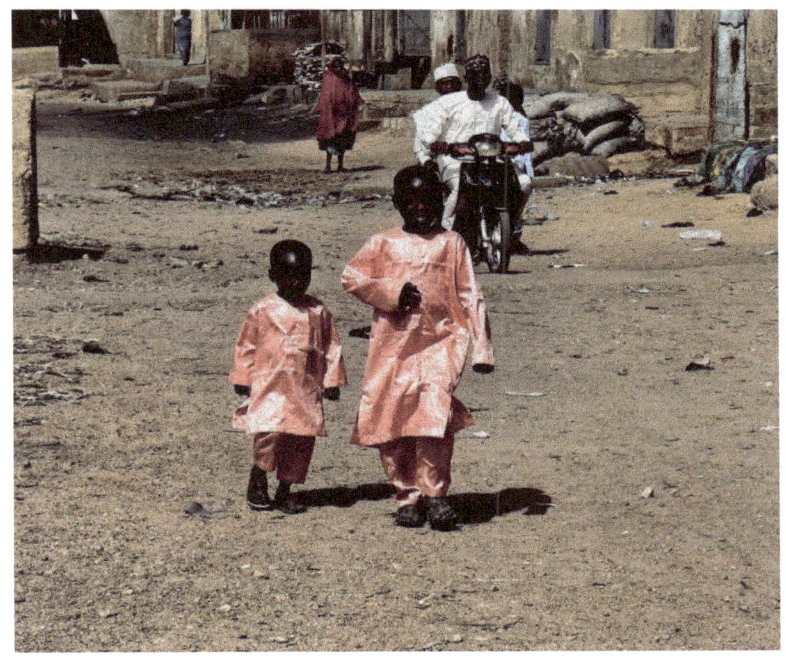

The Tanning Pits

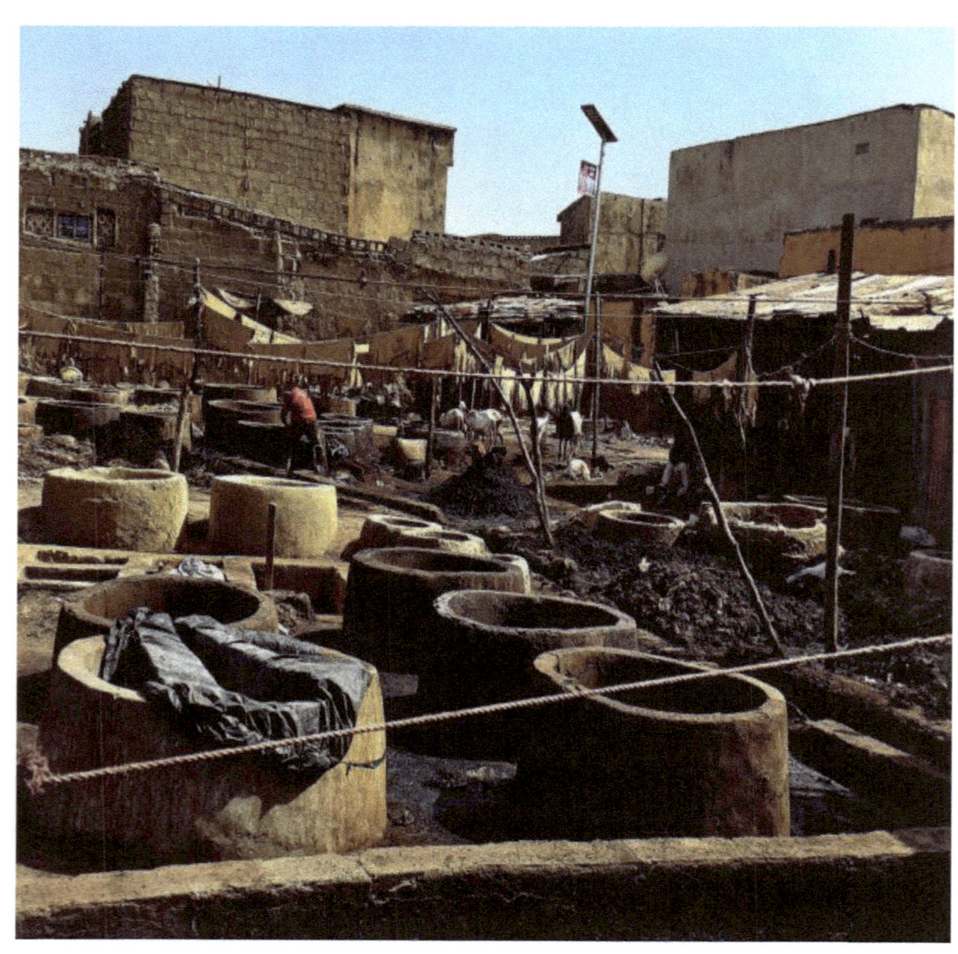

DAY 7

I had the opportunity to visit the Kantin Kwari Market, recognized as the largest textile market in West Africa. The market's history is closely linked to Kano's significance as a regional center of trade. Like the Kurmi Market, the Kantin Kwari Market was established during the Trans-Saharan trade era.

In 1904, the old market was replaced with a new structure to enhance revenue generation for the Native Authority. As we navigated the streets, I was impressed by the numerous shops displaying racks filled with textiles and exotic fabrics. Men and women briskly moved through the streets, balancing bolts of fabric on their heads.

That day, I searched for hats with my guide, and we met up with a merchant who led us through the complex network of shops. Ultimately, we settled in a fabric shop where the merchant had shop owners come and present me with various hats available for purchase. I selected several Nigerian-style hats and then continued on my way.

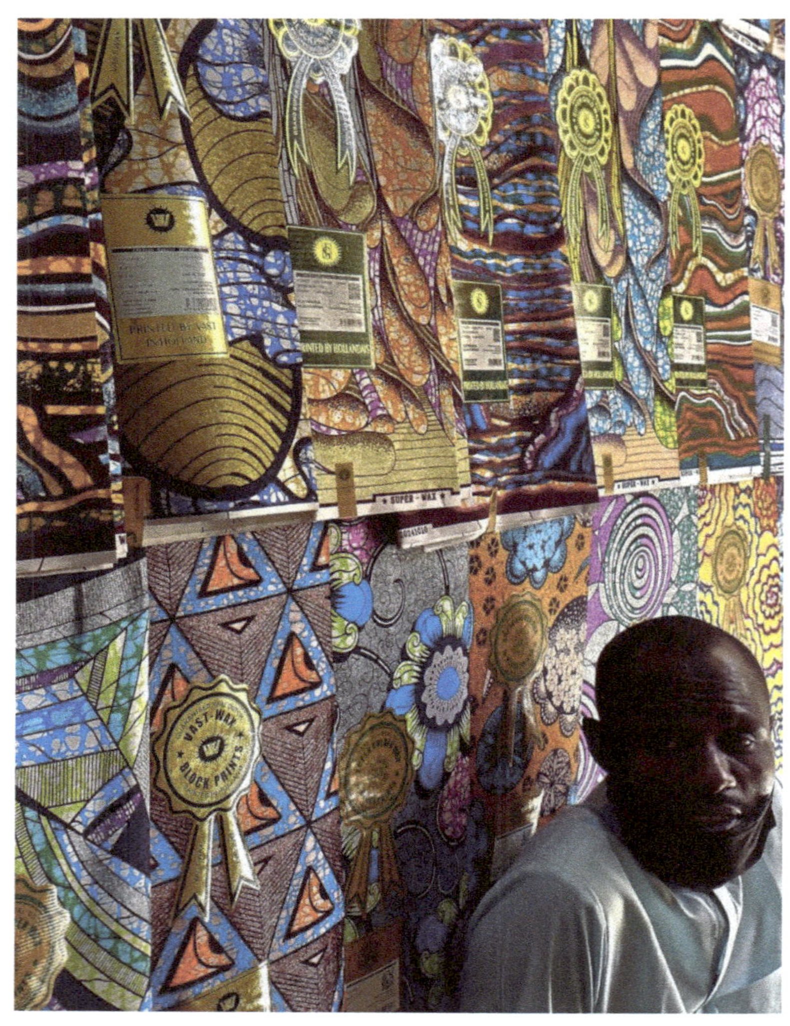

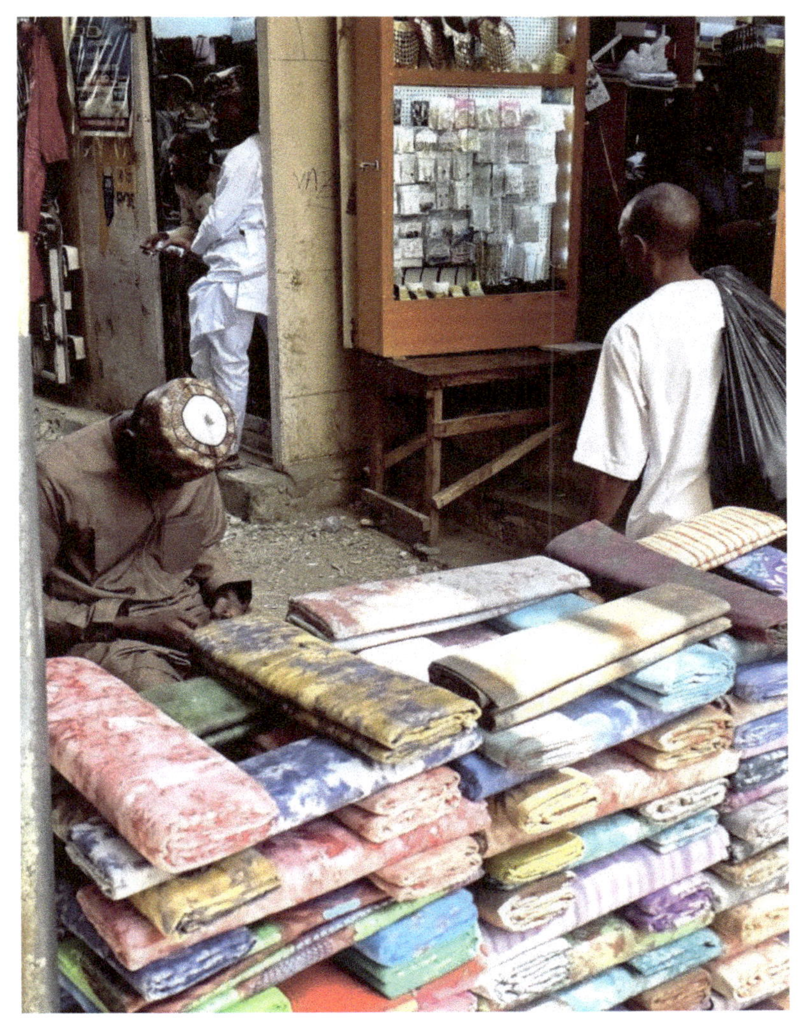

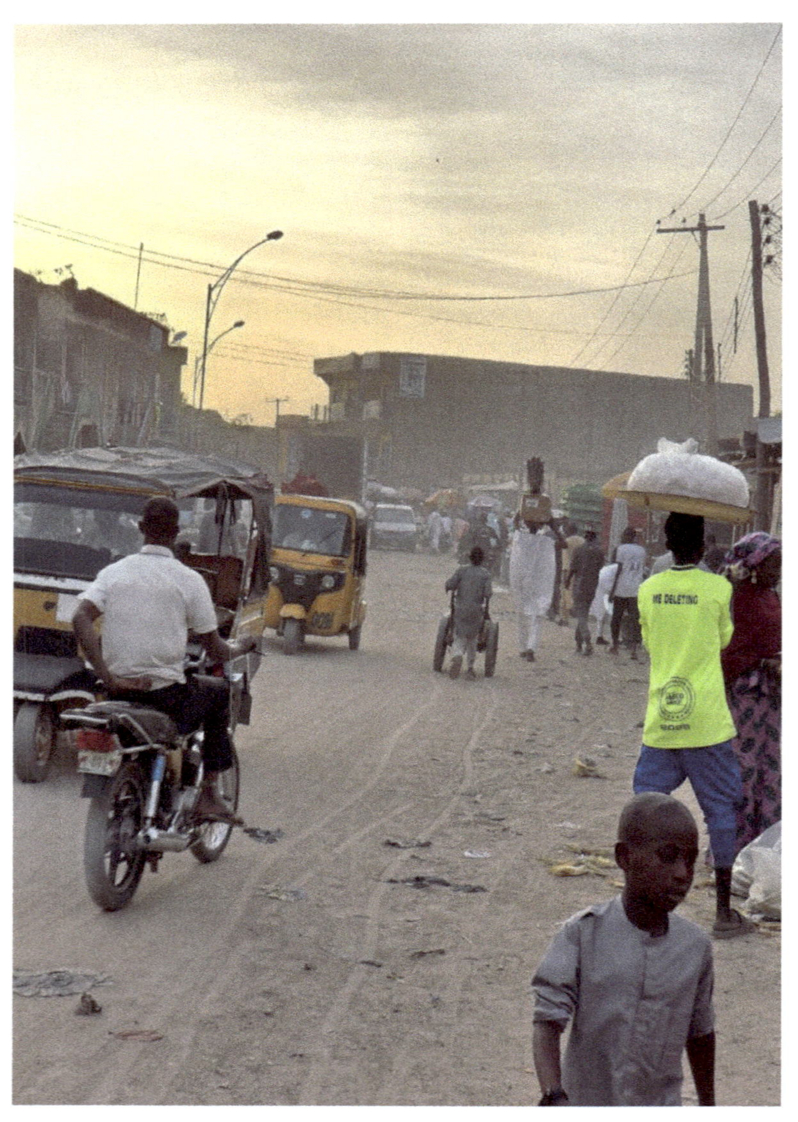

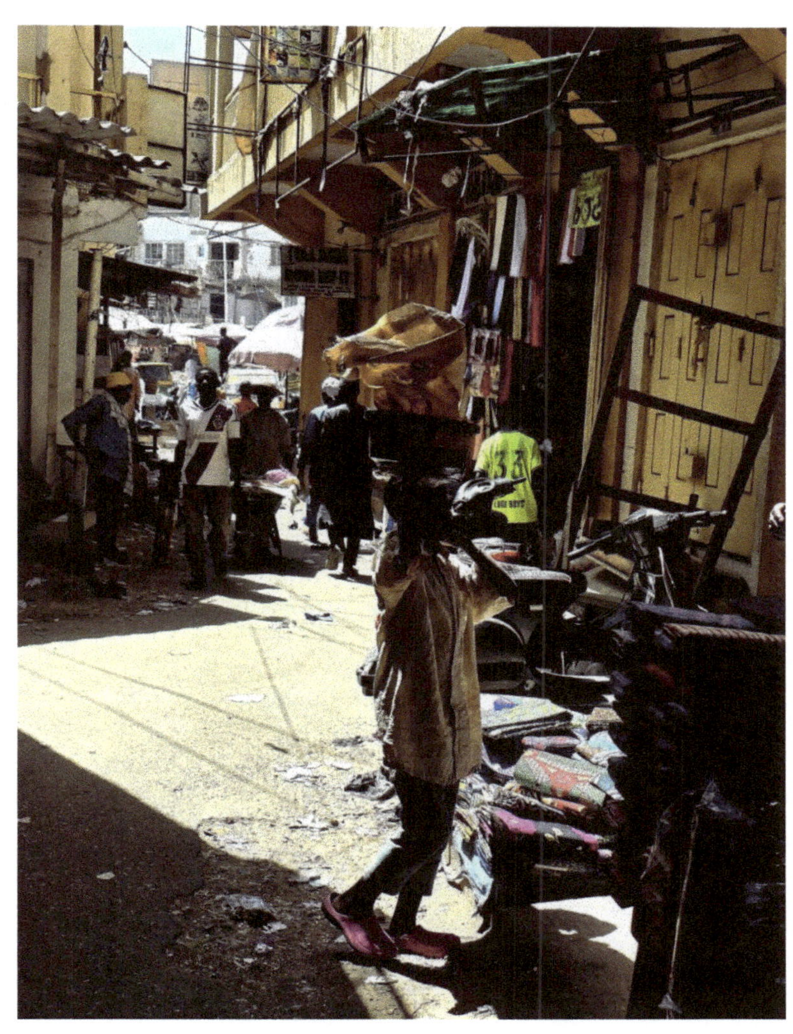

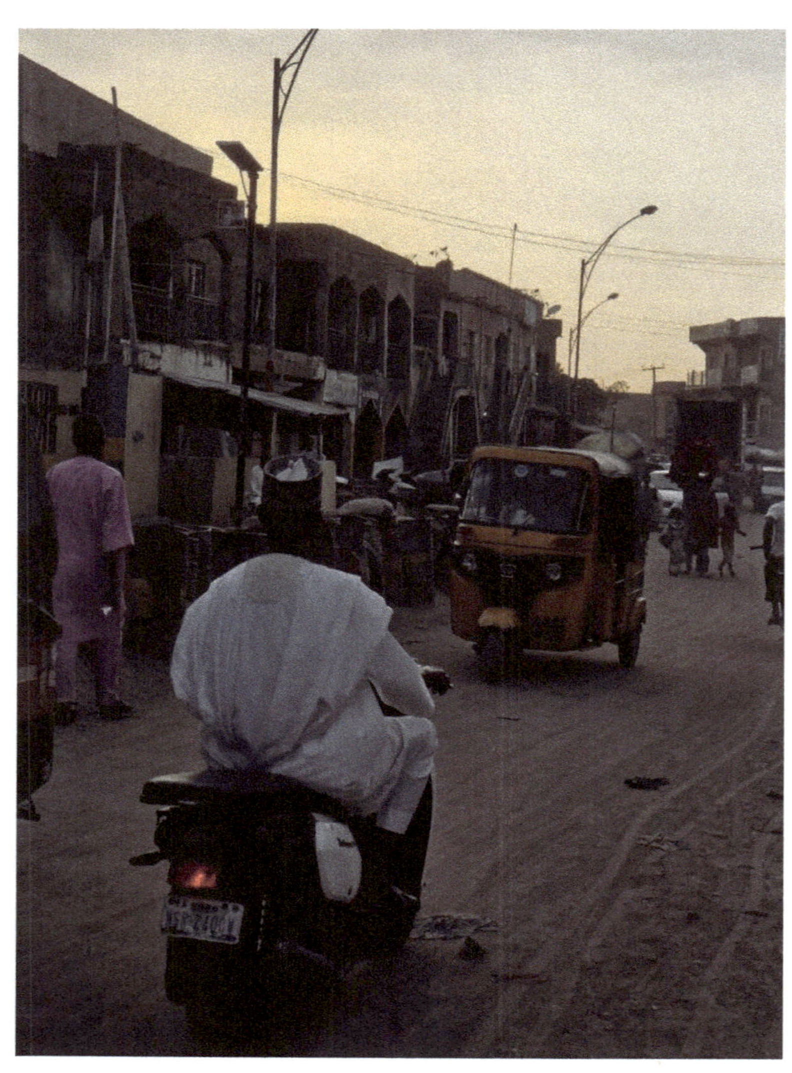

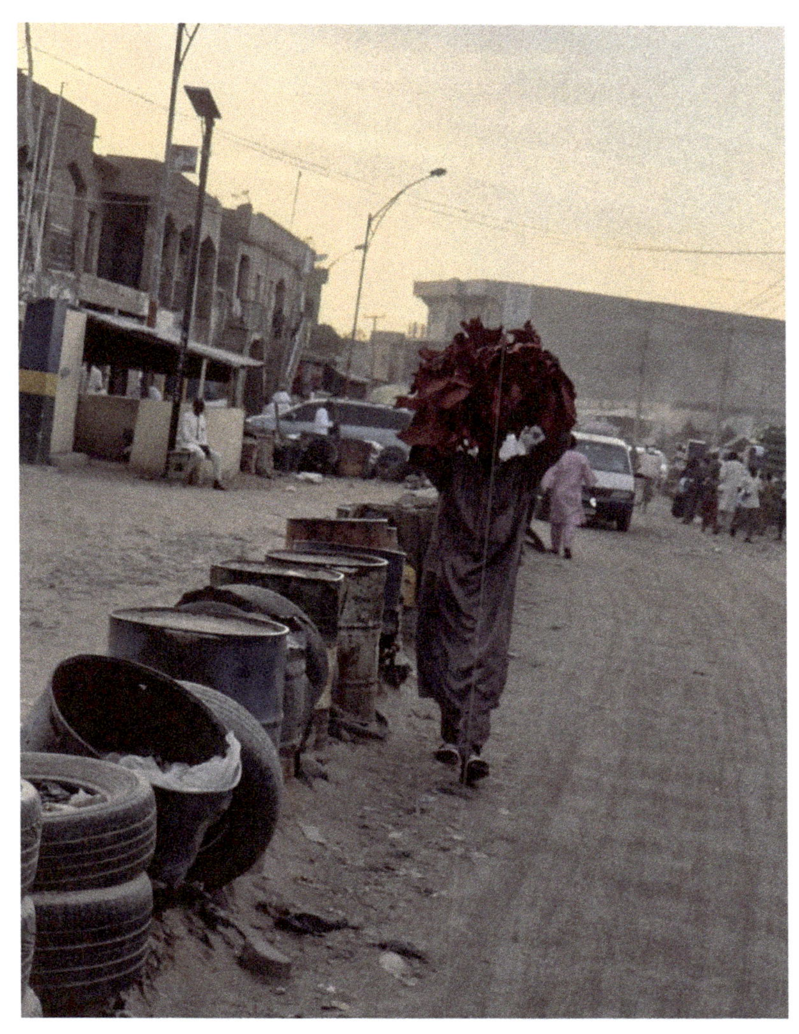

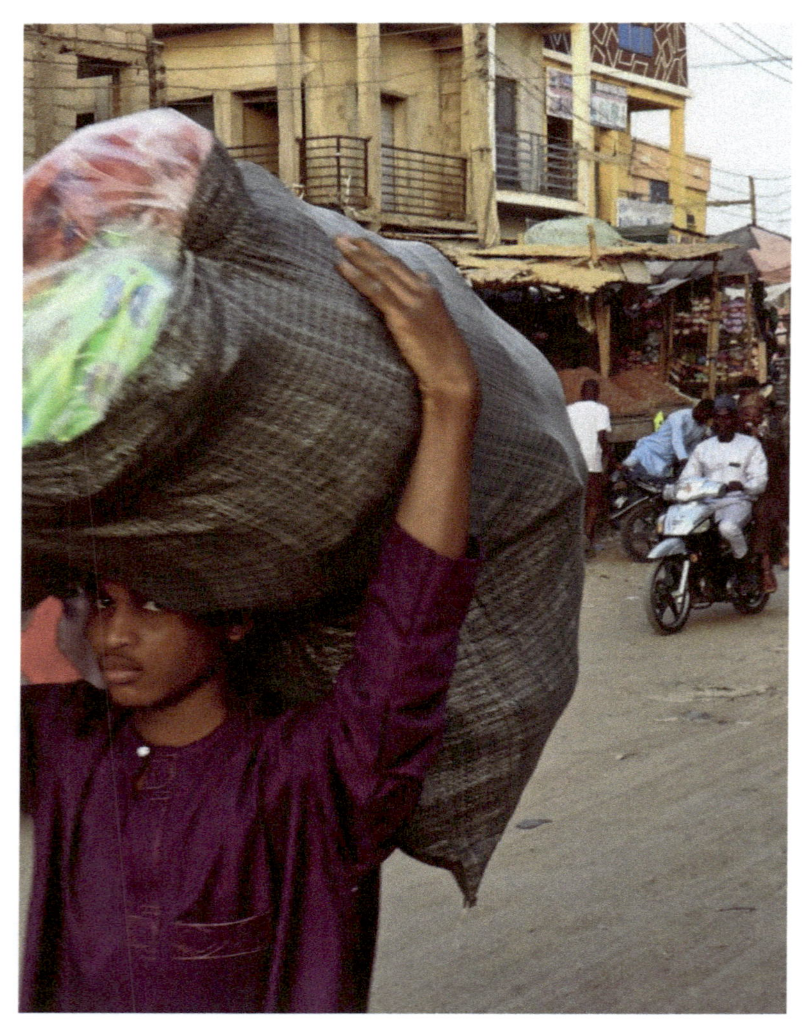

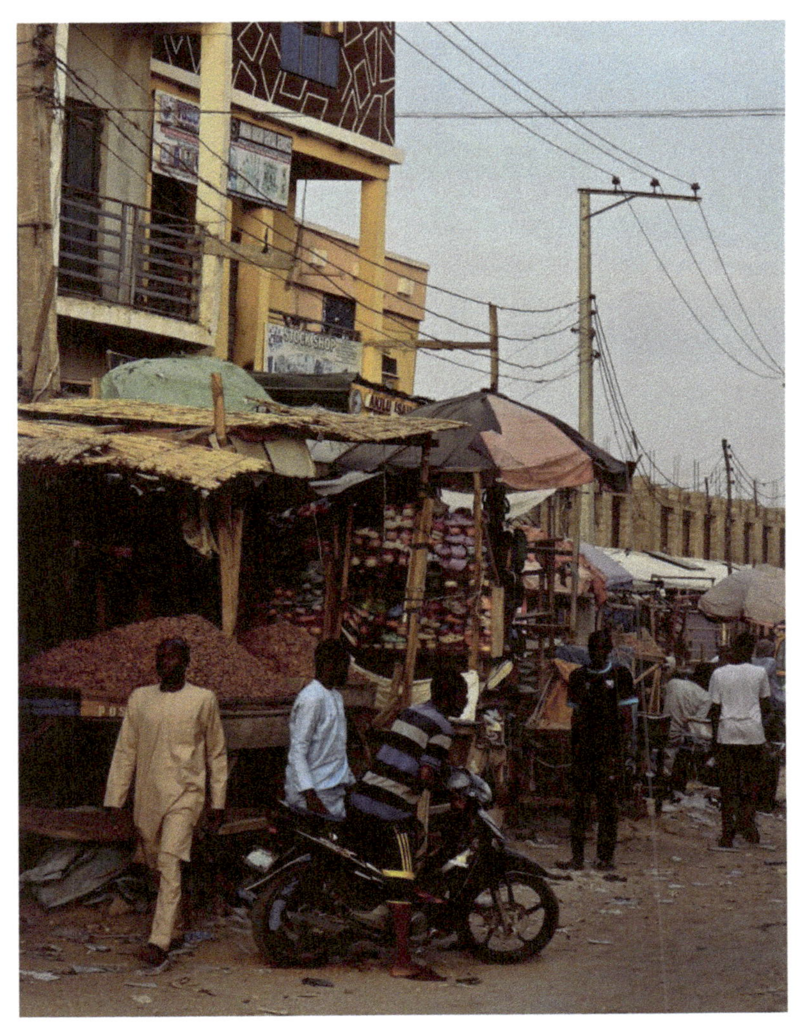

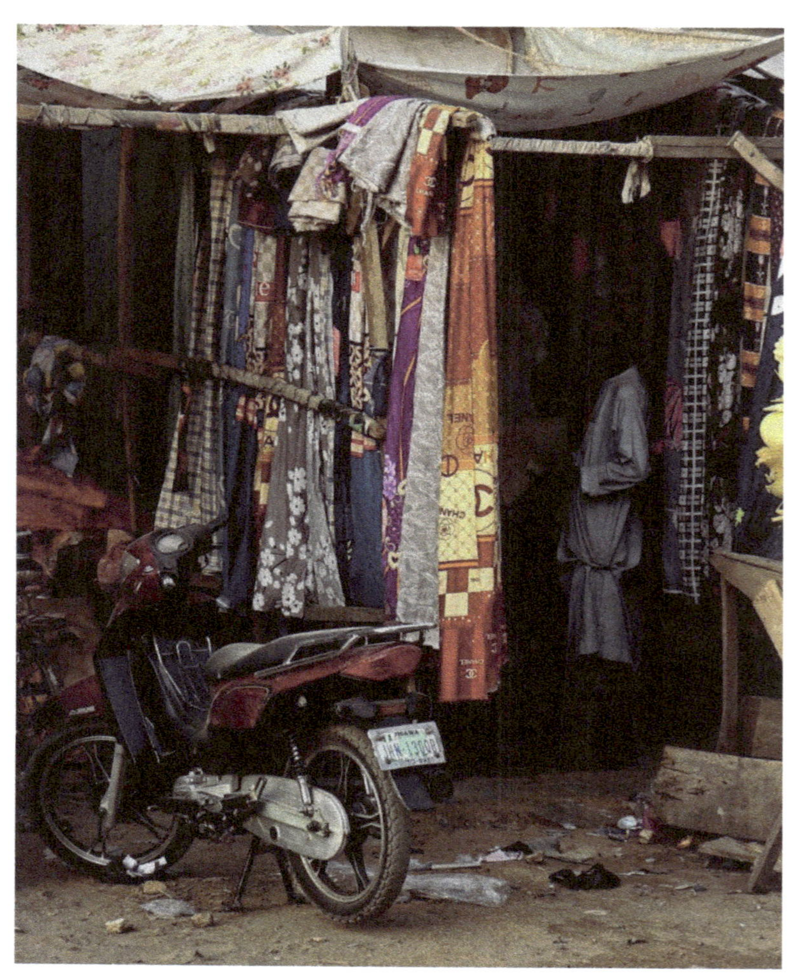

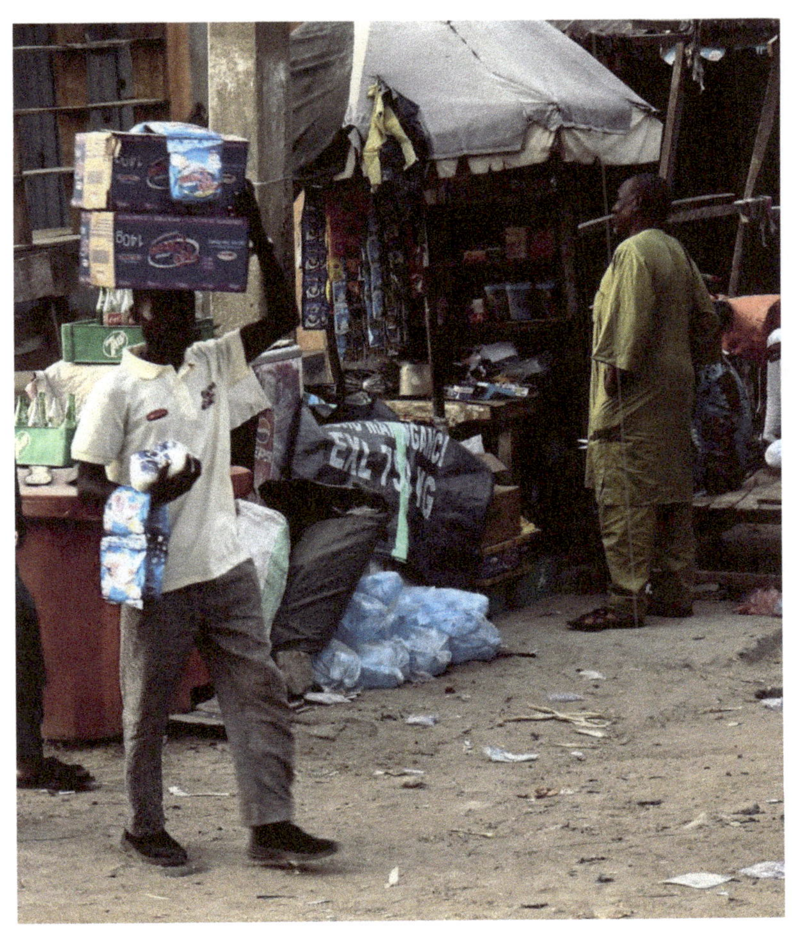

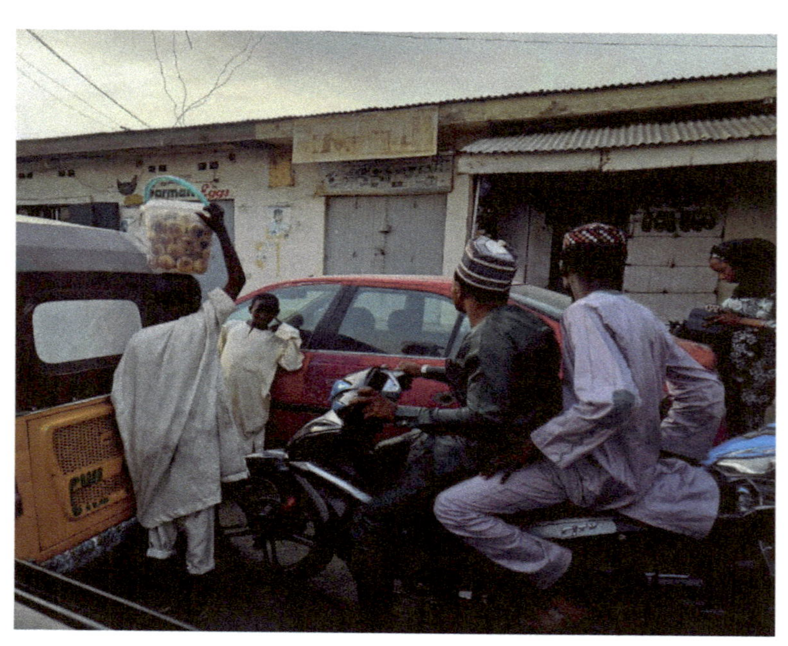

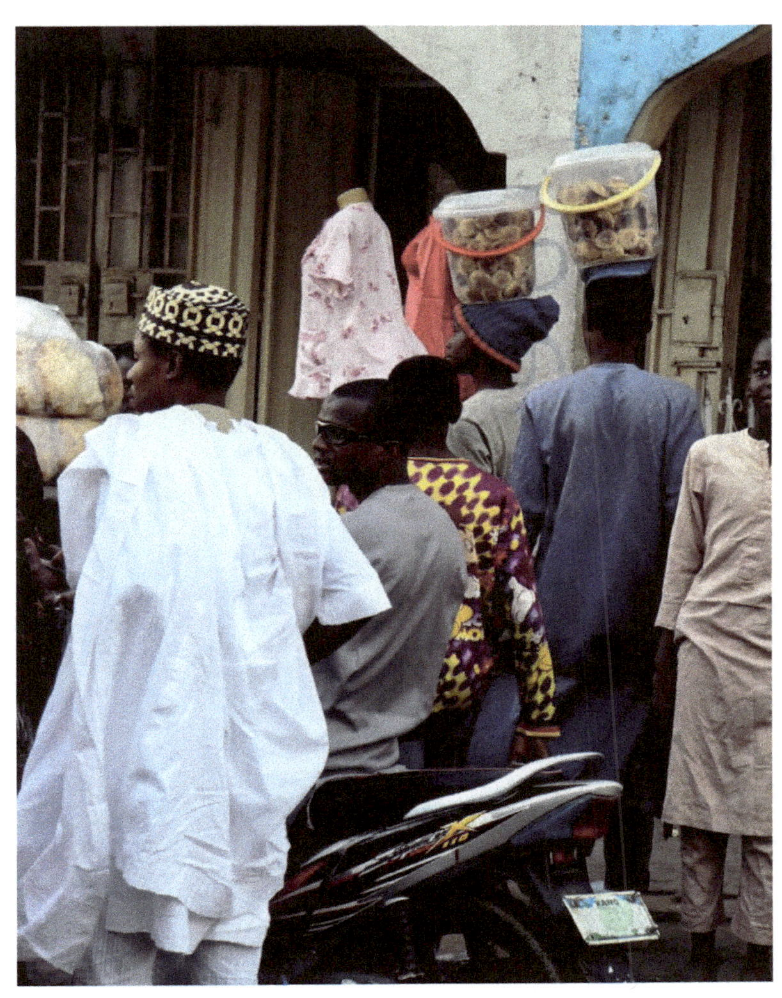

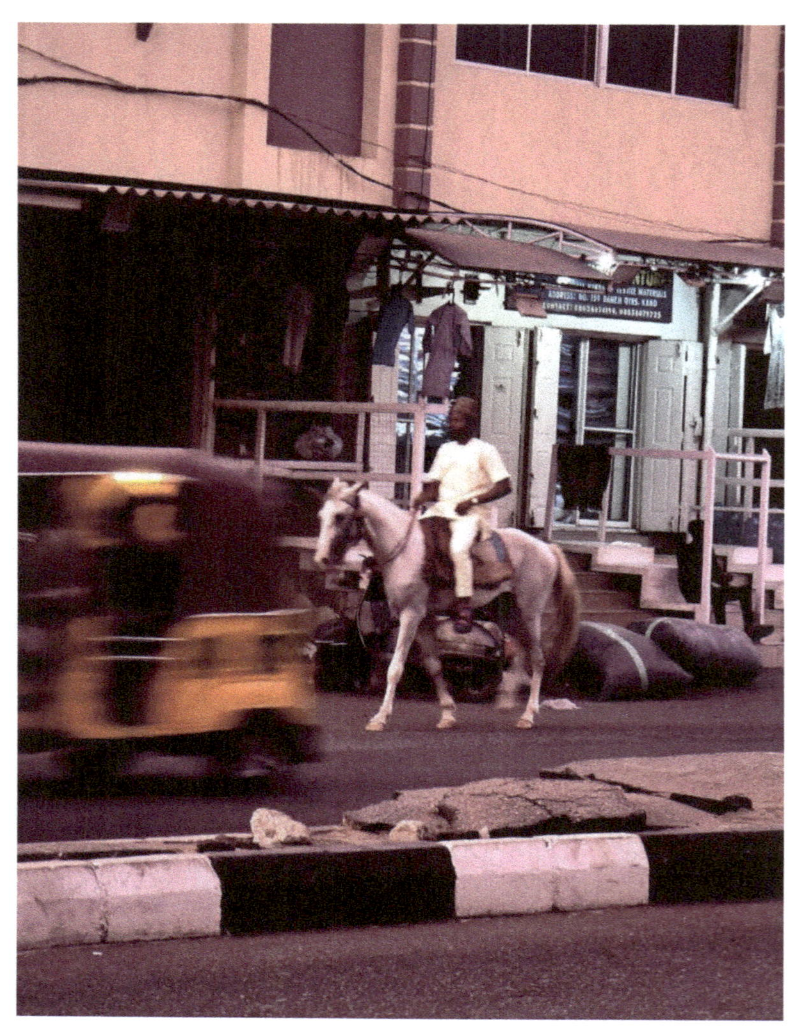

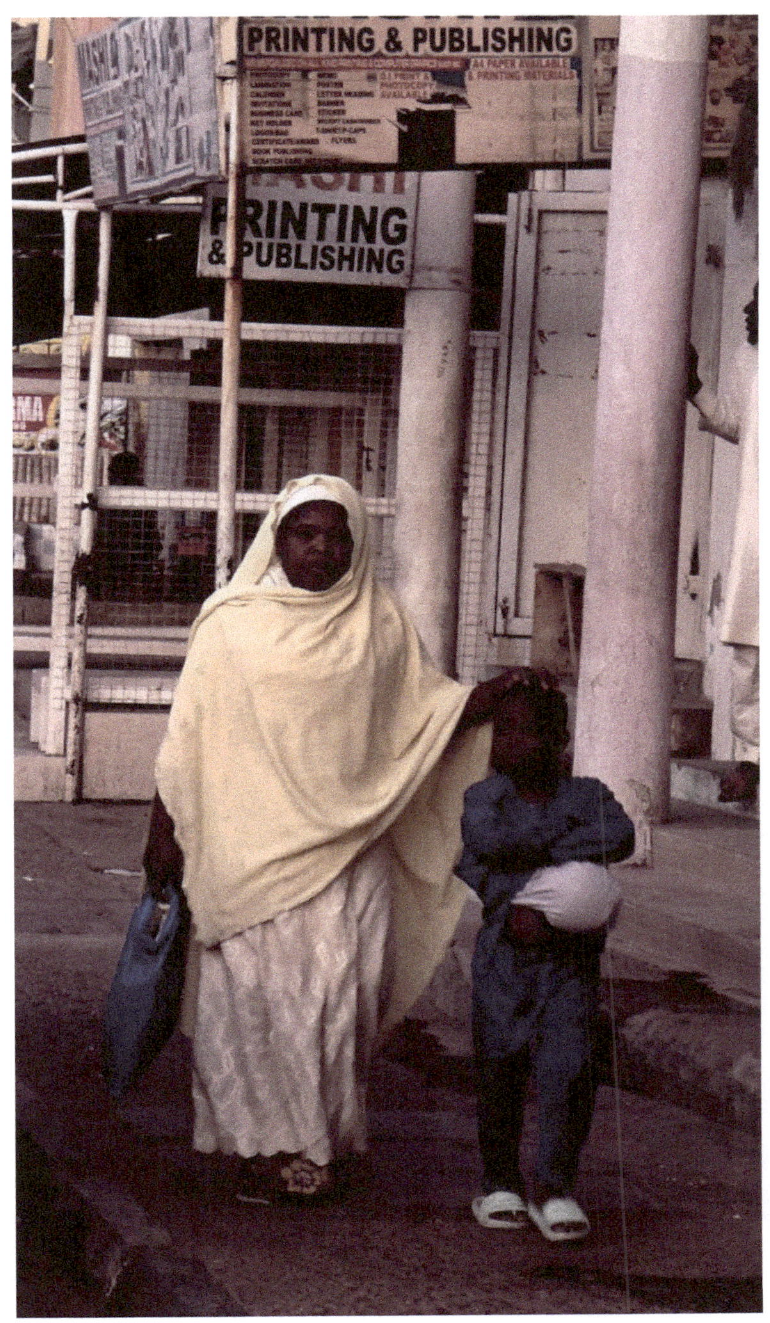
PRINTING & PUBLISHING
A4 PAPER AVAILABLE
& PRINTING MATERIALS
PRINTING
& PUBLISHING

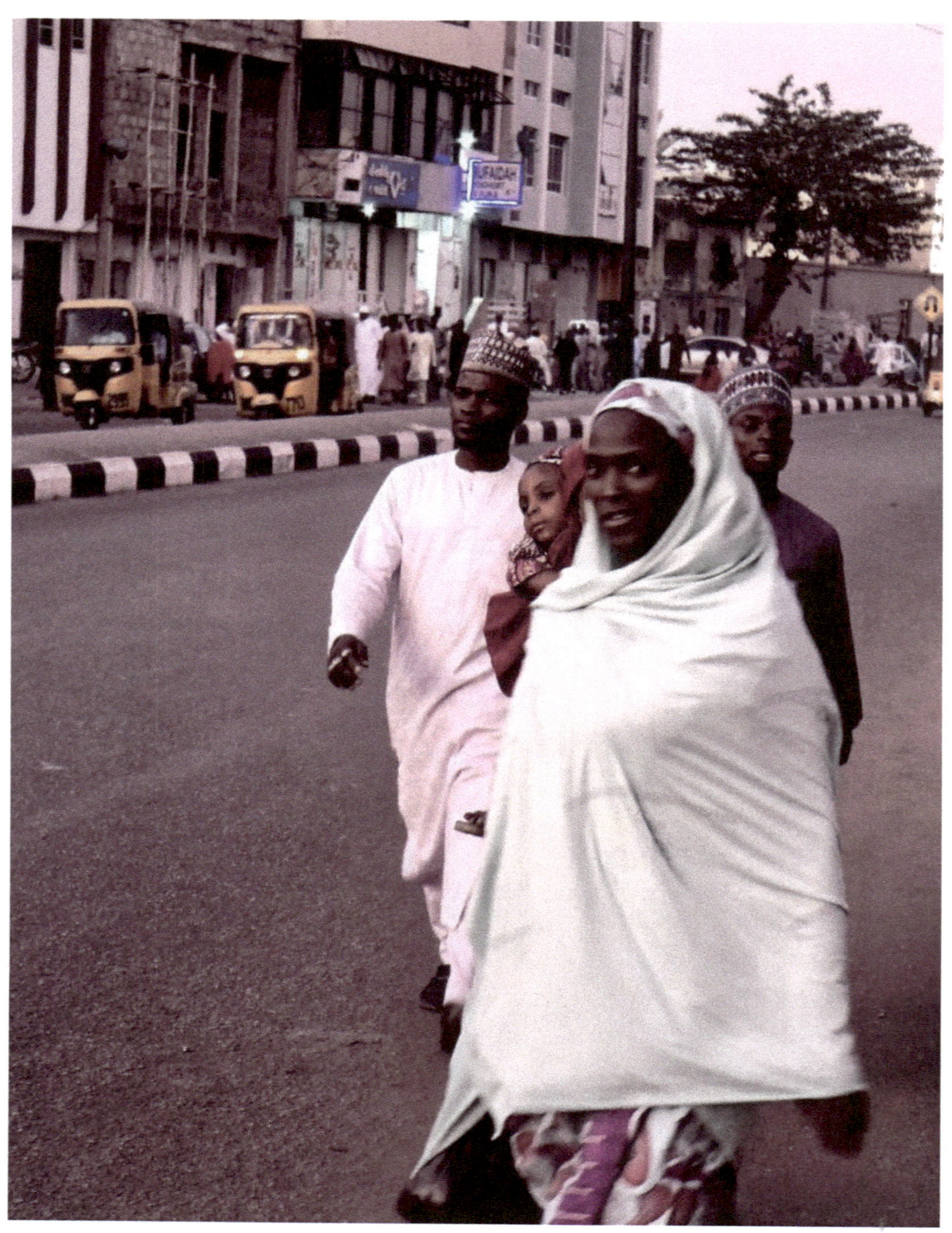

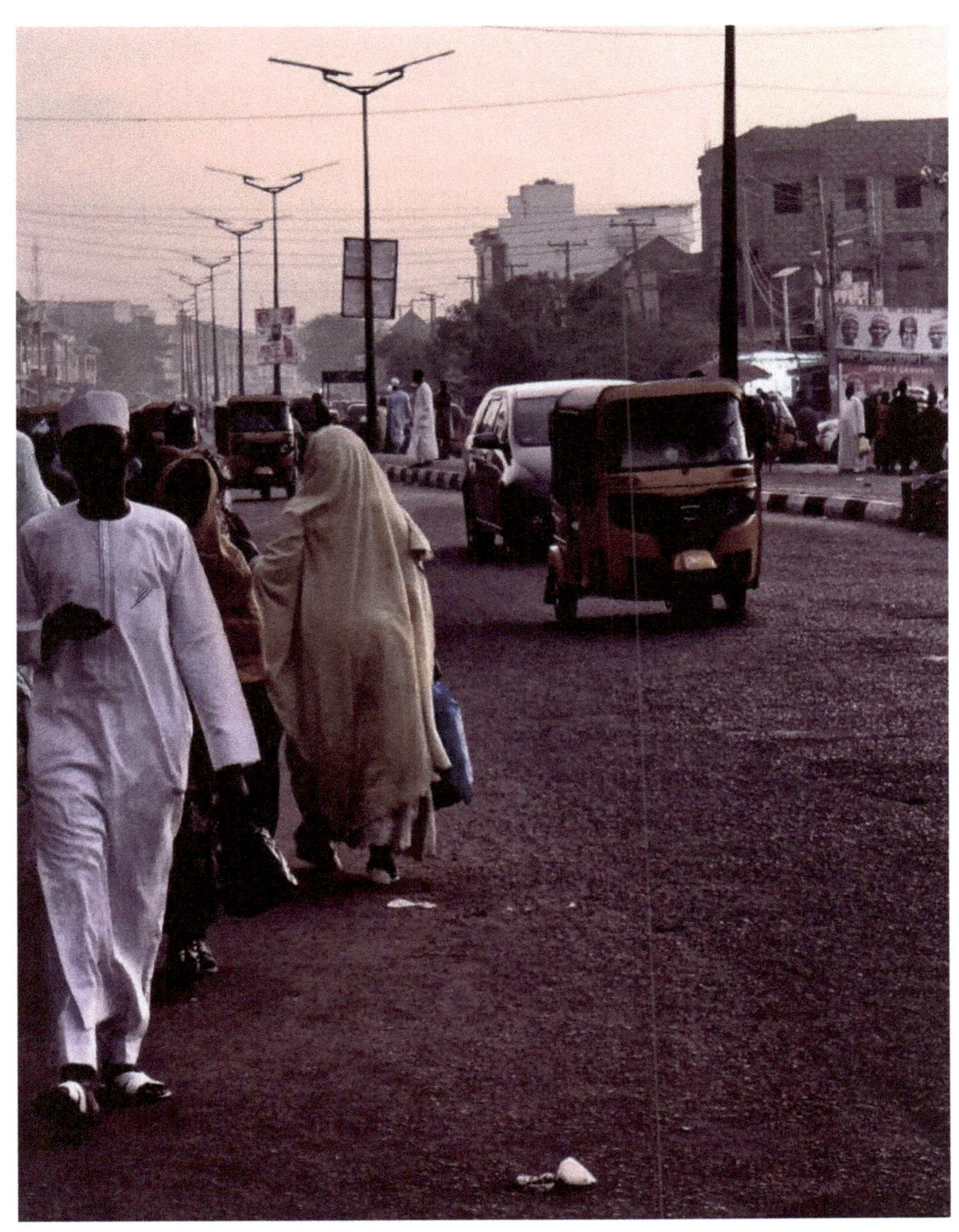

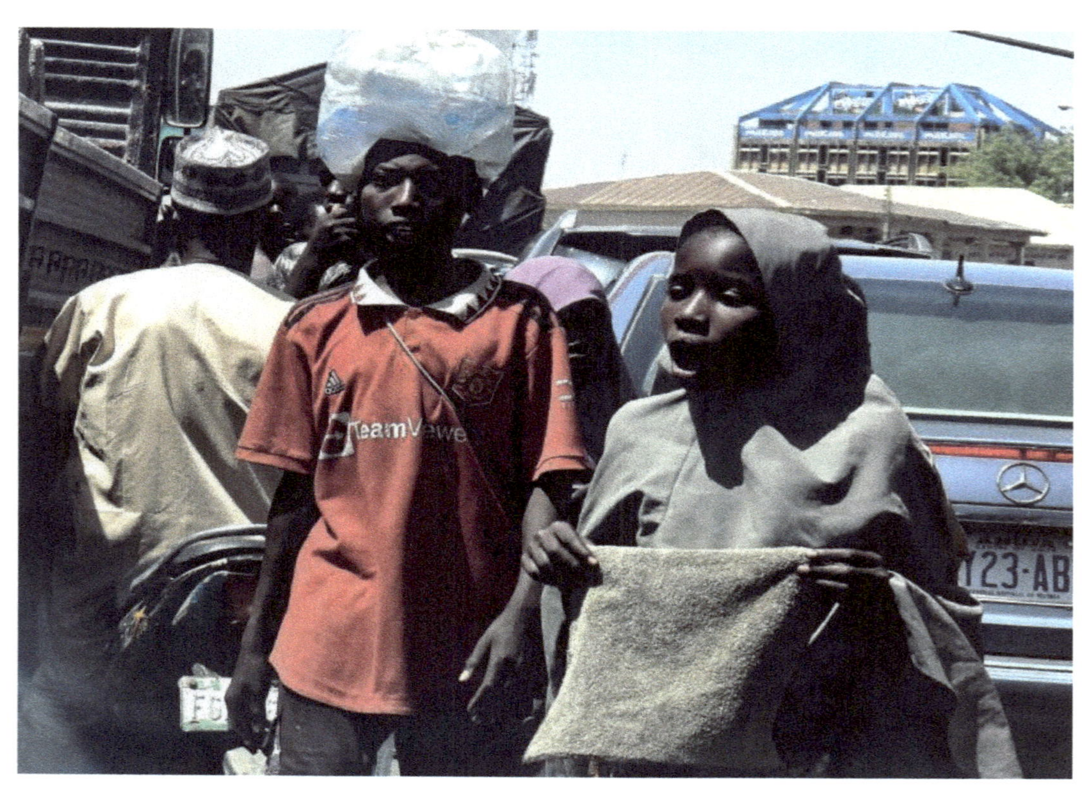

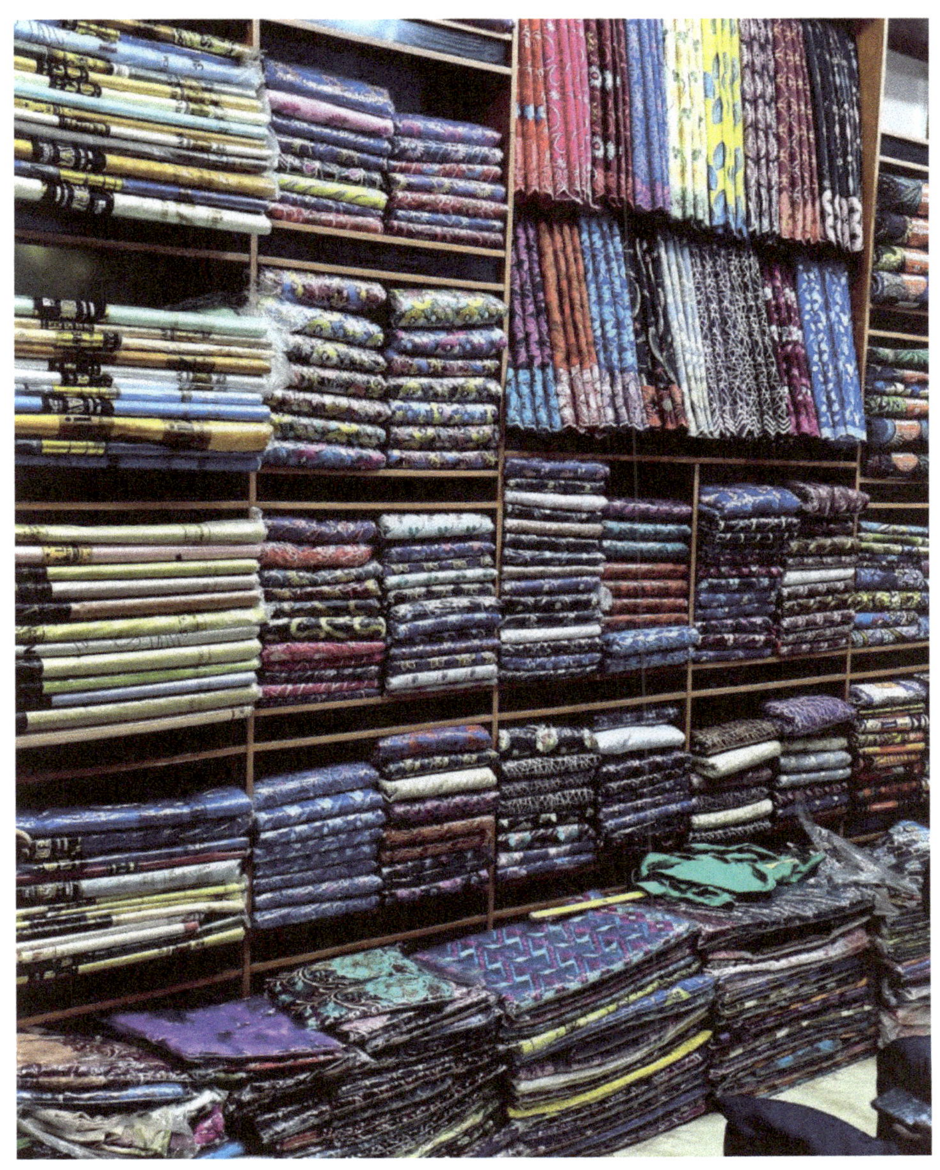

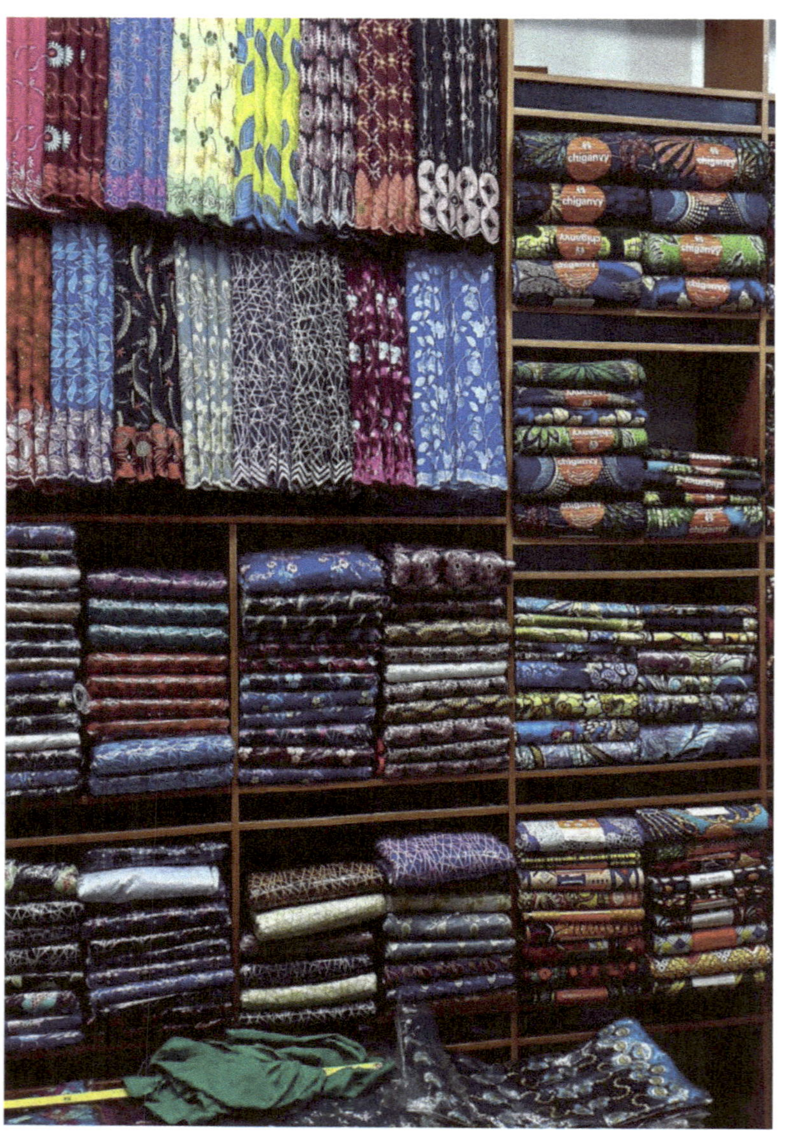

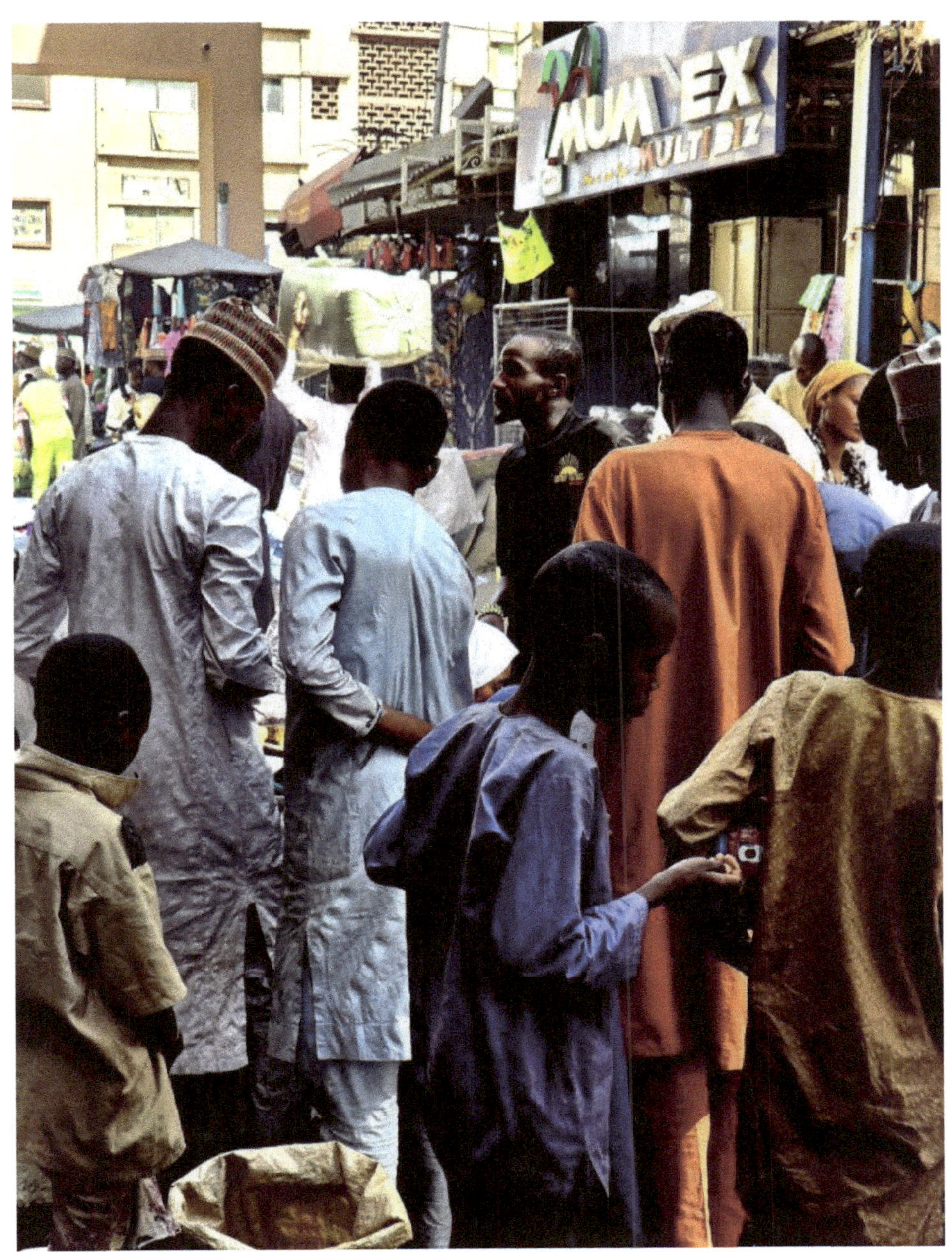

MUM EX
MULTI BIZ

DAY 8

On my final day, I was scheduled to meet with the Emir; at least, I hoped to meet His Highness. The week had already been tedious, and the passing of the Emir's Uncle, a high-ranking member of the Royal Court, had put a host of unanticipated demands on the Emir. My week had been extraordinary; I was grateful for all the remarkable events I'd experienced and the amazing sights I'd seen. I was disappointed that I hadn't witnessed the full Durbar that I'd been so excited to see, but the experience in this ancient Emirate had been fantastic. I did some sightseeing during the day and stopped by a small shop to have alterations made to a garment I'd purchased.

As the end of the day drew near, I received a phone call: the Emir would receive me at 7:00 pm. Earlier in the day, I'd insisted that I wanted to buy a Babbar Riga fitting for an audience with the Emir. My host assured me that I already had clothing that would be appropriate, but I wasn't satisfied. As they typically did with any request I made, they indulged me. It wasn't long before pictures of several beautiful Babbar Rigas were sent to my phone… I immediately selected an extraordinary black and gold Babbar Riga. As I was preparing for my meeting, a knock came to my door; it was Muhammad, my driver.

Muhammad came into the room and laid out the Babbar Riga; it was even more beautiful than the pictures. Muhammad helped me put it on correctly and assured me I had achieved my goal of being presentable to the Emir of Kano. During the ride to the palace, I was quiet and honestly a bit apprehensive; I'd never actually met royalty before, and I didn't know what to expect. Ahmad, my host, must have sensed my nervousness; he quietly assured me everything would be fine. Soon, we entered the palace grounds; I'd been to the palace before, but never beyond the front gate and the outer palace court. I was surprised when we went through several gates before parking at a building toward the back.

As I entered a large waiting room, I realized dozens of people were already there. It became clear that the Emir was receiving people, and my heart sank. It was already late; I could only imagine how tired he must have been. I began to doubt I would meet him. Before long, a courtier entered the room; he came and bowed in front of Ahmad and me. He advised us that the Emir had instructed that I should be given a tour of the palace. I was dumbfounded. I hadn't expected any special consideration, and honestly, I didn't imagine my visit was very significant. The consideration humbled me, and I didn't want to waste time. The courtier and a palace guard escorted us though hallways, court rooms, large formal chambers and more. We entered the Emir's stables, where I had a chance to see his beautiful horses… It was all so regal; and I still don't have adequate words to describe everything I saw. The courtier explained things to me as we went from one area to another: The palace was ancient, like so many places I'd seen. It had survived invasion attempts and assault by the British when they colonized Kano… the ancient walls and large ornate doors told a story all their own.

After the tour, we returned to the waiting room. Another large group had arrived to see the Emir. All I could do was wait, but it wasn't long before I was summoned. I followed my host and the courtier down a corridor and into a large, beautifully appointed room. Sitting on a large sofa was the Emir of Kano. He waved for me to approach. I walked toward him with my head bowed, "Please sit; I apologize for not receiving you earlier; it has been a challenging week." His Highness was so gracious as he motioned for me to sit. We talked briefly, and then he said, "I had hoped to show you more of the palace, my gardens, and my libraries." I was astonished; I'd hoped to meet him, perhaps shake his hand, and I fully expected to be dismissed after that. In my wildest dreams, I didn't anticipate the Emir taking time to meet and talk with me… as I was still processing what he said, he surprised me again. "I'll tell you what, I have another group or two to receive. Give me a little time, and we'll take a tour."

I stood in stunned silence and bowed my head; I followed the courtier to another room, where we waited briefly to be summoned again. It wasn't long before the Emir sent for us. He and I talked for a bit, and then he said, "Let us walk." We casually walked through the halls and corridors of the palace.

The Emir graciously explained in detail the areas we walked through, his gardens, the minor palaces, and more. I was doing my best to take in all he shared with me.

After the tour, we entered an area with a large spiral staircase. I followed His Highness up the staircase and into a large library, where he explained that this was one of his private libraries. I sat and quietly listened as he shared some of his family's history and his childhood in the palace. His grandfather was the Emir, His Highness Muhammadu Sanusi II, the 14th Emir of Kano, is a descendant of the Dabo dynasty, established in the early 19th century. His lineage as part of the royal family goes back generations.

We talked for what seemed like forever, and the Emir was extraordinarily patient and gracious. I could not have imagined I'd ever have such a remarkable experience. Before I left, we walked to a balcony off of his library.

We looked over the grounds, and he explained the minor palaces and other buildings to me. It was an extraordinary experience that capped one of the most amazing journeys of my life… the Emir and I shook hands before he retired to his private chambers, and I left the palace.

Gidan Rumfa – The Emir's Palace

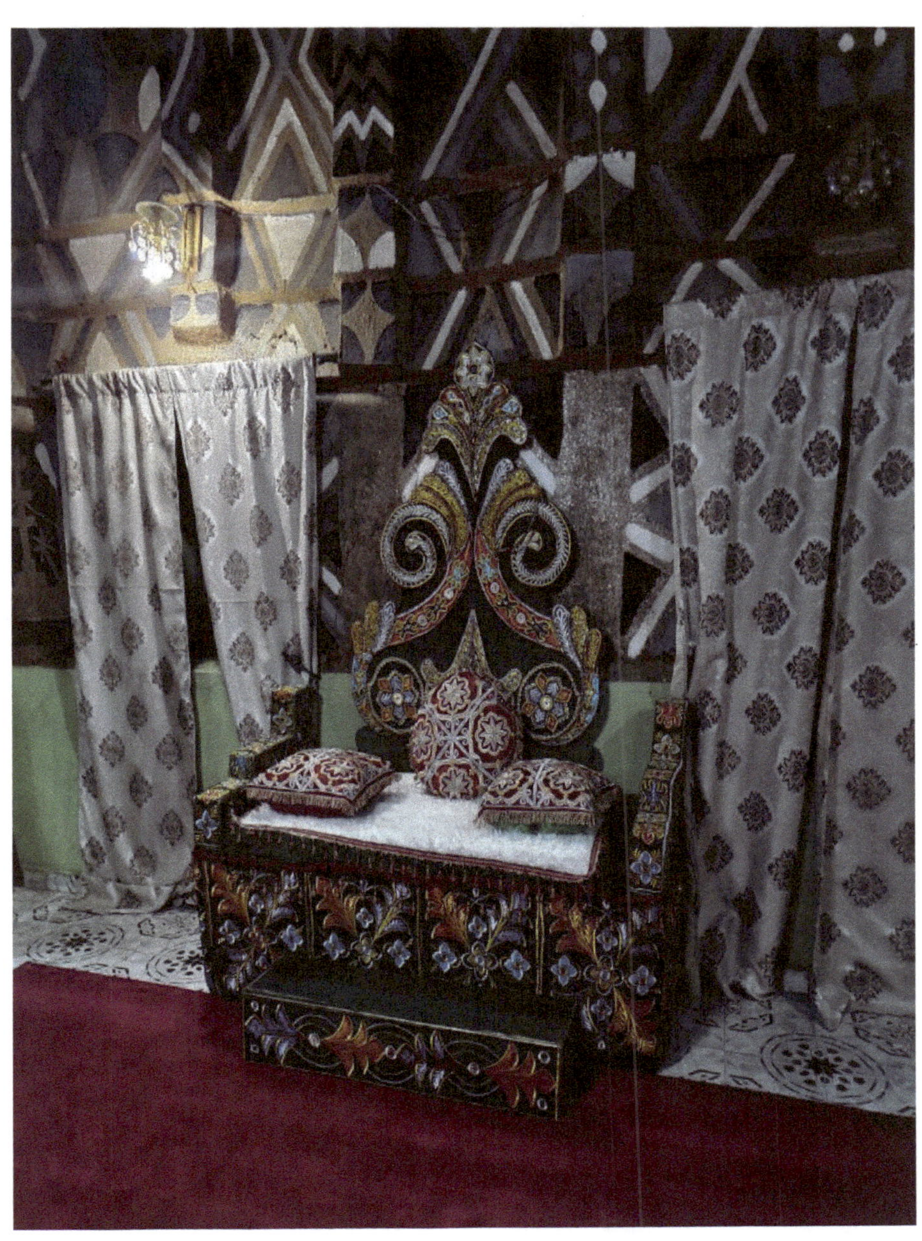

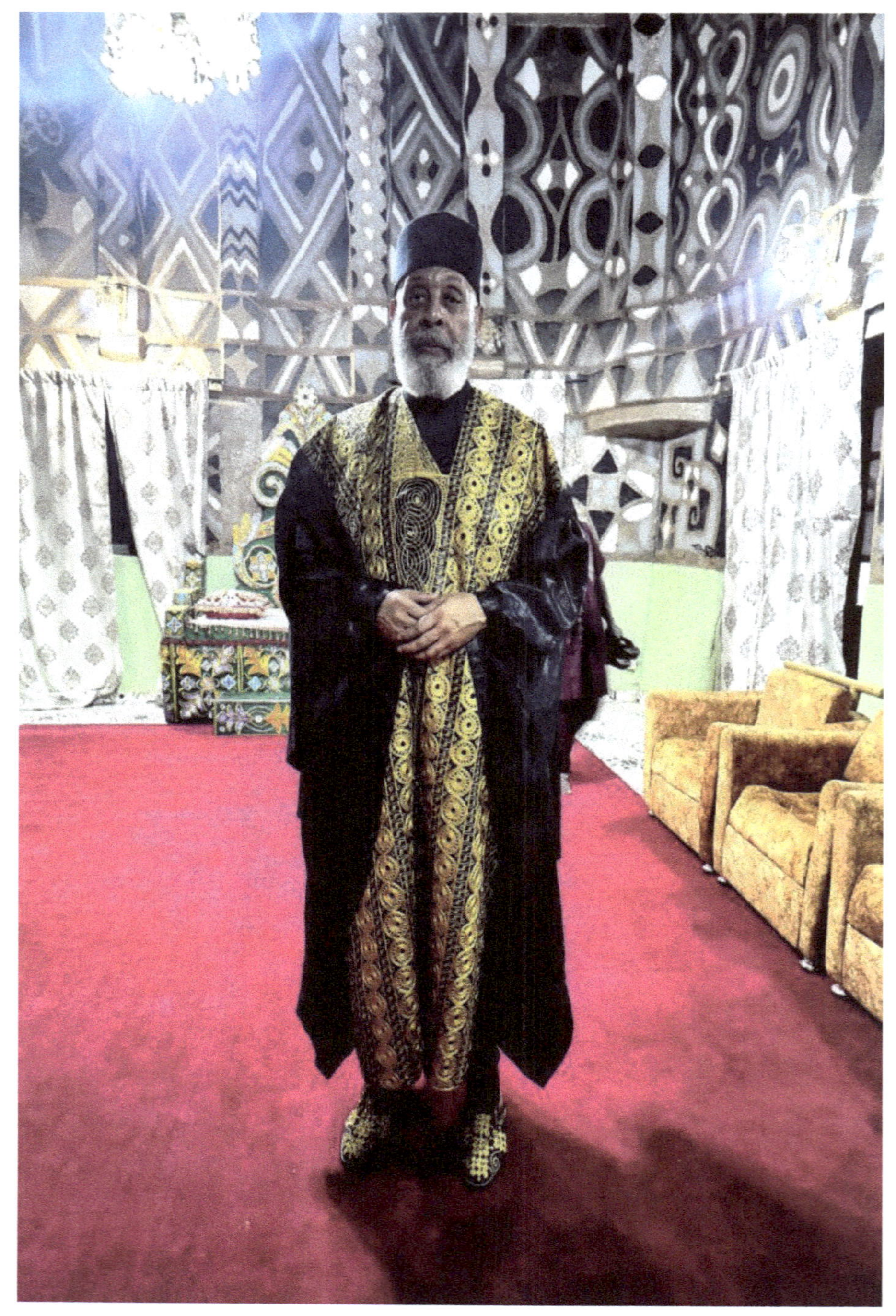

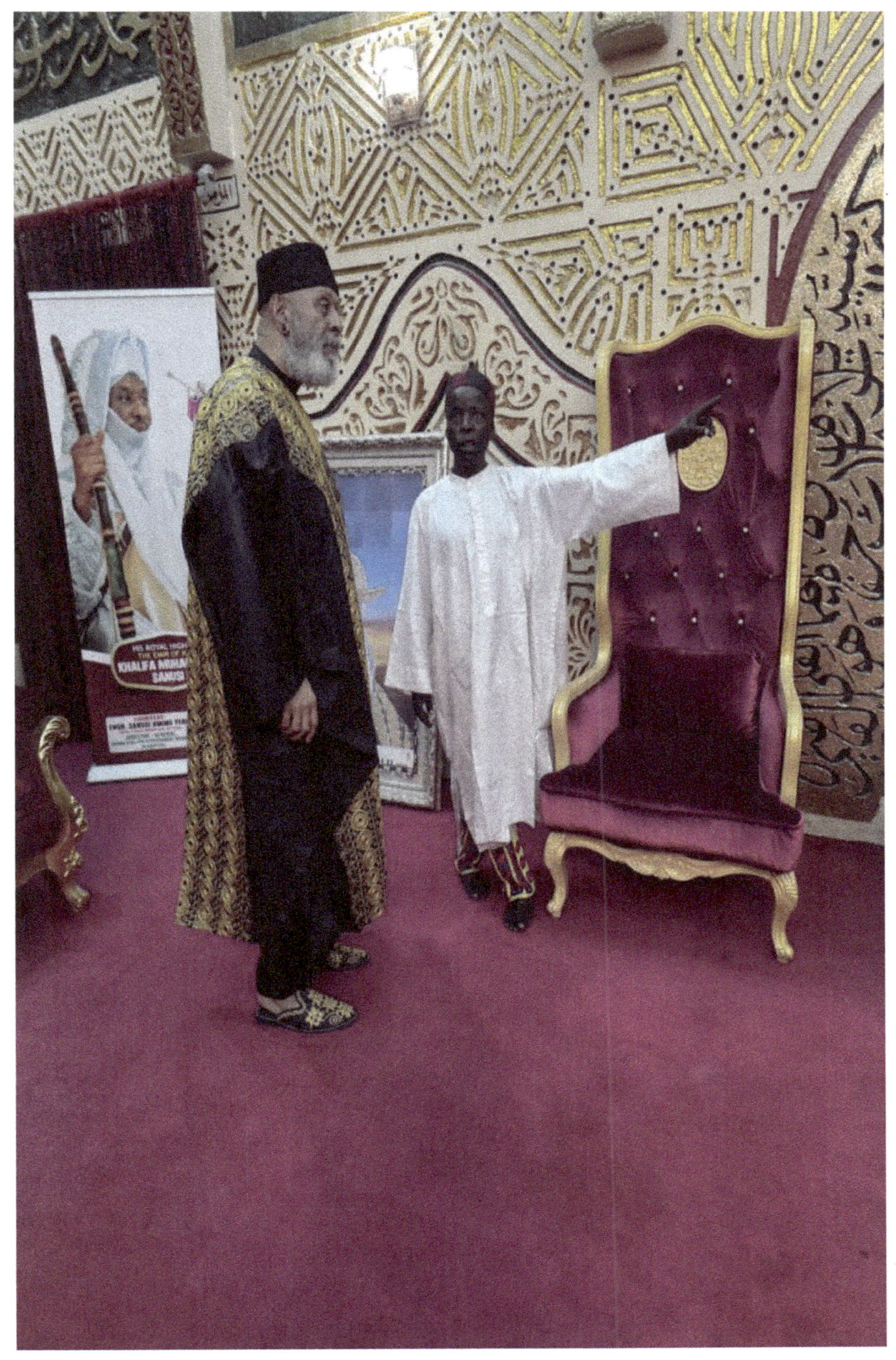

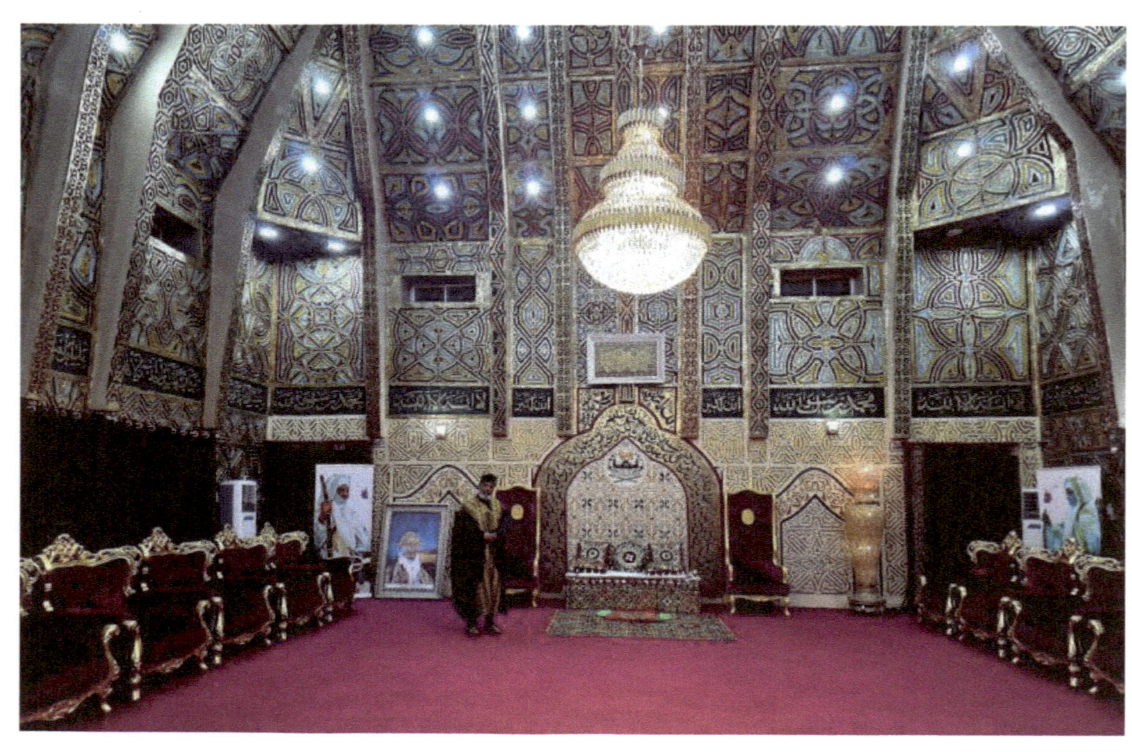

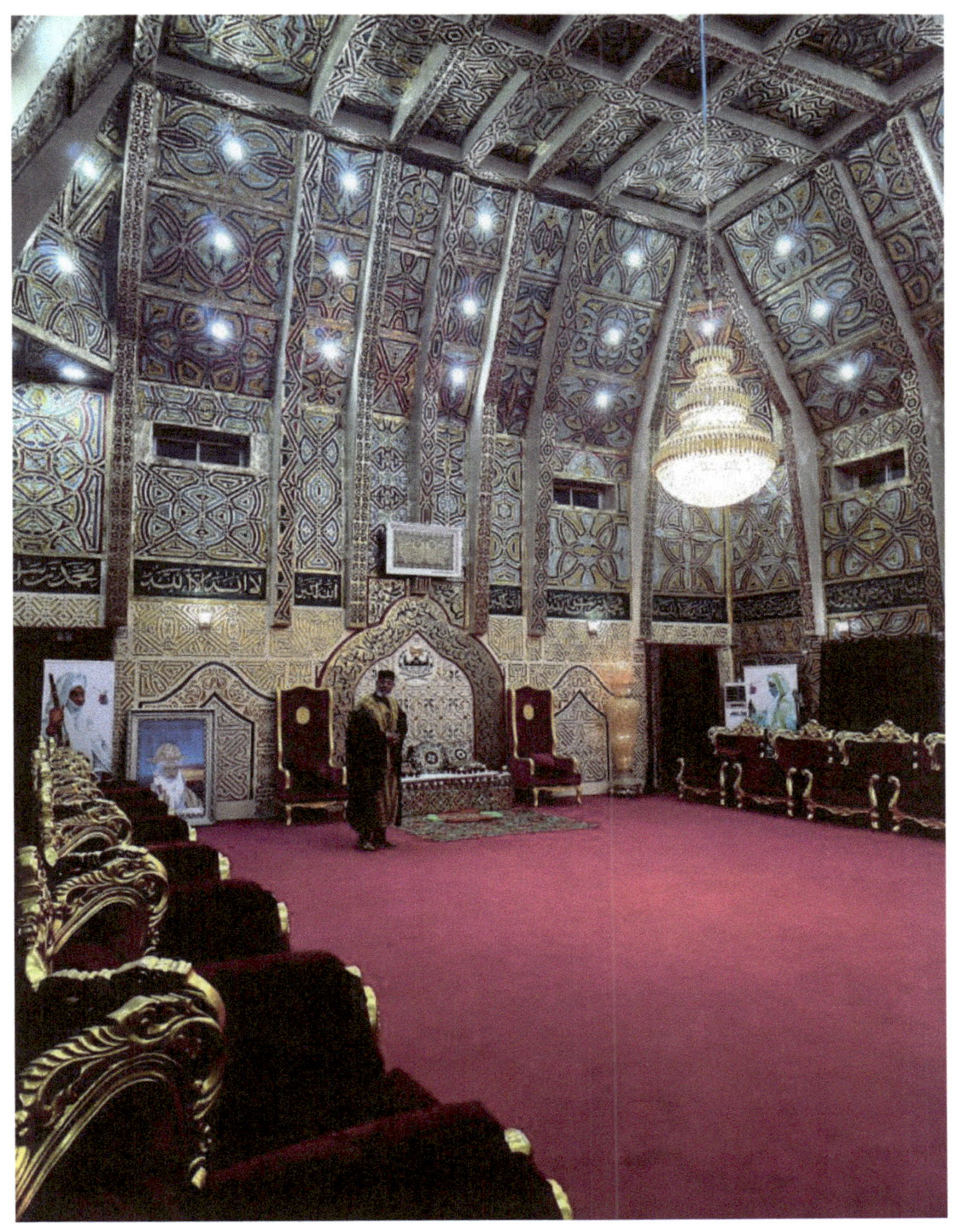

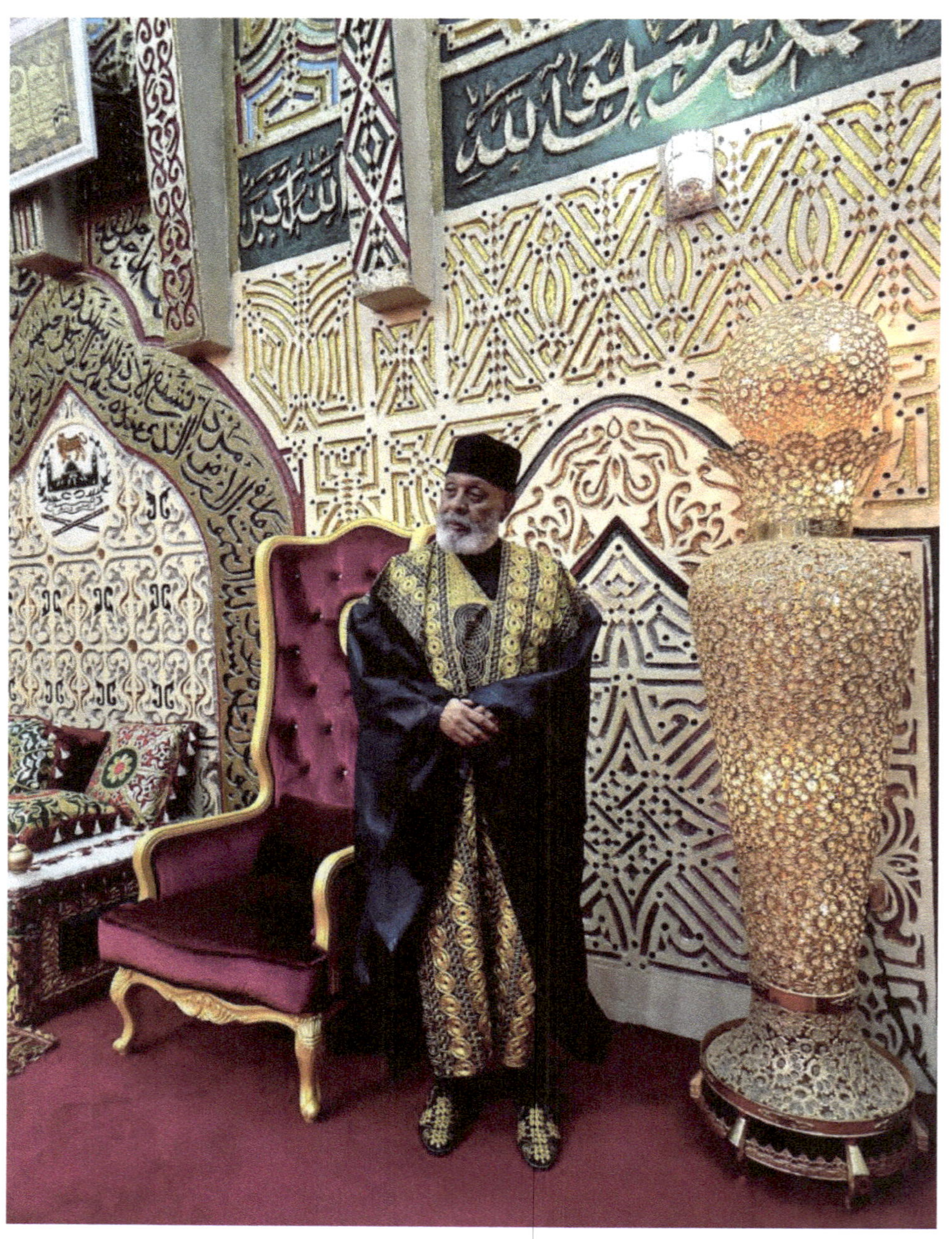

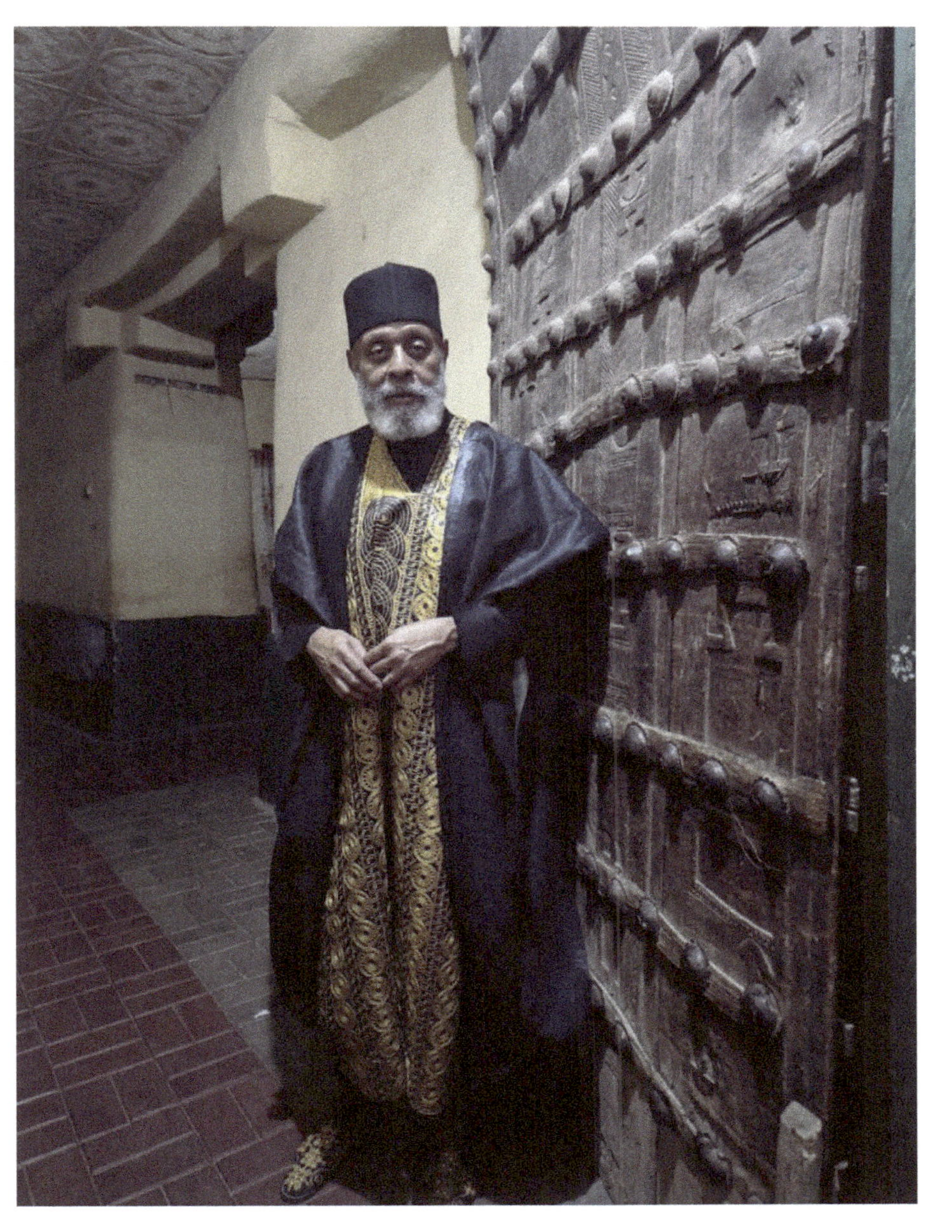

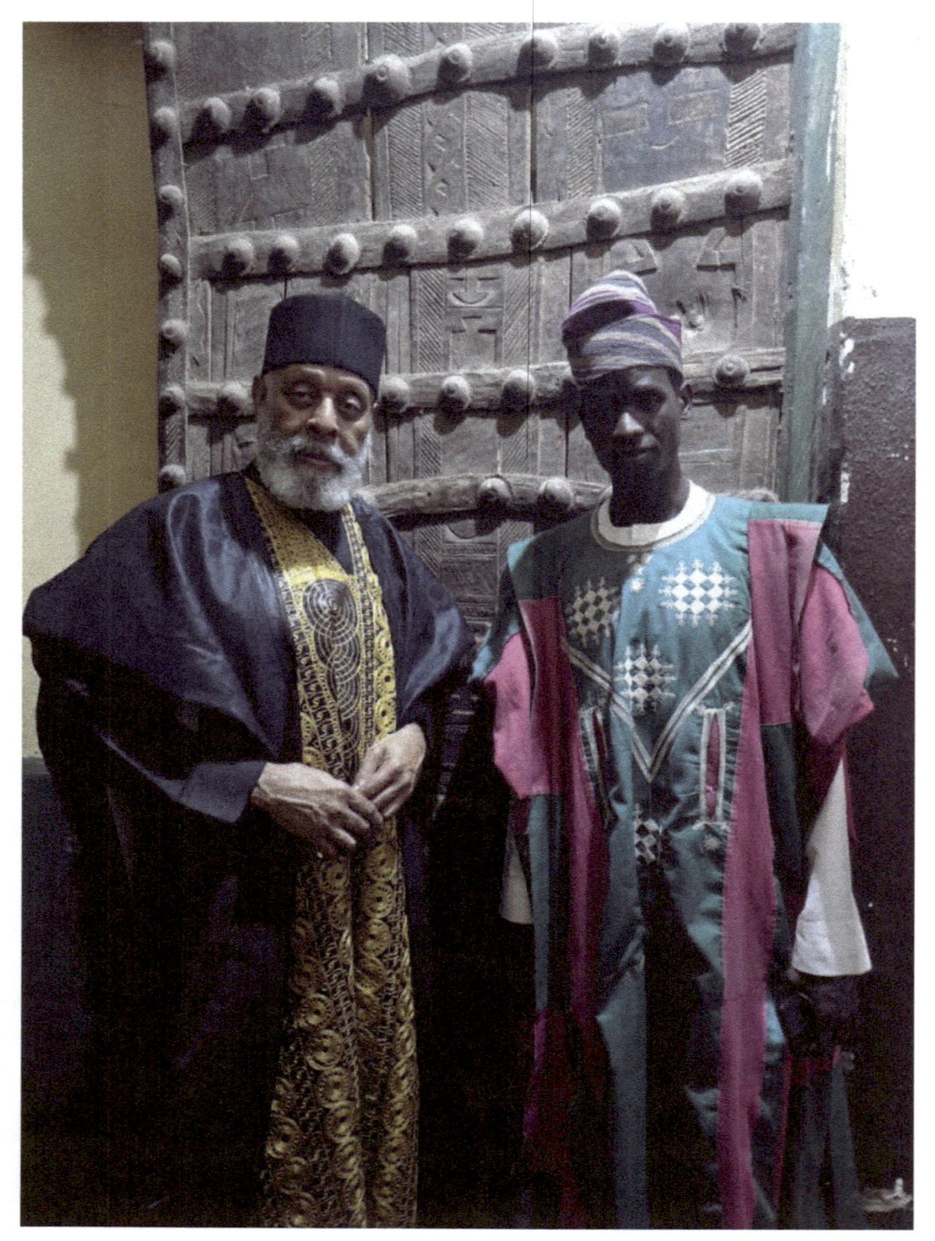

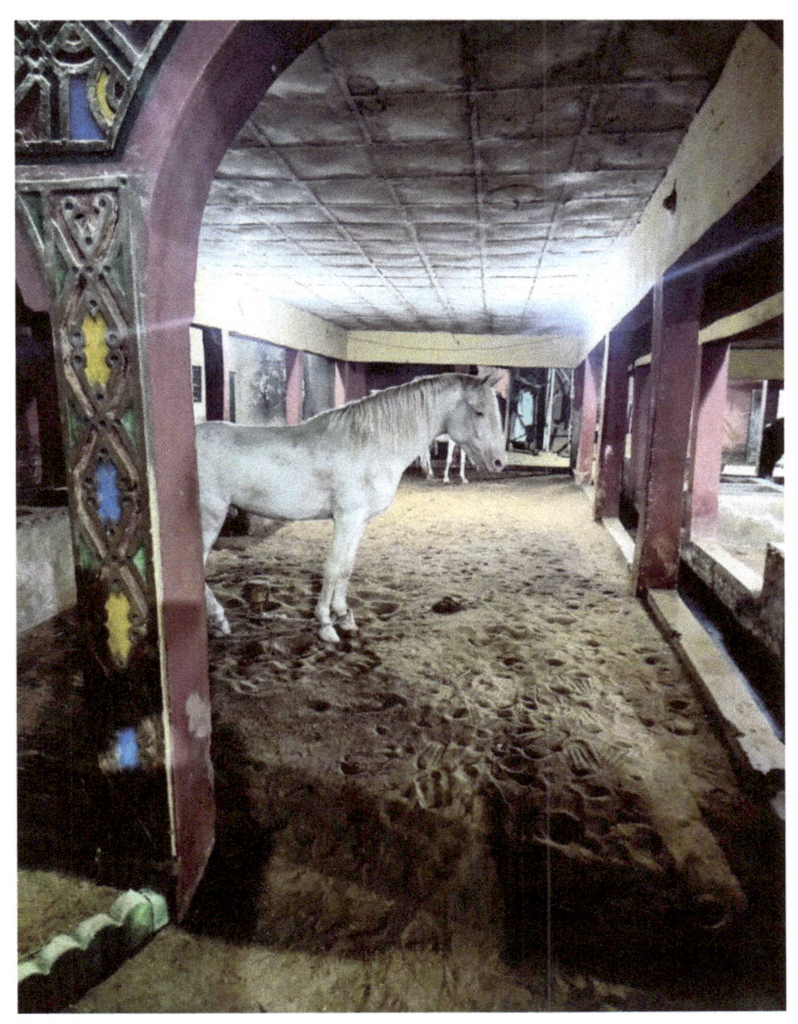

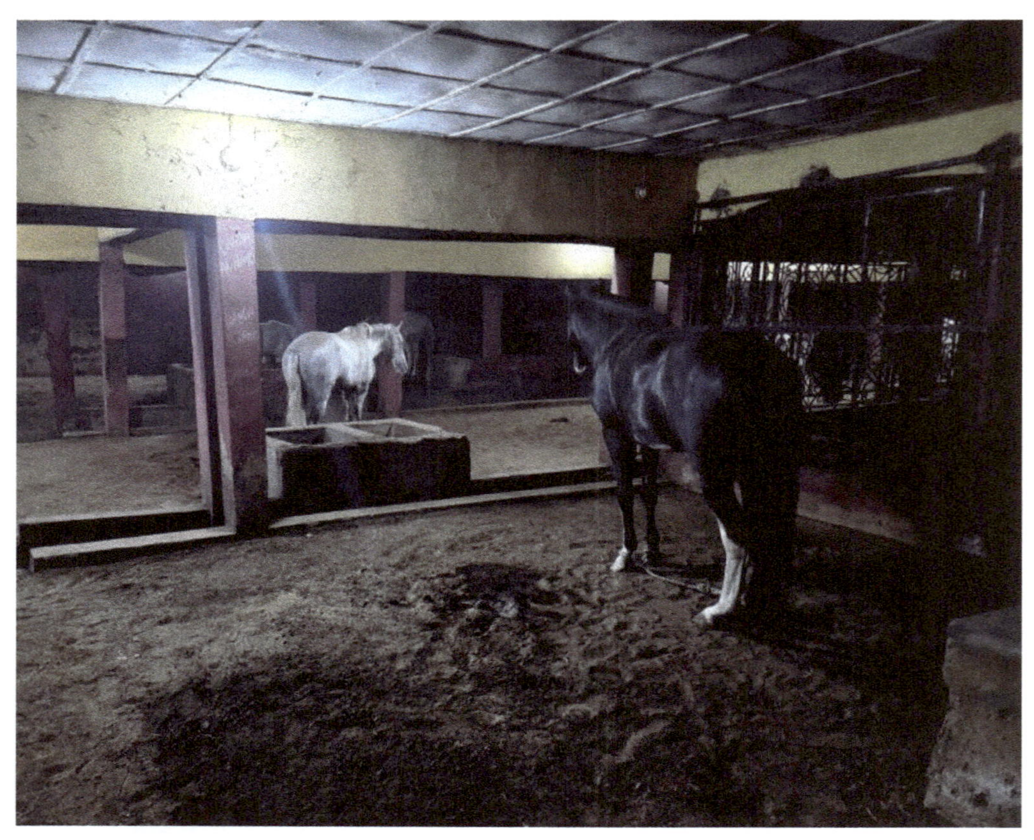

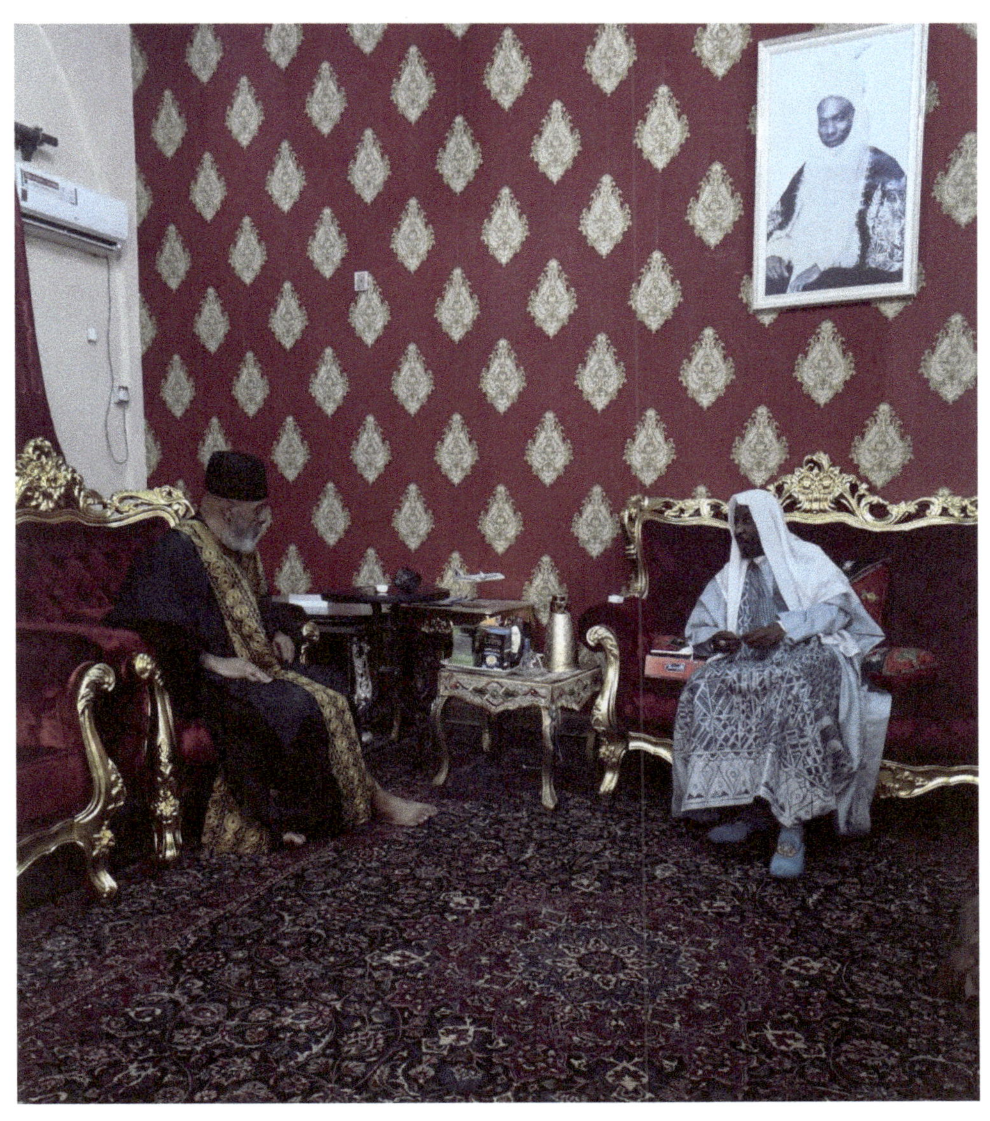

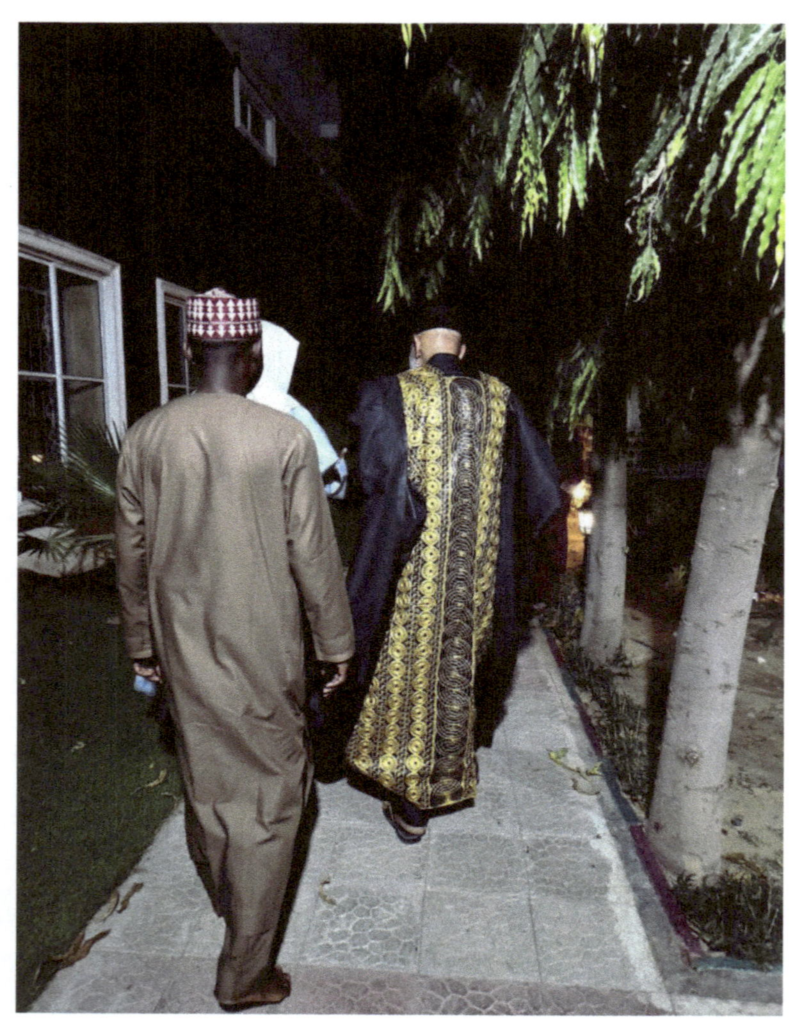

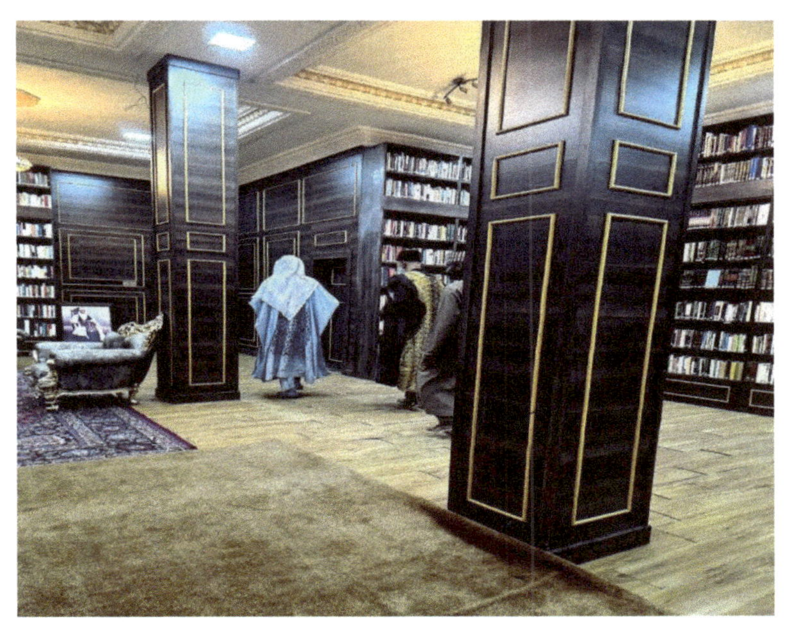

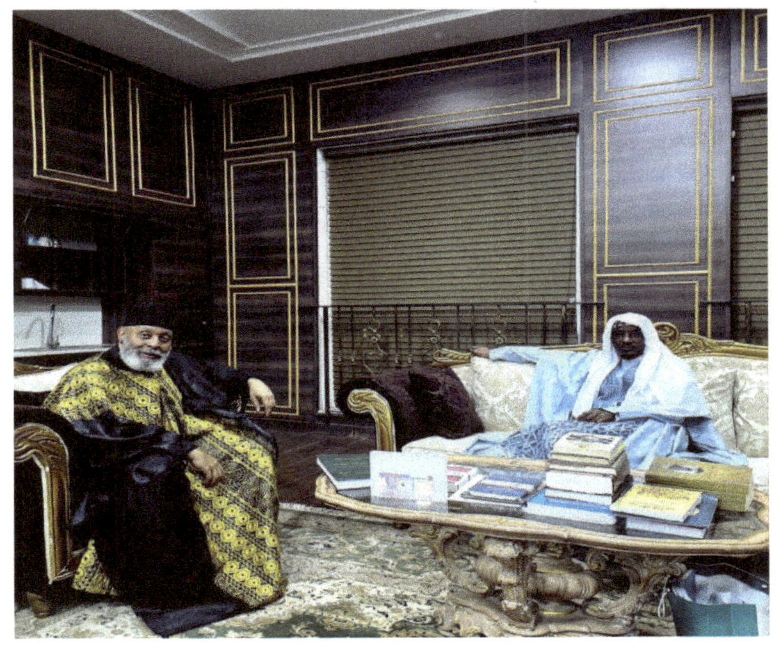

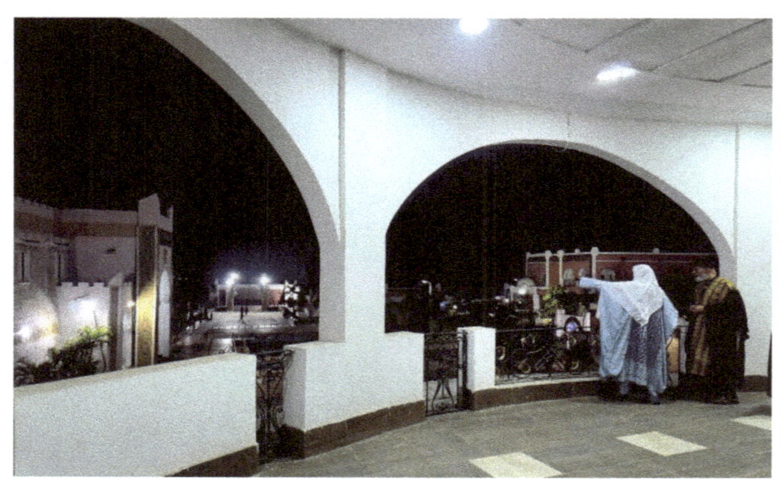

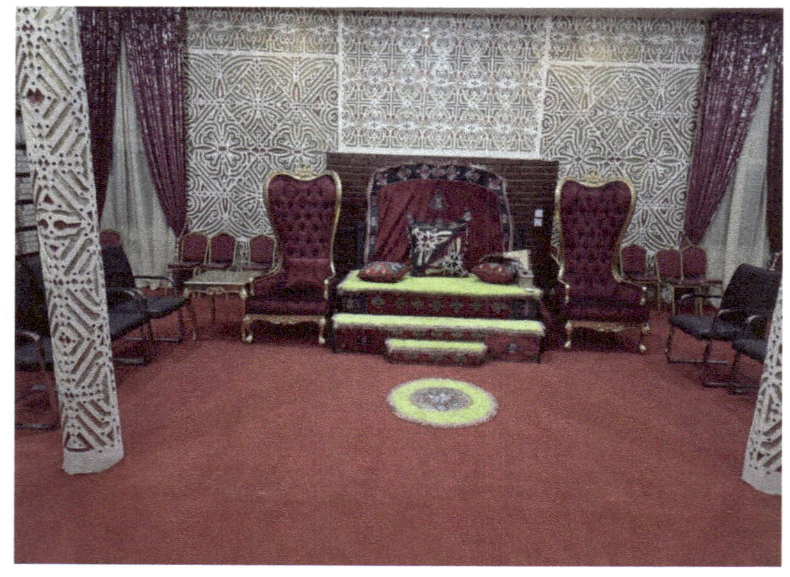

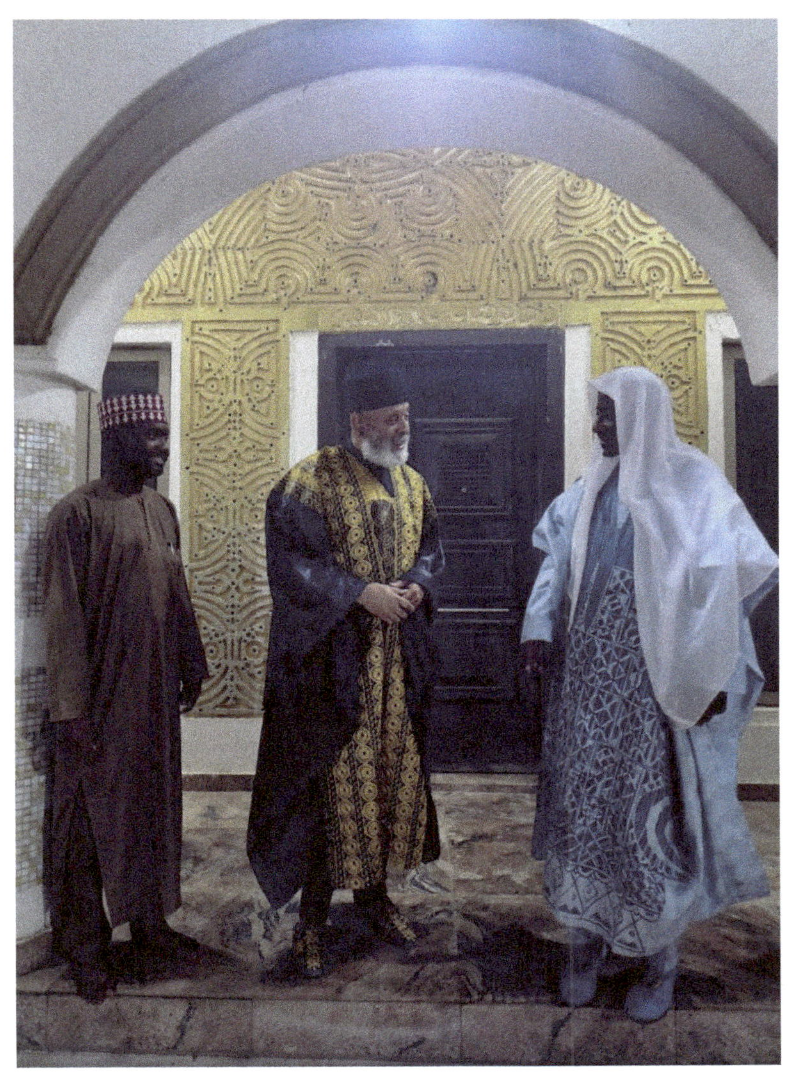

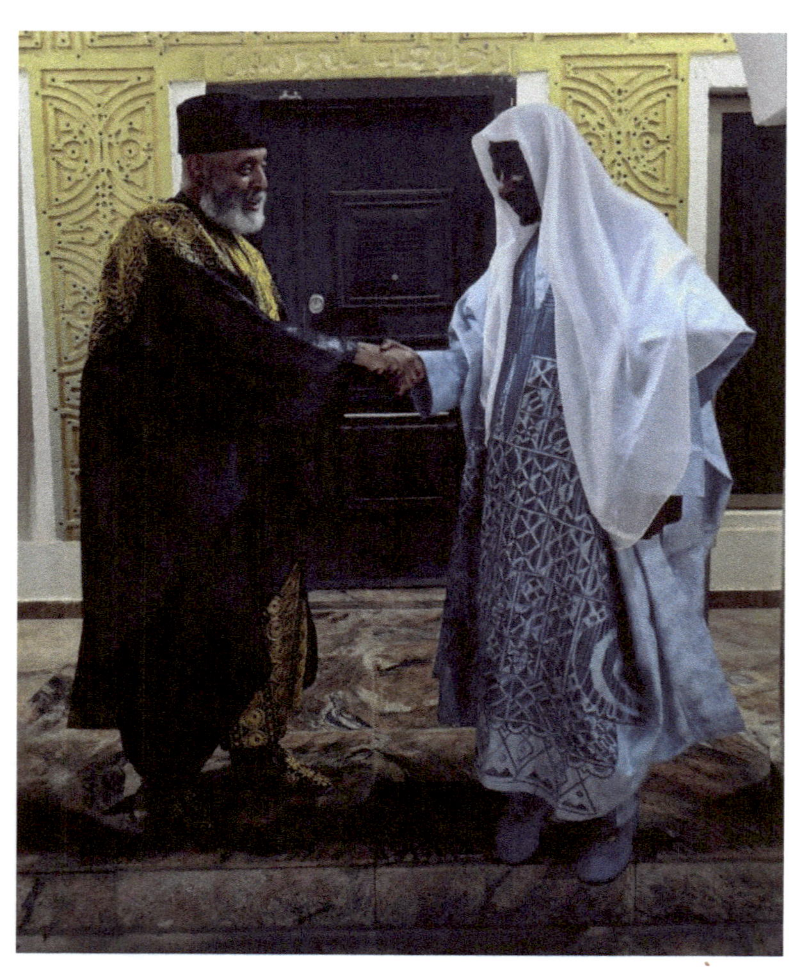

PICTURES OF KANO

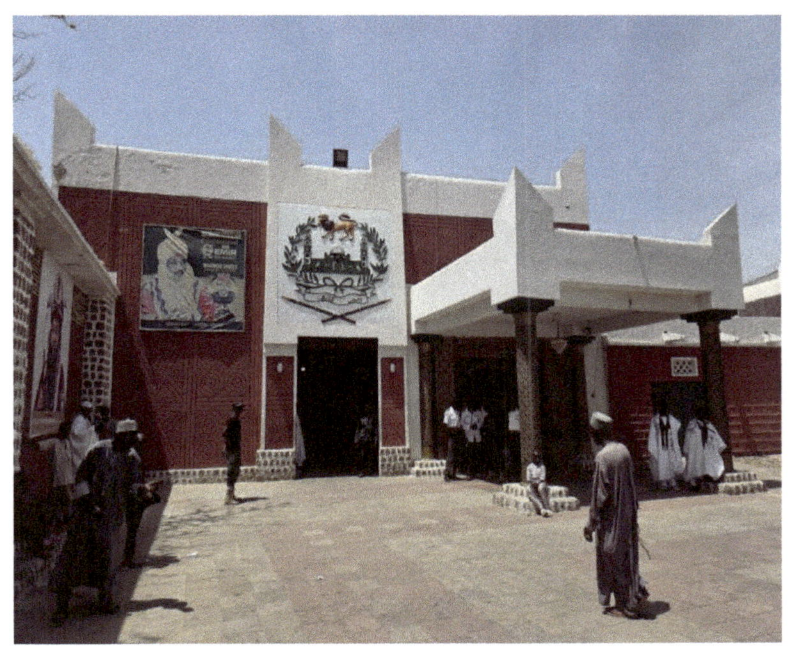

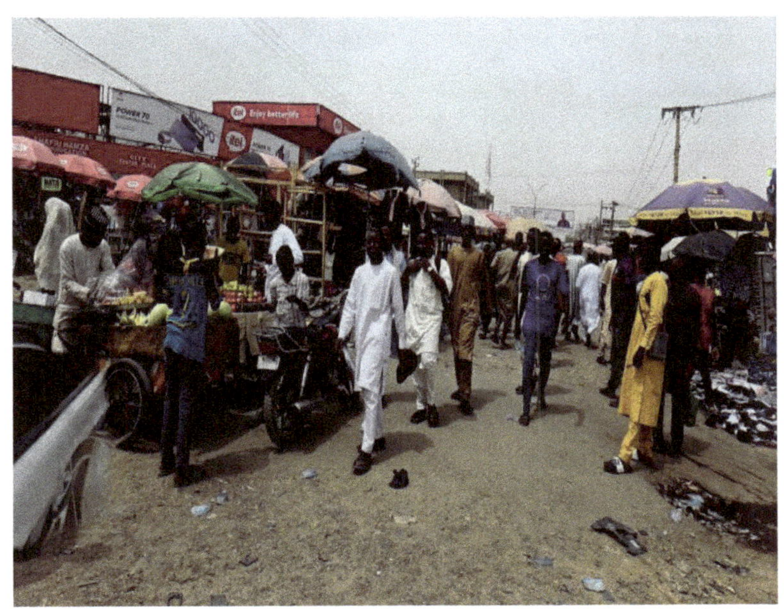

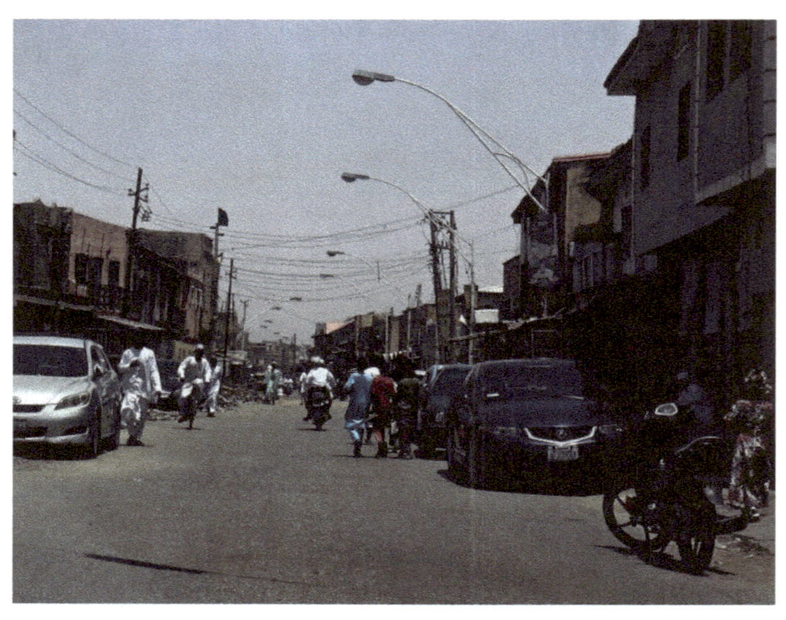

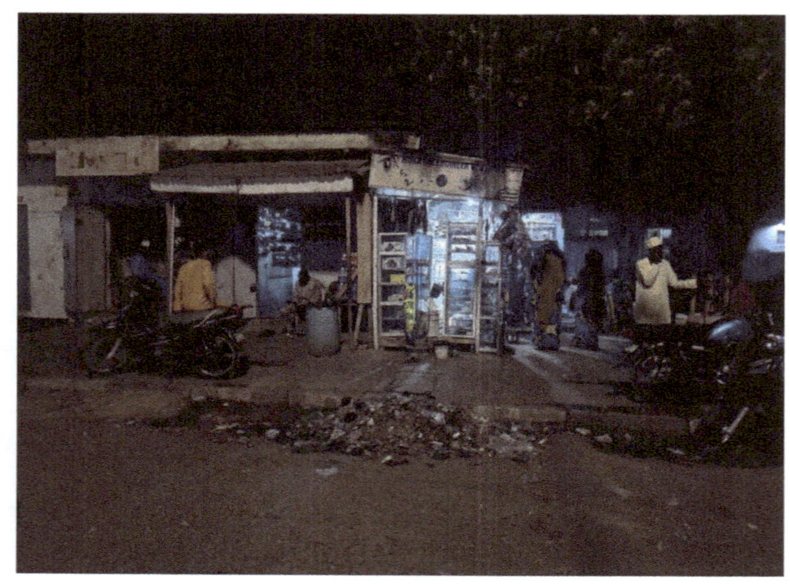

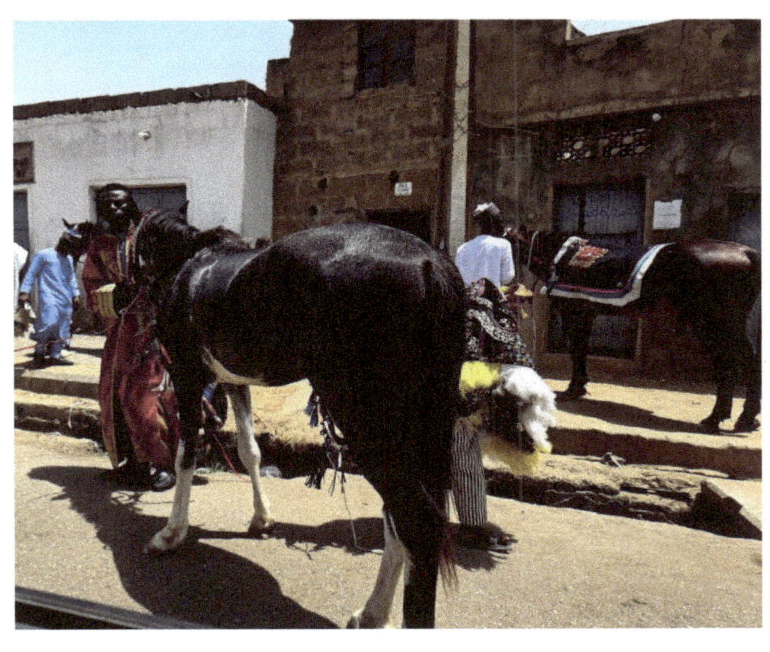

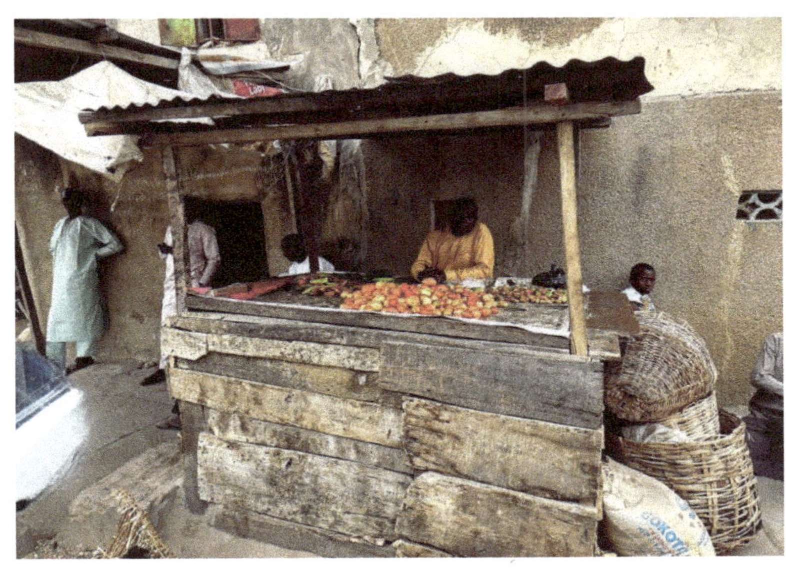

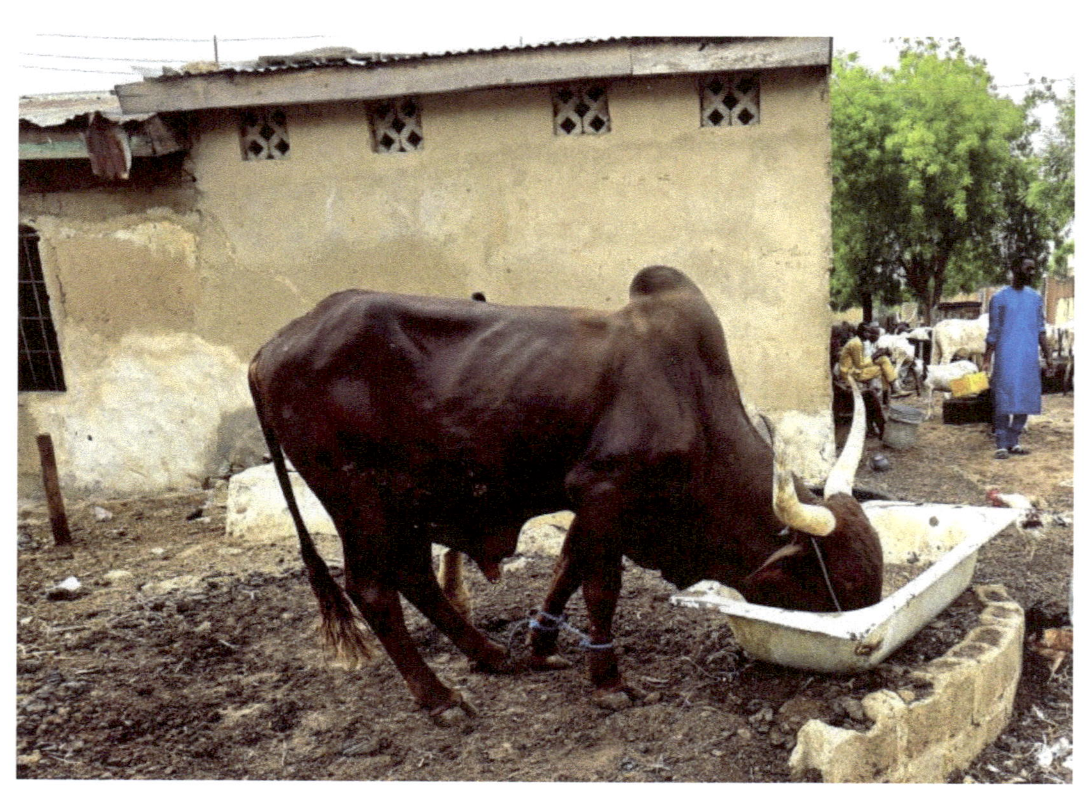

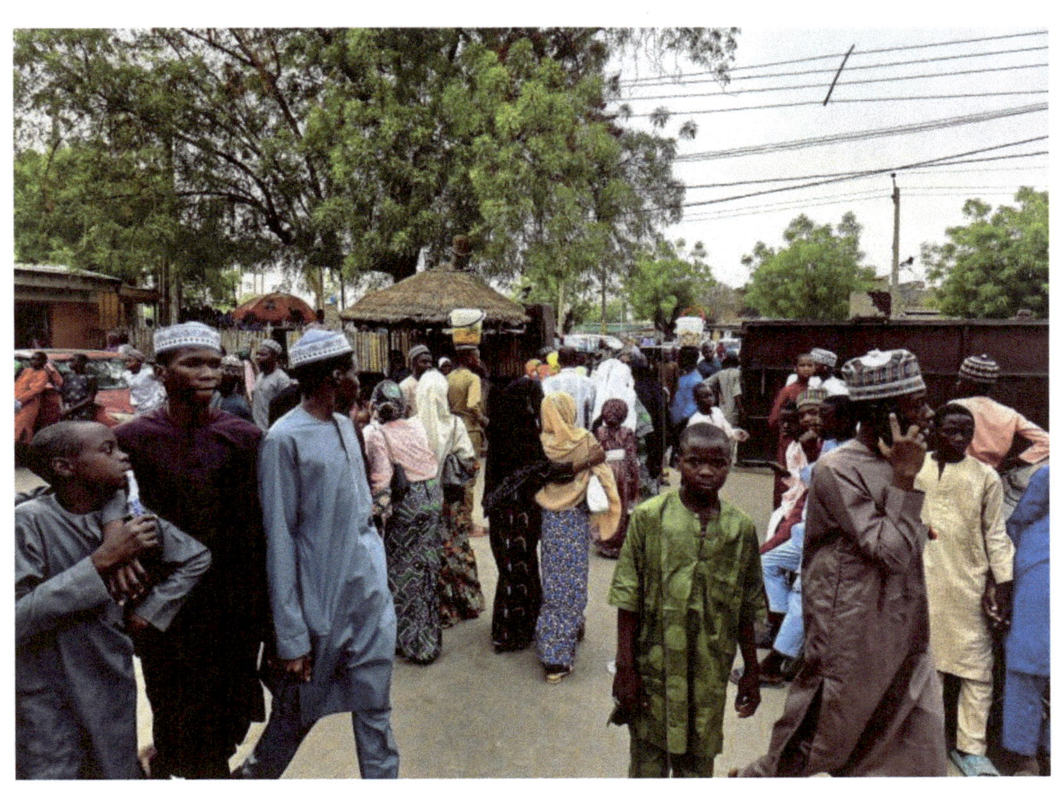

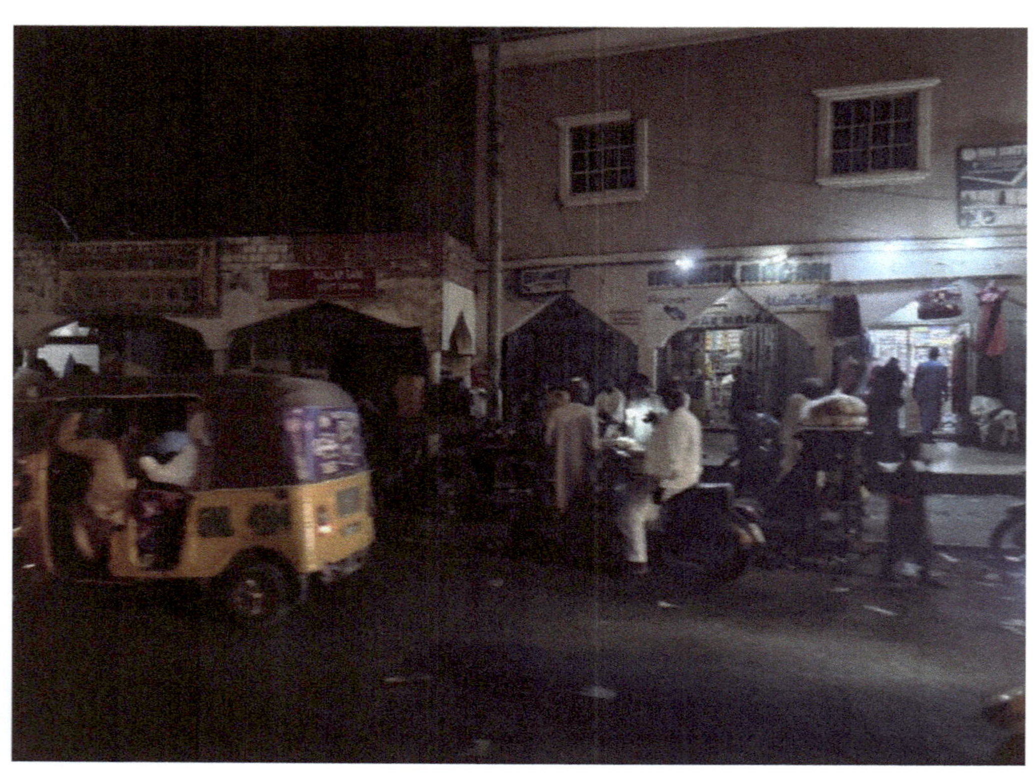

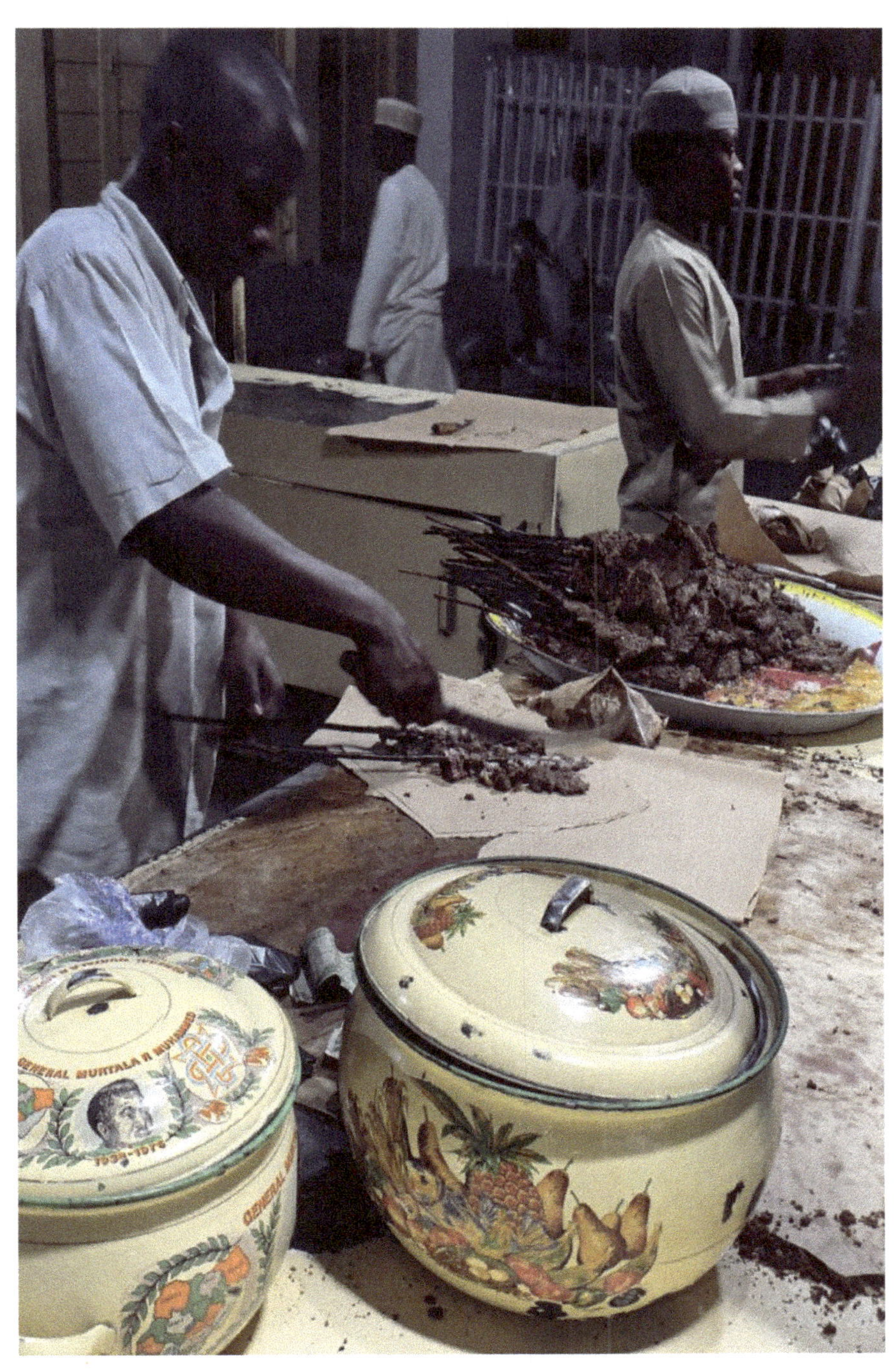

GENERAL MURTALA R MUHAMMED

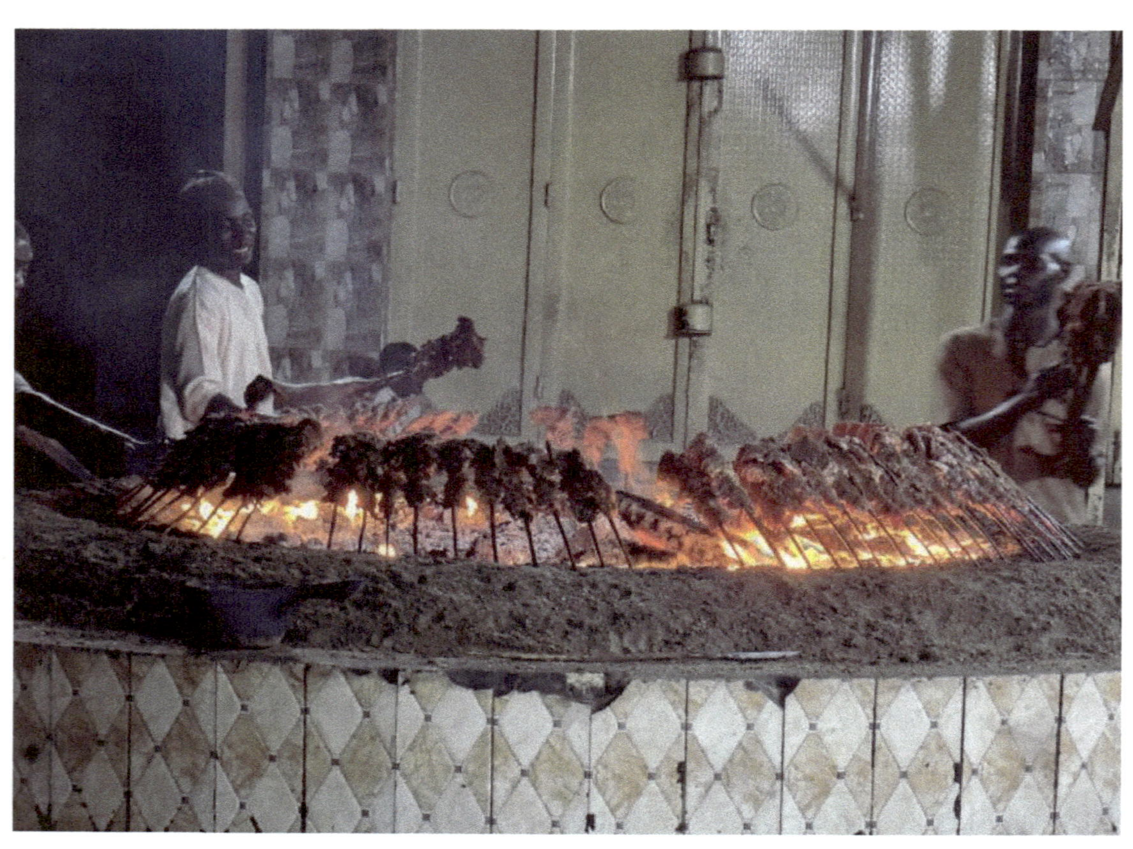

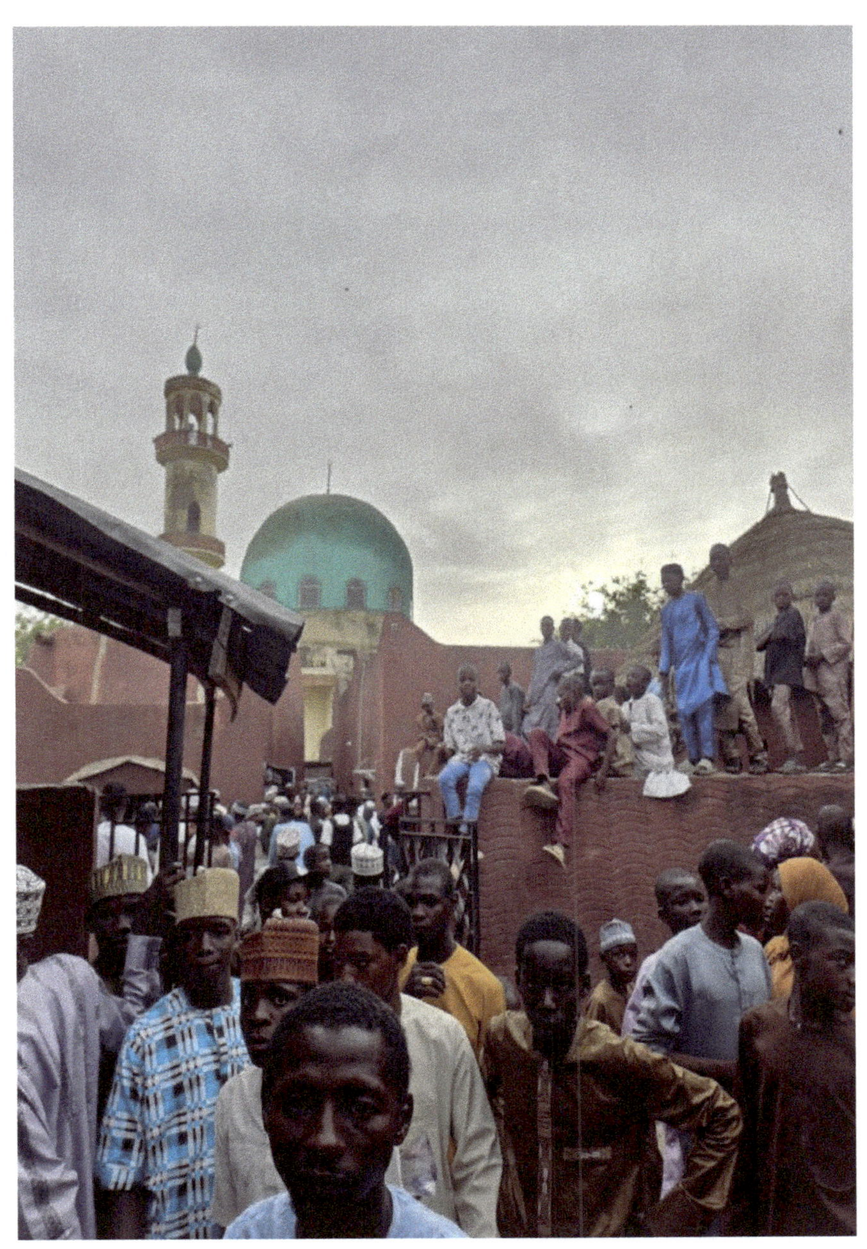

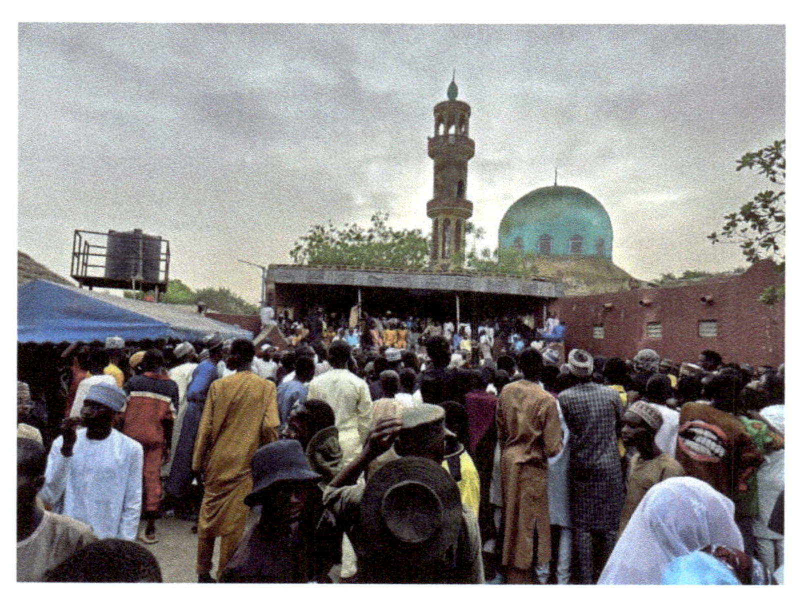

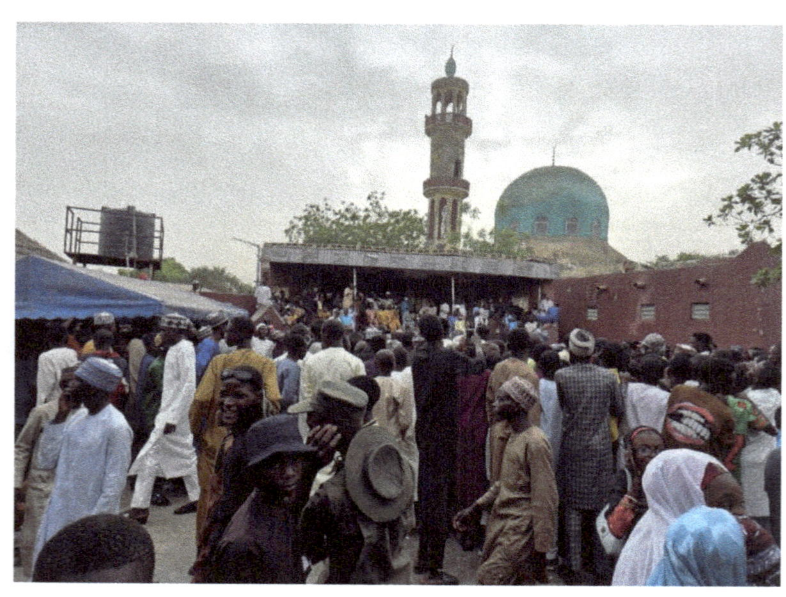

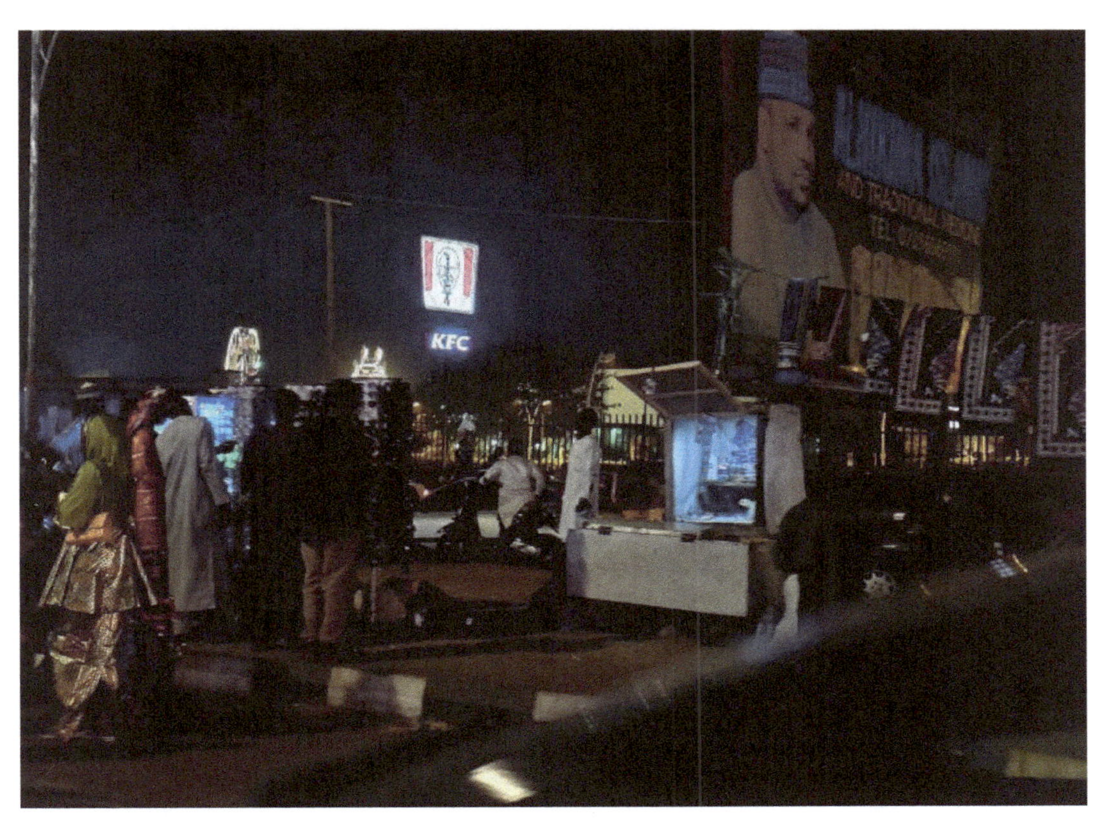

KFC

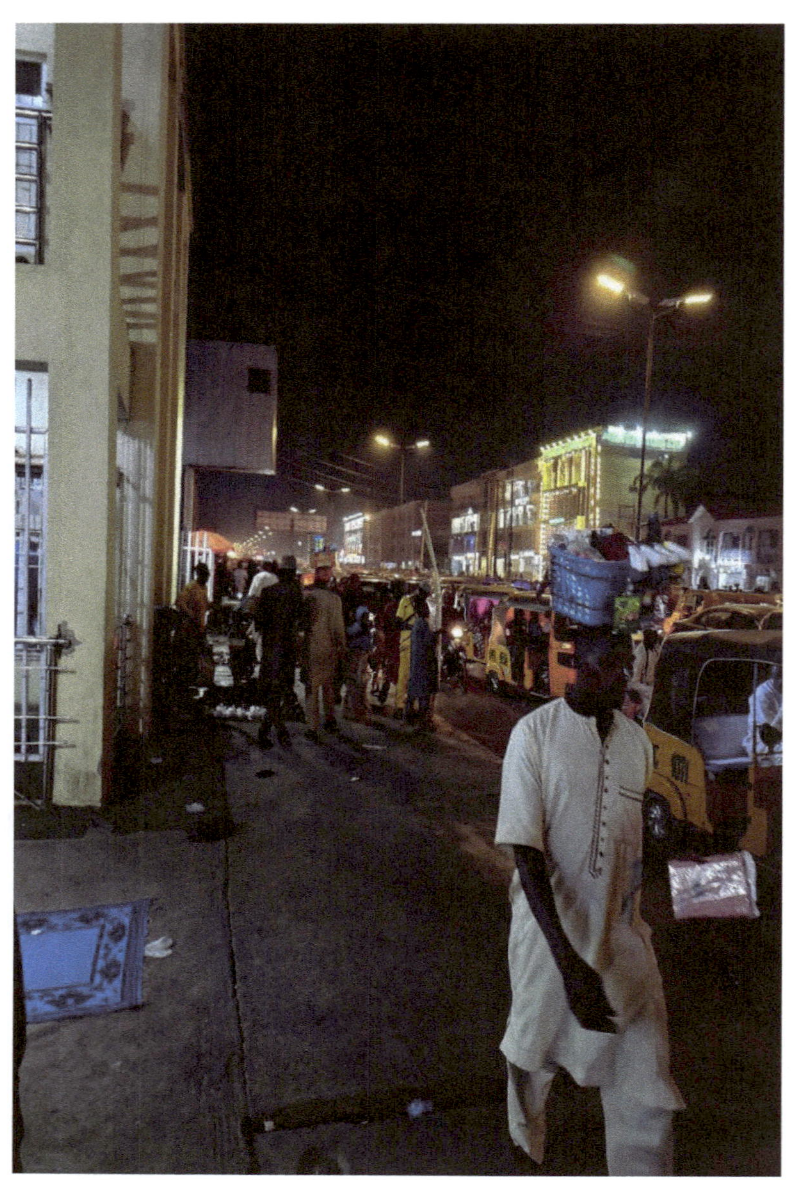

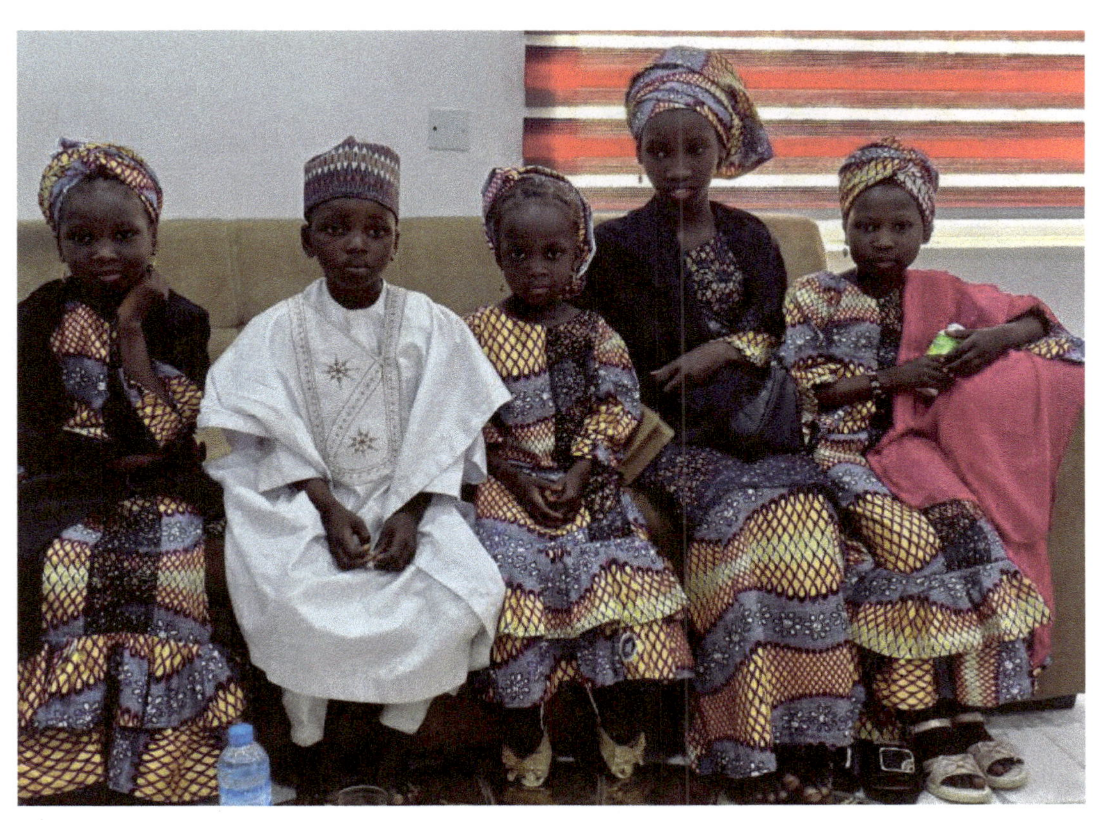

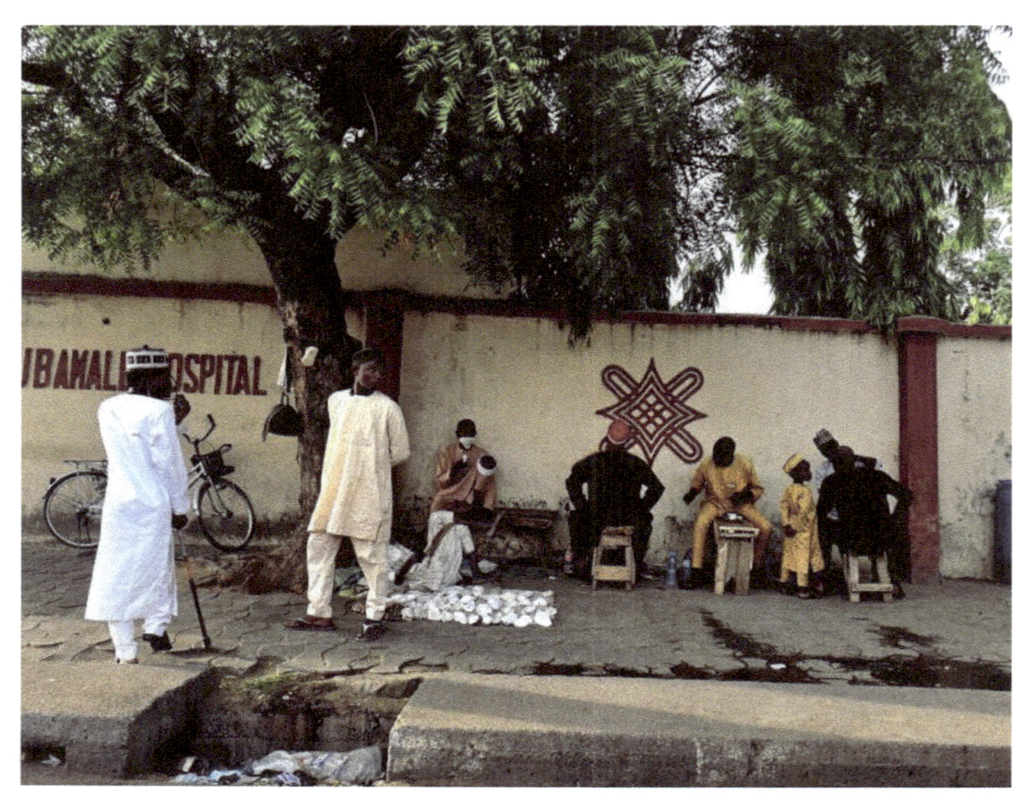

BAMALI OSPITAL

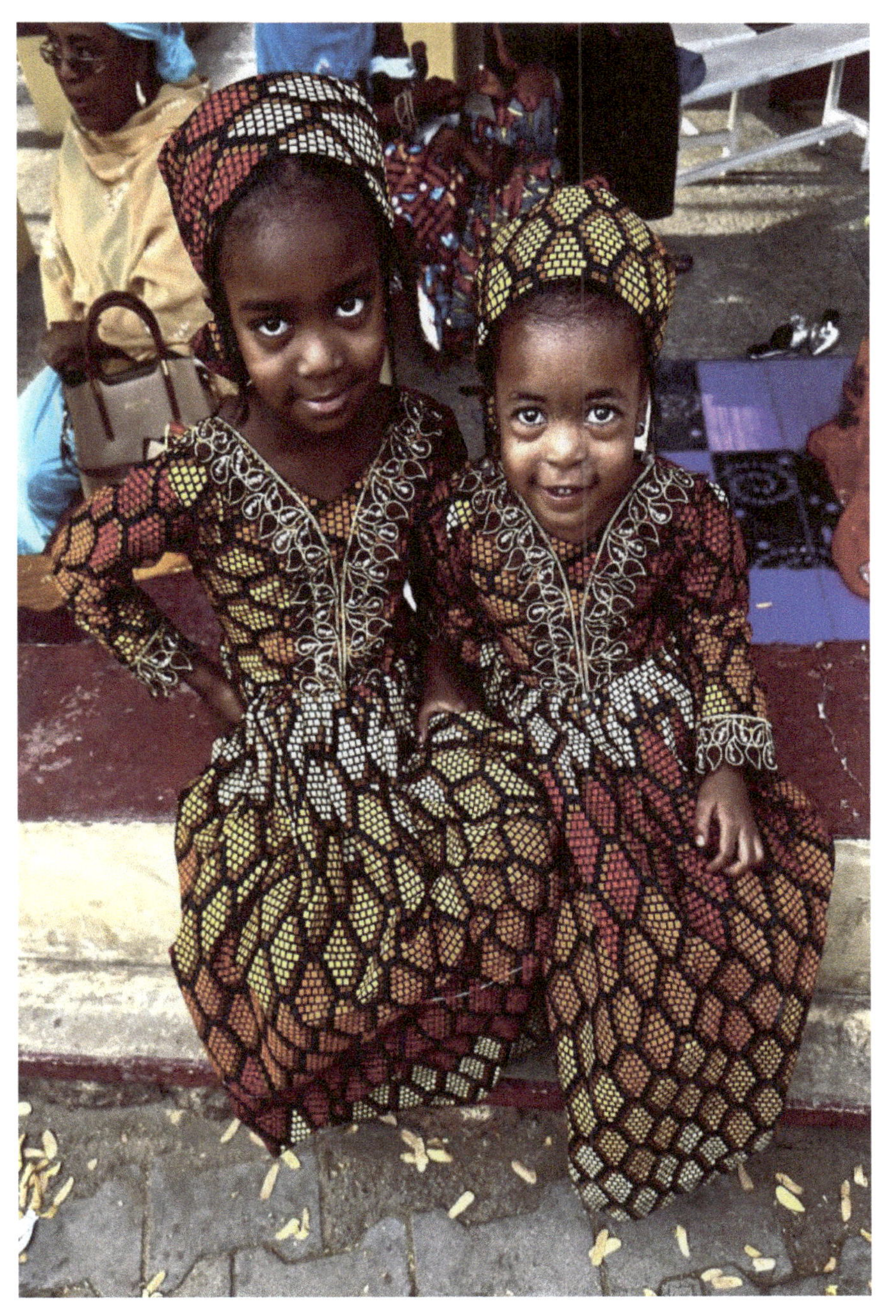

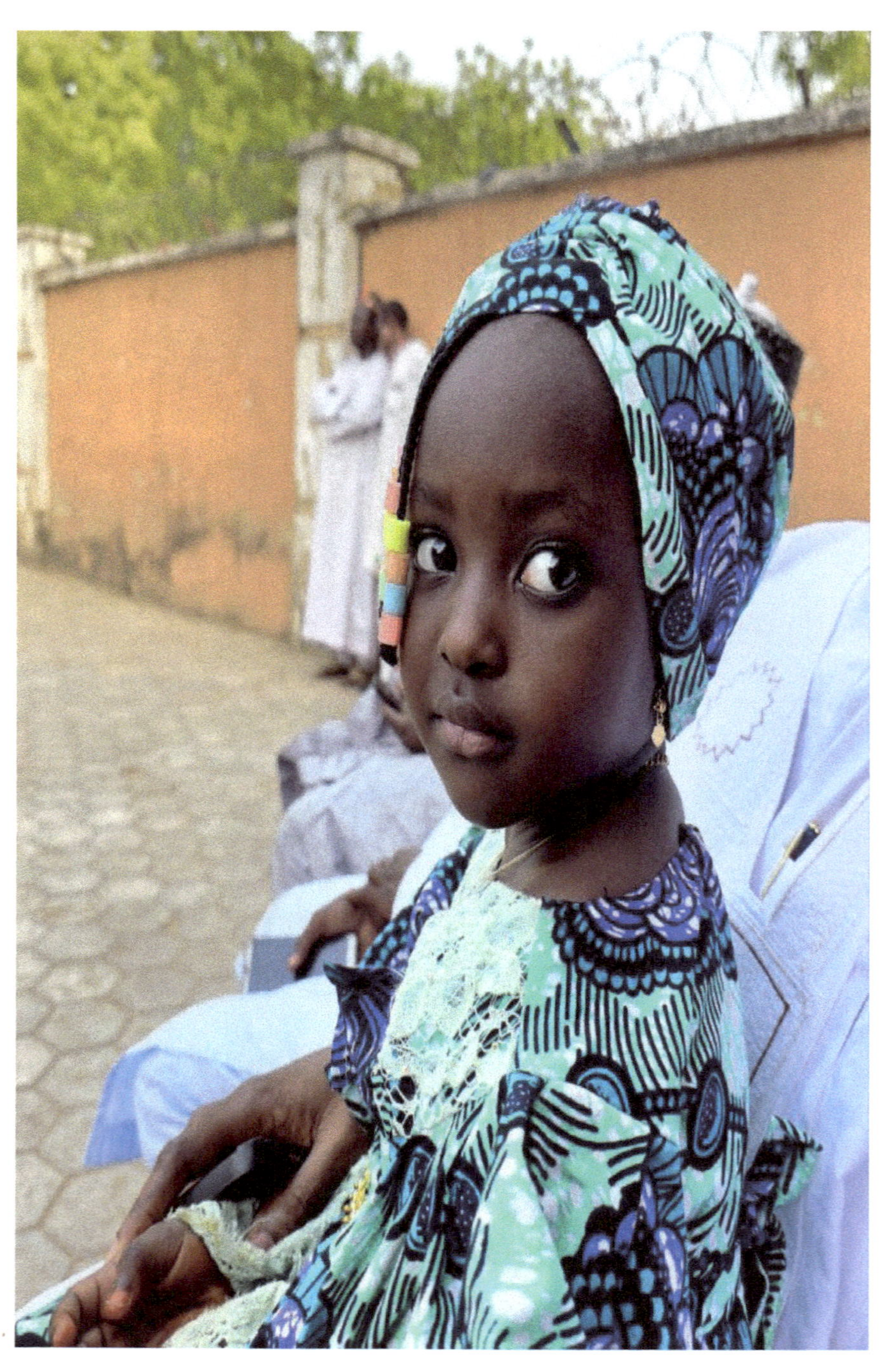

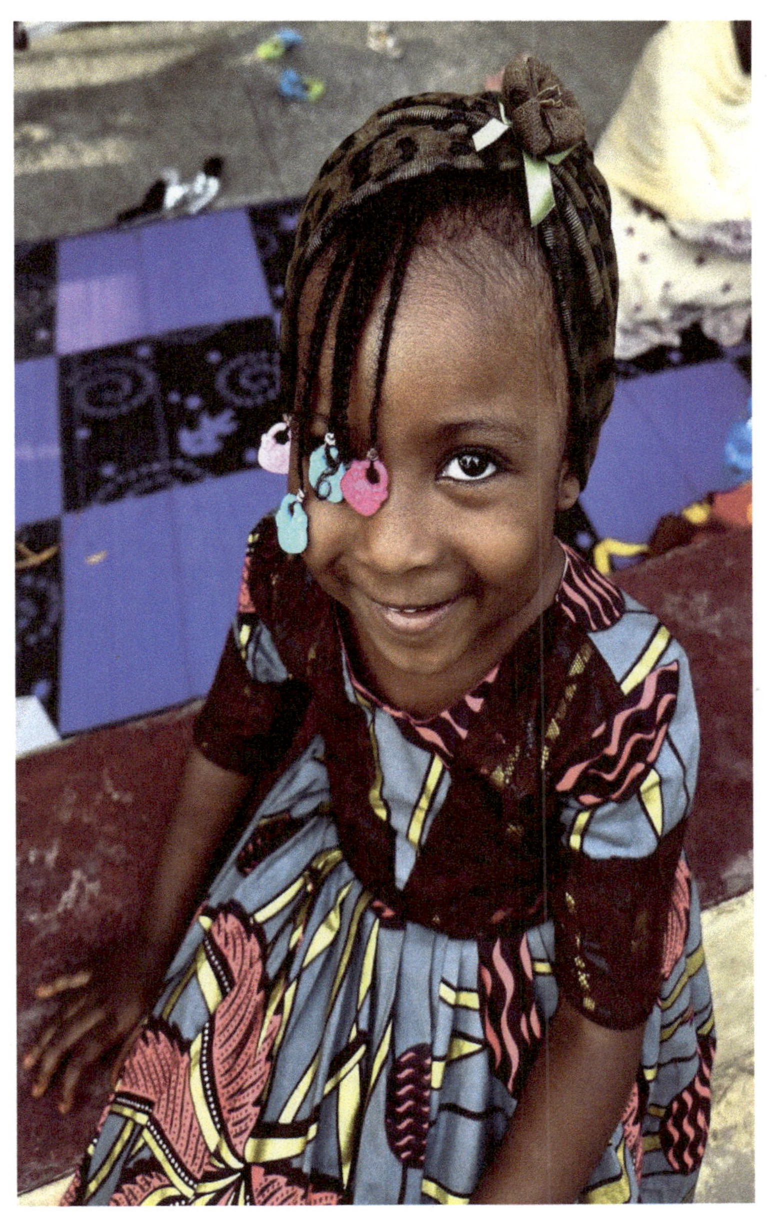

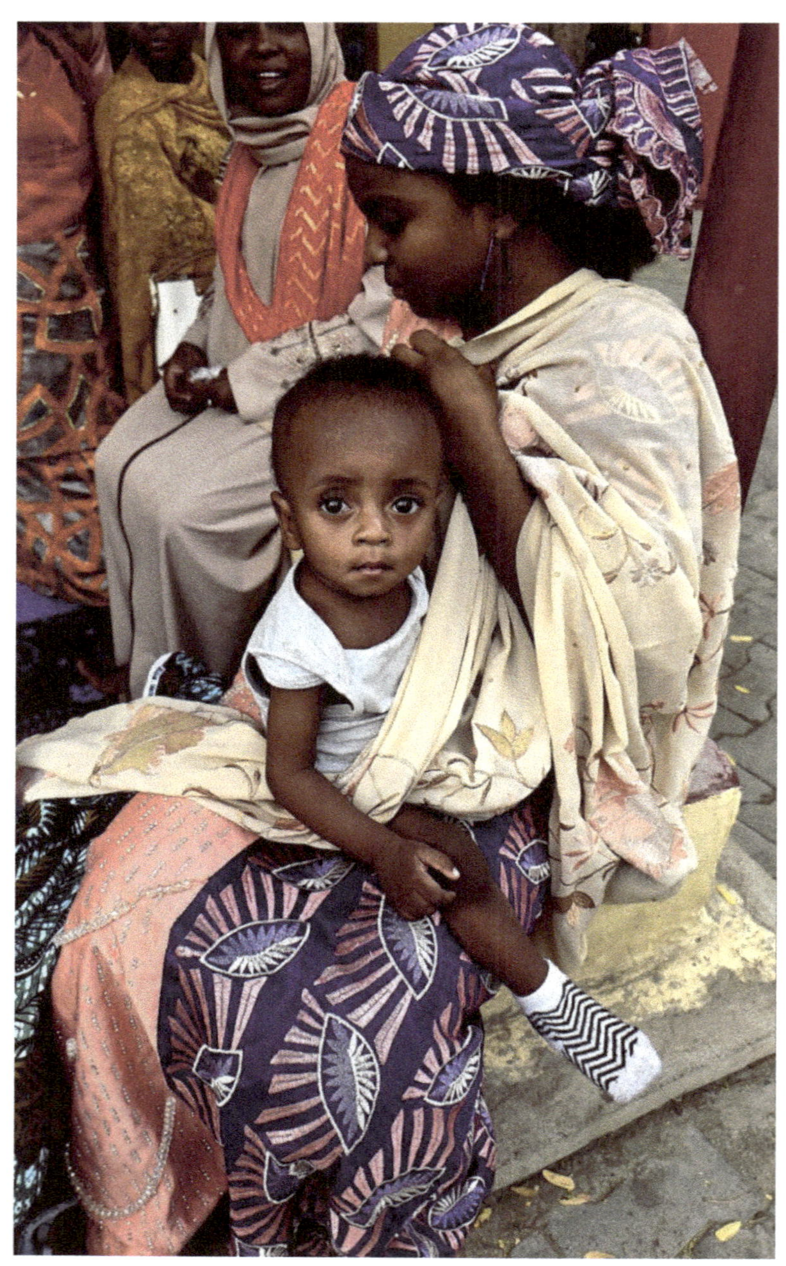

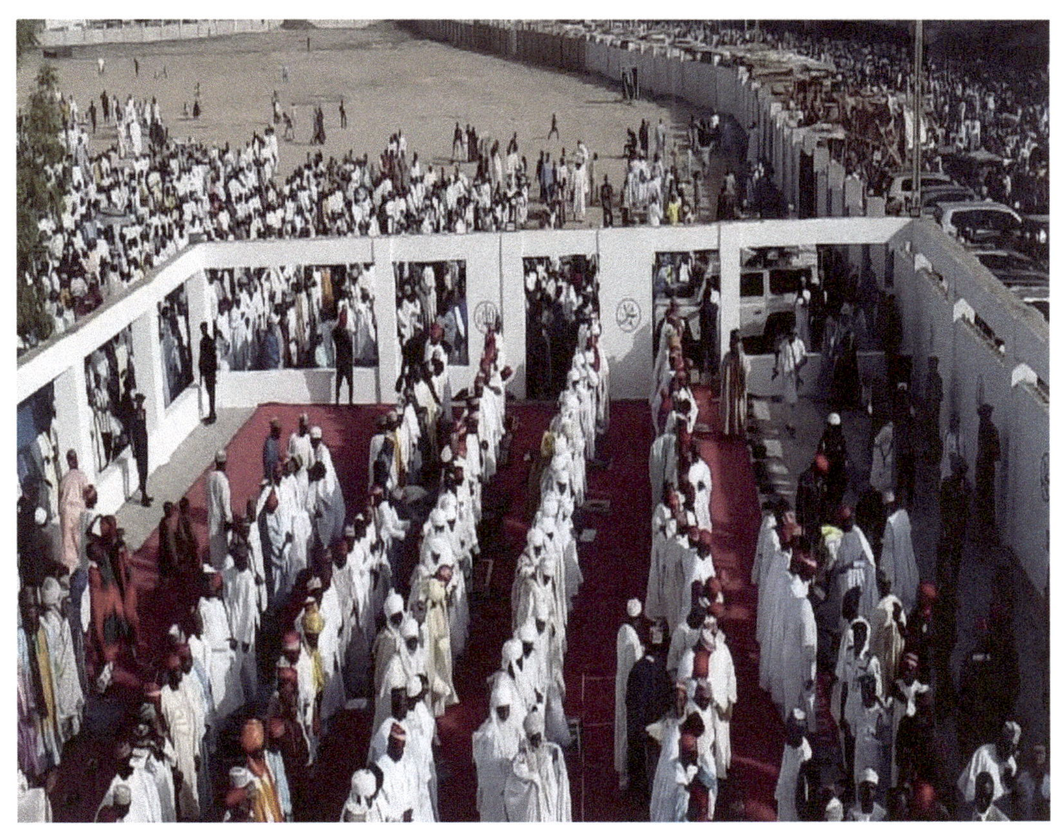

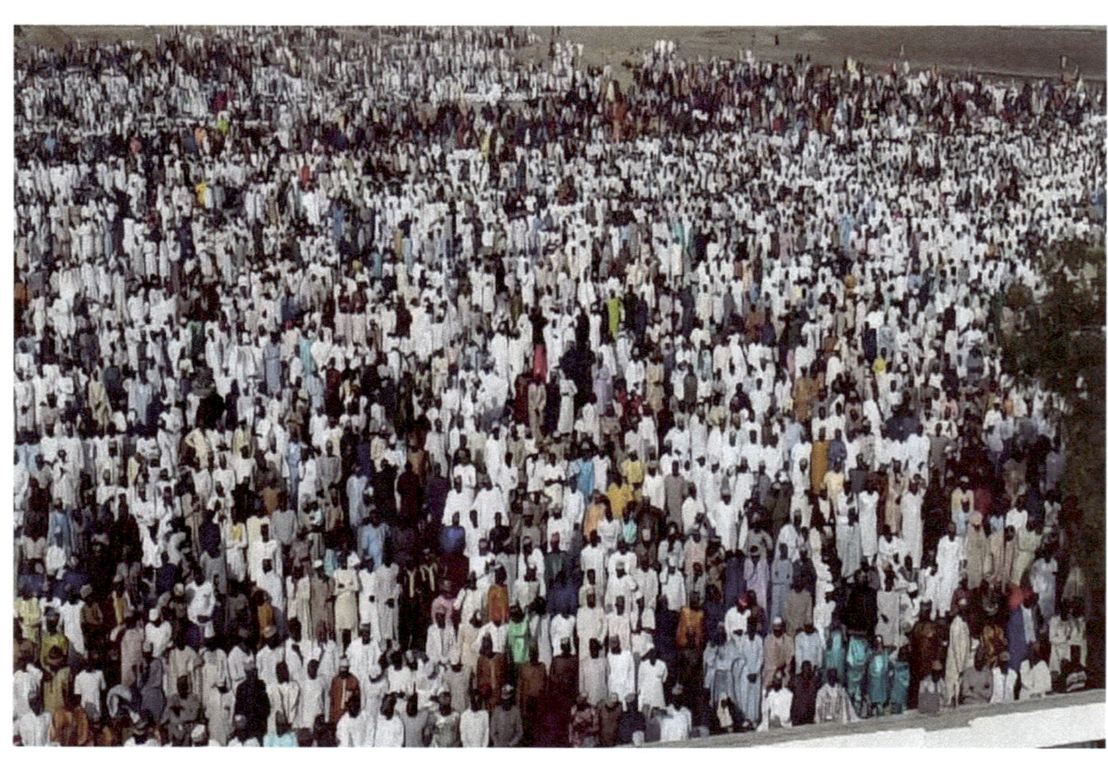

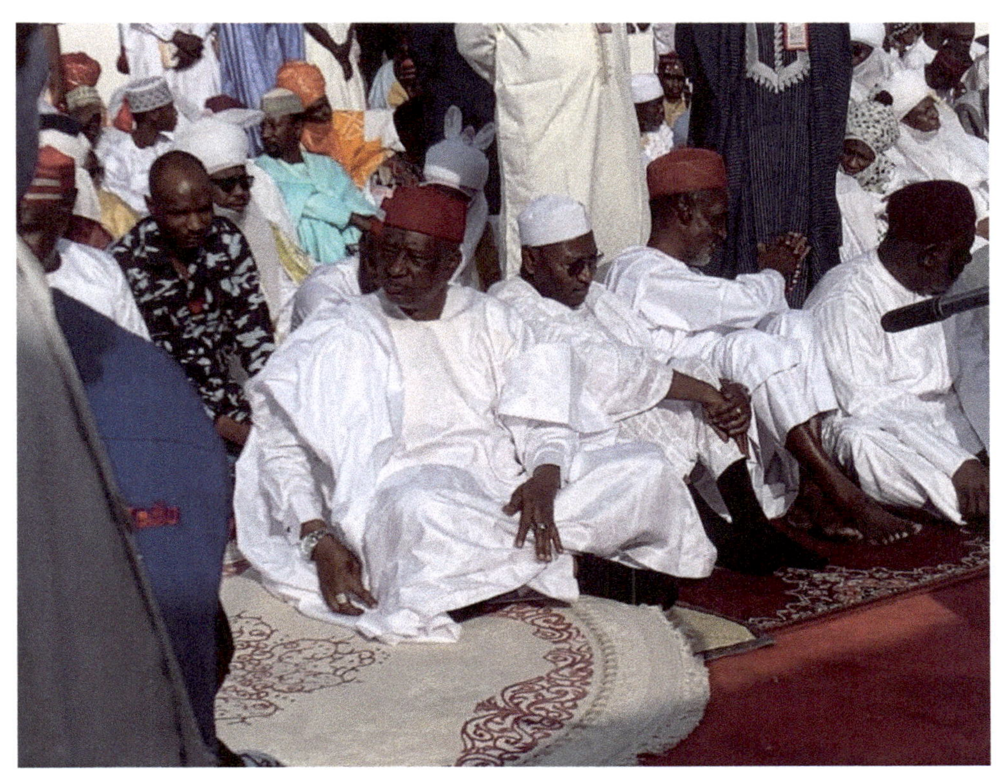

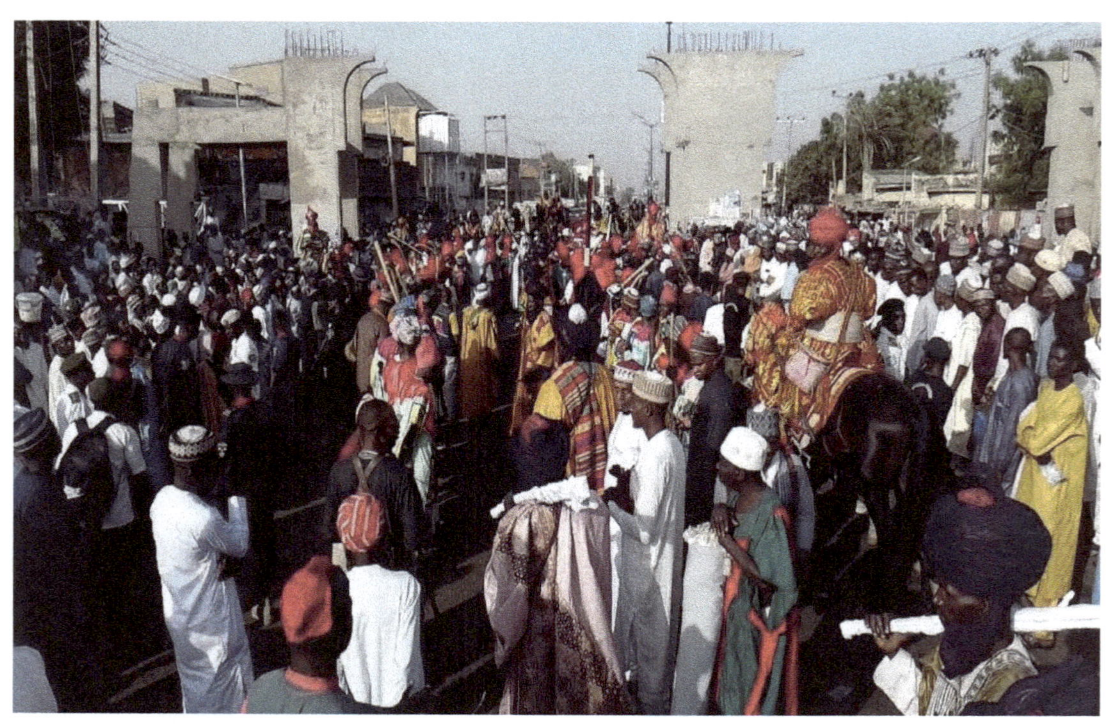

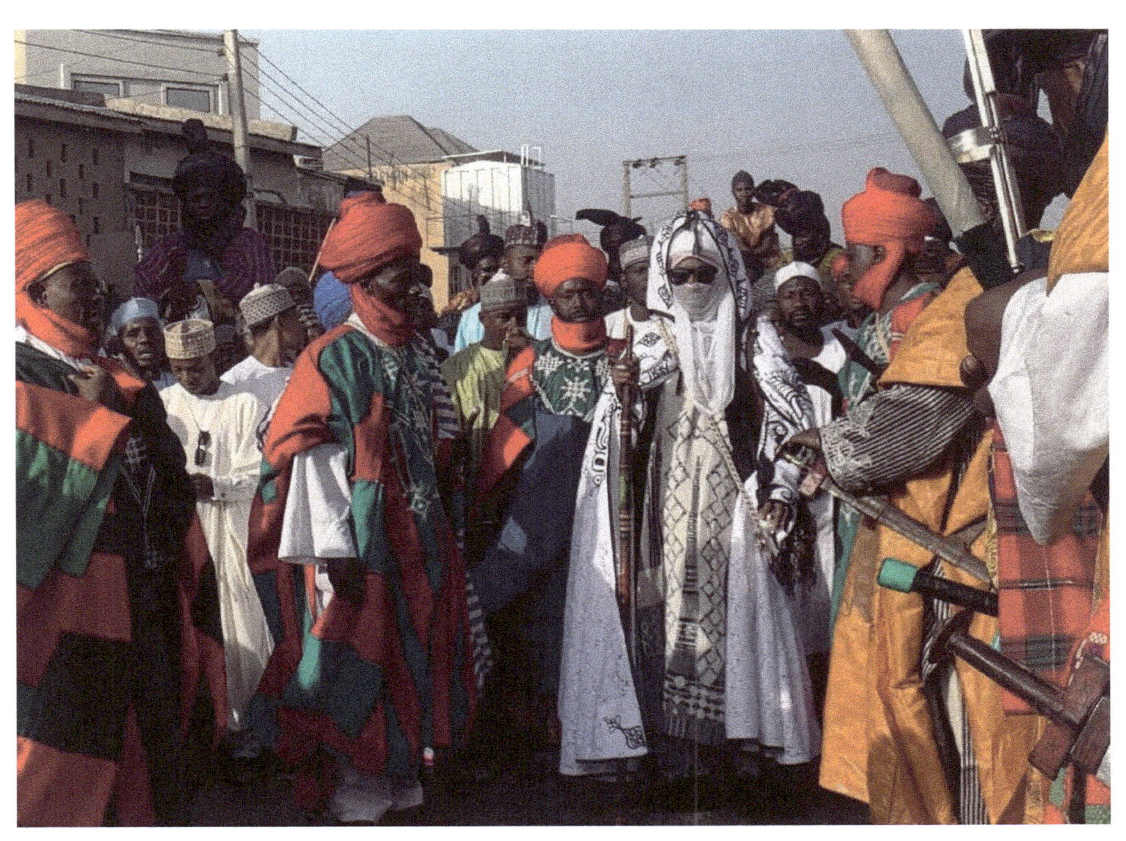

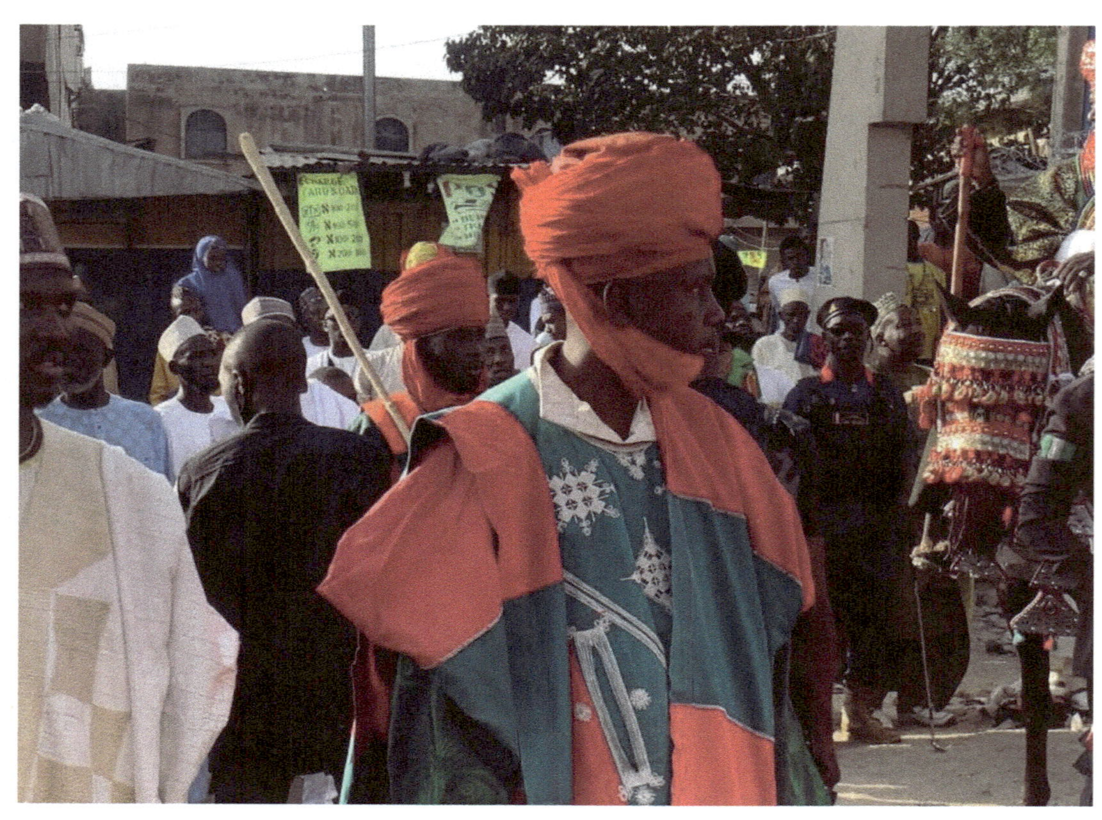

REWARD
CARDS DAD
GTN N100 2
N50 50
N100 20
N200 00

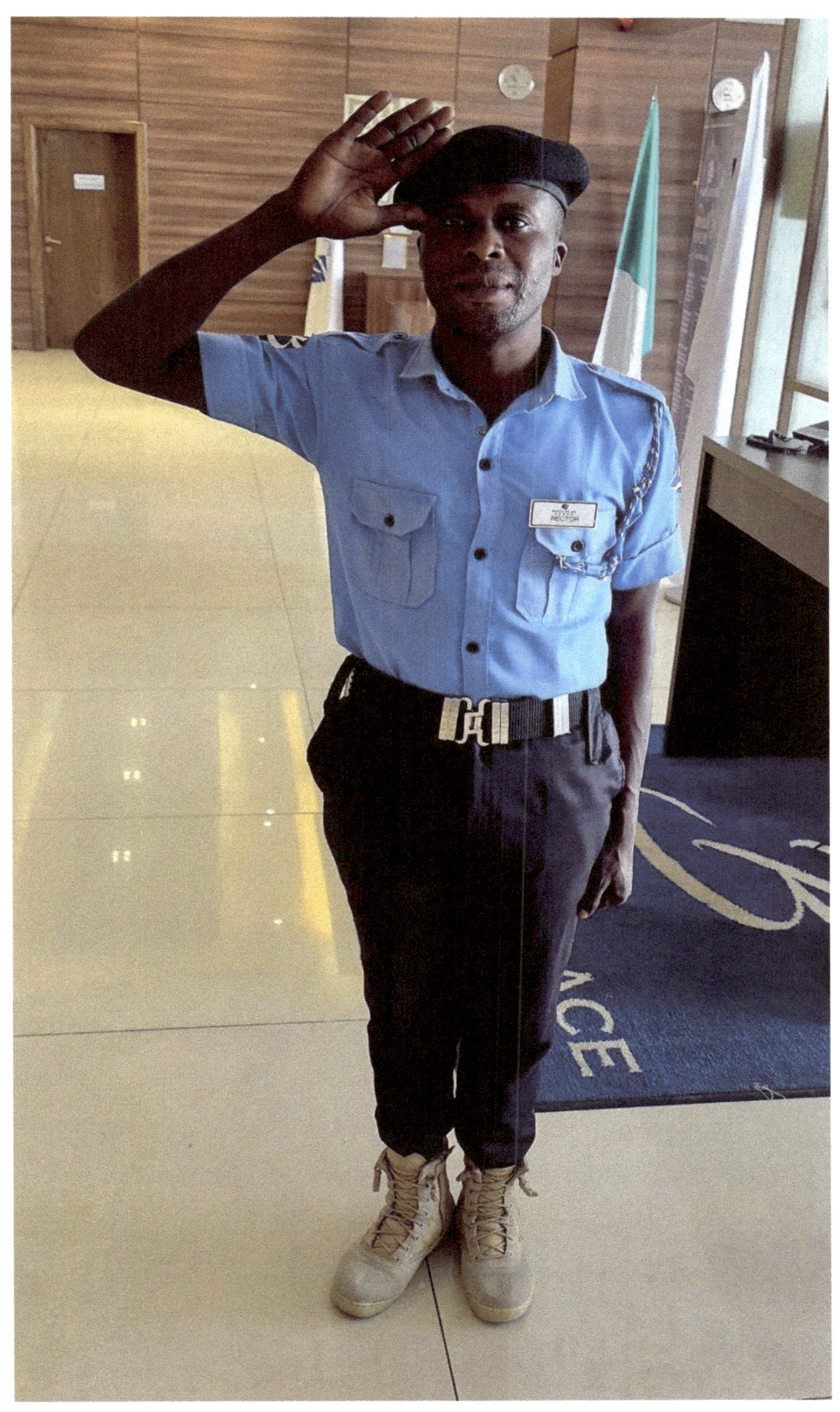

DISCOVERING KANO – SUMMARY

What began as a trip to further explore and understand Africa resulted in my discovery of an ancient region in northern Nigeria previously unknown to me. Learning about my own Fulani heritage intensified my interest in the rich history of the Hausa states that once constituted the Bakwa Kingdom. Although I knew a little about Islam and Muslim practices, I had never been to an Islamic state. Visiting Kano provided insight into a world rich in tradition, history, and cultural identity. Even though I was disappointed by the cancelation of the Durbar Festival, the trip enriched me in ways I could never have imagined.

Observing Eid al-Fitr events and Sallah celebrations in the northern Nigerian city-state offered unique insights into Hausa Islamic traditions. I was captivated by the men's beautiful turbans and Babbar Rigas (big gowns) worn at official gatherings. My host, Ach. Ahmad Abba Yusuf was incredibly gracious and patient with me, despite my many questions. Meeting Governor Abba Kabir Yusuf was a highlight, and I never imagined His Highness, Emir Muhammadu Sanusi II would personally take me on a tour of his palace.

I learned so much on this trip; walking through markets that have been essential to Trans-Saharan trade for over a millennium provided me with insight into historical African commerce. Haggling with Hausa merchants taught me about their trading practices, unique, but not unlike my shopping experiences in other African open-air markets. I thoroughly enjoyed observing Hausa craftsmen as they created items and garments by hand; I was impressed by their skill and use of age-old techniques. It was fascinating listening to the Dye Master as he explained the indigo dying process, an ancient method exclusive to Kano, still in use today.

Discovering Kano offered me a glimpse into an ancient North African Emirate, providing me with further information and insight into the incredible richness and diversity of Africa.

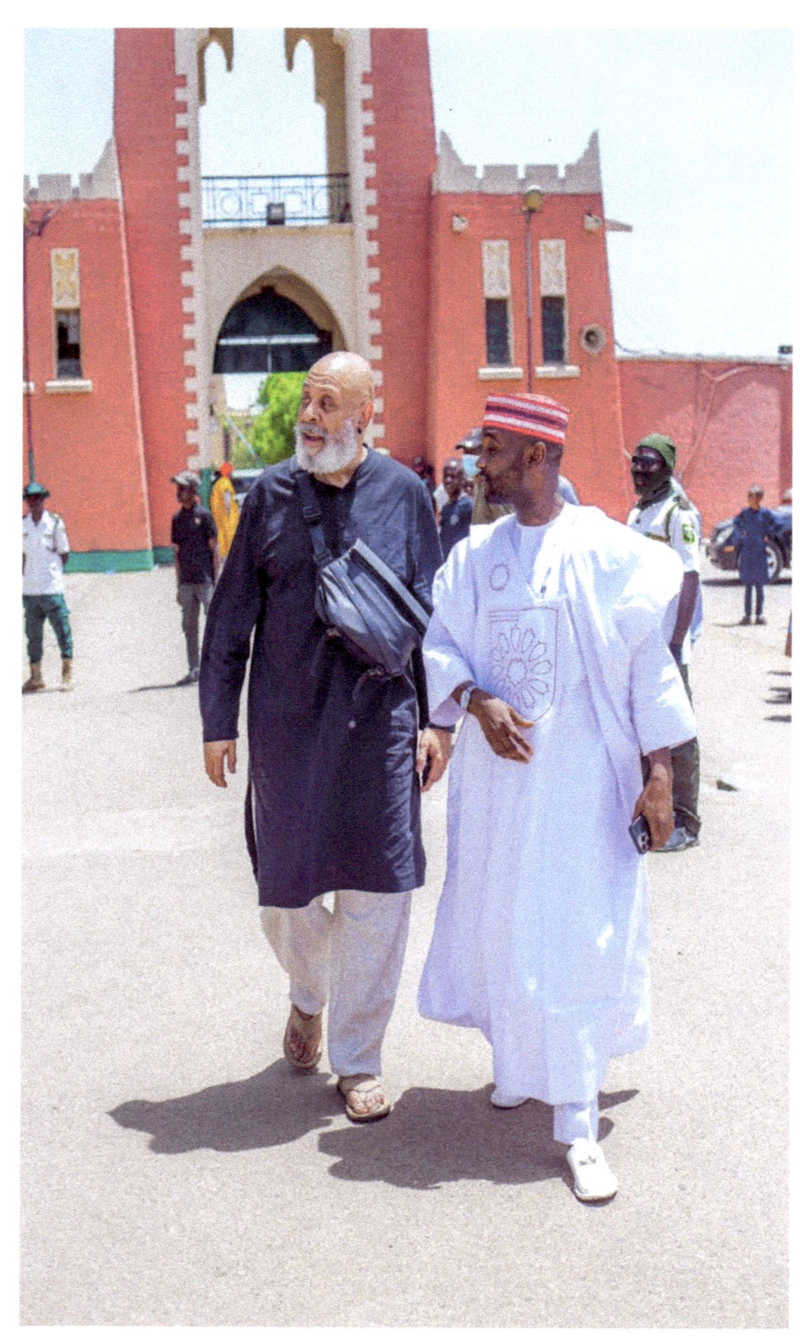

www.ingramcontent.com/pod-product-compliance
Lightning Source LLC
Chambersburg PA
CBHW041110090726
47602CB00020B/52